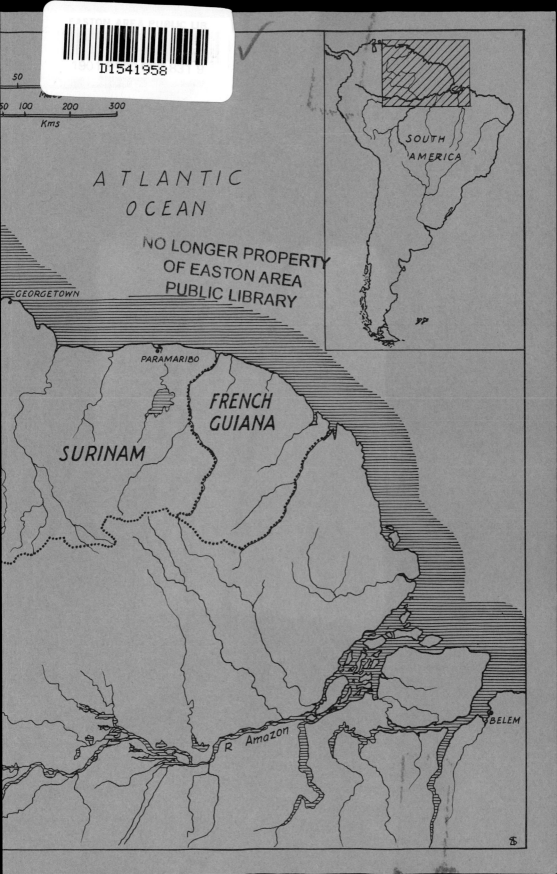

ATLANTIC
OCEAN

GEORGETOWN

PARAMARIBO

SURINAM

FRENCH
GUIANA

R Amazon

BELEM

SOUTH
AMERICA

50

50   100   200   300
Kms

The Last Great Journey
On Earth

The Last Great Journey On Earth

by

BRIAN BRANSTON

WEYBRIGHT AND TALLEY
NEW YORK

I dedicate this account to
'Sir' Wally Herbert
who, though his Country neglected to honour him,
thereby doing no honour to itself,
will always be to me and many others
'Sir Wally',
taking his place in the history of Polar Exploration
by leading the first expedition to cross from the
New World to the Old via the North Pole
on foot;
an epic journey of 3620 route miles
taking one year and four months;
a journey which, had he and his three companions
not been pipped at the post by the
Men Who Circled The Moon,
must inevitably have been called
THE LAST GREAT JOURNEY ON EARTH.

Contents

Illustrations

KEY TO ACKNOWLEDGMENTS

1 Adrian Cowell
2 *Geographical Magazine* © IPC Magazines Ltd
3 Schlenker

CHAPTER ONE

The Start of the Adventure

WE 'lifted off', as the hovercraft pilot called it, from the cluttered-up slipway of the Amazonas Engineering Works.

It's as if you are sitting in a bus and a mad garage man starts to inflate all the tyres at once to elephantine proportions. Then you half slide, half fly away. One minute you're on land, the next you are buoyed over water. Behind you, an aeroplane propeller is creating a tremendous buzz. In front, until it gets drawn through the blades, the steamy dank air hangs about like wet washing.

That misty morning the racket of the hovercraft's engine whammed and cracked from the steel-blue surface of the Rio Negro. Twelve miles south of us, at the junction of the two rivers, the dark waters of the Negro butted up against the yellow-ochre Amazon without mixing: two hundred miles north lay the equator, and we sped obliquely towards it.

It was just after half past six on the morning of Thursday 11th April 1968 and the sun was a late spectator. We were late ourselves – ten minutes – and the pilot didn't like it. When Captain Clarke said, 'Lift off at six-thirty', that's exactly what he meant. Ten minutes late at the beginning of a journey we knew would last at least a month: well, it just wasn't good enough. It didn't matter whether you were going on a twenty-minute hovercraft trip from the Isle of Wight to Southsea, or as now, starting a 2000-mile drive from Amazon to Orinoco, to the

Caribbean Sea. 'Lift off is lift off, gentlemen; and that's all there is to it.'

Somewhat chastened, we sat – seventeen of the twenty of us – rather like overgrown boys in a too-small school bus. The three who hadn't got seats had to dispose their bottoms on angular boxes of stores and piles of luggage at the back. One of them, our sound-recordist, young Peter Smith, preferred standing in the aisle, leaning against a seat with his neatly rolled umbrella hooked into the seat-handle behind him. He was reading a week old *Guardian*, and one of the hovercraft crew, Jim Sweeney, winked at me and tossed his head towards the engrossed Peter and shouted above the din, 'Brian! Just like being in the tube back home!'

It was, and it wasn't. For Jim Sweeney himself was shirtless (stripped as ever to the waist), his body golden brown from the tropical sun. And the temperature: even that early in the morning it was crowding the eighties. Soon, the front of the hovercraft would work up to ninety-six degrees Fahrenheit, while the back of the cabin would do duty for a Sauna bath at a hundred degrees. Even so, in spite of his khaki shirt and pants, Peter Smith, swaying against the seat as the hovercraft pitched slightly, would not have looked too incongruous wearing a bowler hat. It would have matched his newspaper and brolly. Of course, when you glanced out of the spray-spotted window, instead of the familiar circle and bar sign of the London Underground or 'Marble Arch' or 'Picca-dilly' you saw receding into the distance the silhouetted palm trees and the shacks of Manaus. Bobbing against the stilts of those shanties built over the water were some very strange craft – at least to our eyes: huge dugout canoes with *toldas*, palm-thatched roofs; river boats like battered old-fashioned stove-pipe hats with two or three storeys above the water line; even an ancient stern-wheeler. There was, too, the American missionary Lyle Sharp's water-plane, dragged out of the river on a cradle, standing stiff-legged like a stork on aluminium floats which were paper thin and rotten at the joints. We of the BBC Film Crew watched that plane recede with a feeling of relief. In some desperation, we had tried to hire it. Later, our hovercraft engineers had told us that on the next landing the struts would have gone through the float bottoms and plunged the missionary and his passengers to the depths. And I really mean depths, for the Negro hereabouts is twelve miles wide and cor-respondingly deep. Deep enough to take ocean-going liners.

I could still glimpse the little knot of people who had risen early to see us off. There were Peter and Mrs Jane Eyre; Colonel Winstanley from Rio; a pale girl (with that fragile transparent look some Euro-

peans get in the tropics) from the World Health Organisation; David
Pirrie, the local manager of the Bank of London and South America
and British Vice-Consul; and a priest from the Salesian Mission to the
Indians conspicuous in his long white cassock. There they waited for us
to go out of sight, incongruous and European, watched themselves by a
couple of curious vultures perched on the roof of the Amazonas
Engineering Works. They were surrounded by rusty iron boats on
stocks as they stood there in the slipway among the rails, cradles, rubbish, lush tropical weeds and beams for propping up beached shipping.
Behind the spectators the early morning streets of Manaus, for once
bare of pedestrians (as I knew, having just taxied through them), were
rather like a smelly farmyard, with chickens, dogs and buzzards all
despondently picking over the night's refuse. Still farther behind, beyond the criss-cross grid of better streets, the fine houses of the long-
dead rubber-barons and the newer office blocks and banks, unfolded a
thousand miles of trackless jungle. For Manaus is an island city, an
island in a sea of forest. No roads lead into Manaus, and very few lead
out. The dirt tracks that do lead away stop after ten or twenty kilometres, blocked by a solid wall of trees.

What the farewell party could see of us by this time probably resembled a buzzing cocoon of river spray, for we were overloaded, what
with food, camping gear and extra fuel, and a good deal of the engine's
power was being used by the fan to force air under the hovercraft's
skirt and raise us from the water. Our forward speed was slowed by the
extra weight, and so the compressed air blew out, turning the river
surface to spume which preceded us and hung round us in a cloud.

A hovercraft is rather like a single-decker bus, with the passenger
cabin set on a gigantic saucepan lid. Hanging down from the edge of
the saucepan lid or 'plenum chamber' is a heavy, thick, yet flexible
plastic skirt – a bit like a mighty tyre inner-tube with a slit all round
the bottom from which a continuous blast of compressed air is allowed
to escape. The machine's aero engine drives the fan which thrusts a
cushion of air all round the bottom. Of course, the craft floats even when
no air is forced downwards. Its base is like a hollow raft, being divided
into twelve buoyancy tanks. In full working trim, not overloaded, and
with its cargo properly distributed, a hovercraft of the Winchester
Class like ours can do sixty knots and has a fuel consumption at forty
miles an hour of about a gallon a mile. Its forward motion comes from
the thrust of an aeroplane propeller at the rear set between two giant
air rudders. There is a certain risk in stepping along the catwalks on
either side of the cabin while the craft is moving: the minor risk is that

you would slip and put a foot through the thin aluminium skin of the plenum chamber, damage which in these remote parts we would find difficult if not impossible to mend; the major risk, of course, is that you would be blown back into the propeller and come out the other side as crimson confetti.

But, as film makers, it was essential that at least one of us, the cameraman Henry Farrar, should work at intervals outside on the catwalk. Graham Clarke, the captain, had agreed this with me on the understanding that Henry would always wear a safety-harness and be accompanied by one of the two crewmen, Jim Sweeney or John Hoyland. We did, in fact, find this arrangement worked very well.

Alongside the catwalks, resting on trunnions built out over the plenum chamber, were our auxiliary fuel tanks. These long oval tanks were essential. Using only her internal tanks, the craft had a performance of up to 250 miles; with the extra fuel we were able to cover 500 miles.

It had taken six months for the Shell Oil Company to lay fuel dumps of forty-gallon drums of kerosene from Manaus up the banks of the River Negro to the Brazilian border. On the Venezuelan side, Shell had laid dumps from the mouth of the Orinoco River as far as Tama Tama – itself at the back of beyond; between this isolated New Tribes Missionary post and San Carlos by the Brazilian–Venezuelan–Colombian frontier there was a no-man's land about which little was known. Here lay the mysterious Casiquiare Canal, a natural waterway said to provide a link between the Amazon and Orinoco basins. Whether it did or not, we weren't quite sure: even if there was a link, we didn't know if it would be wide enough for our craft or whether there would be impassable obstacles. What we *had* been told about this two-hundred-mile stretch was that it snaked through some of the most pestilential jungle in the world and that half our party would be laid low with fever and dysentery and all of us eaten alive by insects into the bargain.

Of course, it was jungle all the way, and on that fine April morning as I watched it racing by, from water level at this speed that jungle was a new and exciting spectacle. On our right, to the east, bars of red and gold were pushing up the horizon – the banners of Brazil. Ahead of us the hard, unbroken matt surface of the river was a dull silver-grey; here the Negro is anything from five to twelve miles wide. On our left the jungle flashed past close by us, a solid wall of trees, thirty to forty feet high. Far to our right, the forest on the distant bank was simply a dark thin line which divided the darker grey of the river from the lighter grey of the tattered sky. This band of jungle was so remote that individual trees didn't show, except where the heads of tall palms or other larger species pimpled the forest skyline.

In our noisy, sweaty, cramped seats we were cocooned from *the jungle*: that mysterious, vast, terrifying *idea* with which one would sooner or later have to come to grips – two million square miles all covered with trees, one of the most naturally hostile regions (I believe) on earth.

This Amazonian rain forest has been called some uncomplimentary names, but the one that has stuck is 'the Green Hell'. A Brazilian writer, and he should know, called it that during the heart-breaking years when they were trying to build the Madeira–Marmoré railway. Men flocked into the woods from Europe and the States, never to come out again. The jungle was a green hell because its dark, dripping monotony closed down like a trap on hopeless men who saw no chance of escape and were driven off their heads. It was, and is, a green hell because of its killing diseases, malaria, yellow fever, dysentery, beri-beri – you name it, the Amazon has got it. And it is a green hell because, like Dante's Inferno, its tortures never end through daylight and dark: you can start the tally with heat and humidity, and you can complete it with biting insects from mosquitoes to piums to chegoes which can combine to turn your body into a parboiled, itching, aching sore; and in between you can include demons in human form from Indians to white and off-white renegades, and demons in animal form from the grunting, squealing pitilessness of the wild pig sounder to the sly cayman, the South American alligator, dragging men to suffocating death in the foetid river.

There was time to muse on it, for there was little conversation in the cabin. O.K., so the region is a dangerous and beastly one. And before you went into it you were living in an expensive middle-class modern house with an acre of garden on the outskirts of tony Henley-on-Thames with nothing more frightening than the explosive twitter of a startled blackbird in the early morning or a snorting hedgehog at your back door last thing at night. And you're here to make a great film: a film of what must be a unique exploit. A *great* film. A lot depends for you personally on its being a great film, but aren't you inviting derision and contempt by calling your adventure 'the last great journey on earth'? Common sense and modesty caution you against using superlatives like *last* and adjectives overloaded with their own meaning like *great*. 'Well,' you say to yourself, 'I didn't choose this title. Arthur Helliwell (sitting just across the gangway), the *People* Sunday newspaper reporter, or somebody on his editorial staff, wanted that for a title. It's a catchpenny, a circulation-puller. Most people – newspaper readers – are like that. Their daily lives are so routine, so dull they can't bear 'em without a spice of vicarious danger, a shot of sensation, a fix of tedium-destroying melodrama. Or at any rate, that's what editors and ad-men think their reading public are like.' And then you try to justify yourself by saying, 'This *is* 1968, and in a year, or eighteen months at the most, somebody is going to fly round the moon, even land on it. So unless your old pal Wally Herbert (who's up there now in the Arctic wintering on an ice-floe) succeeds in leading his four-man expedition to the North Pole and then down the other side to Spitzbergen, it isn't likely there'll be a comparable journey before a man-carrying rocket leaves earth to circumnavigate the moon.' So that disposes of 'last' and 'earth'. What about 'great'? You go on justifying yourself: 'To be great, a journey ought to be unique. Well, ours is. Nobody has ever attempted taking a hovercraft from the Amazon to the Orinoco before. Then the journey ought to be big: is 1500 to 2000 miles and at least four weeks – with a possibility of four months if anything goes radically wrong – big enough? There must also be danger. We know about disease, wild animals, wild Indians, cannibal fish; there's also the chance of a nasty accident from drowning or being dashed to pieces in the rapids – and we've been told there are at least two bad cataracts, one at Waupés (on Brazilian soil) and a *forty-mile* stretch (in Venezuela) just above the town of Puerto Ayacucho. Enough danger here to satisfy a cat.'

You're brought back to your present condition (chafed knees cramped against the seat in front) by Jim Sweeney pushing a cigarette at you. The craft is whining steadily along like a banshee, and people are beginning to talk above the din. We are skidding across the tarnished silver surface of the Negro River at about forty-five m.p.h., sometimes within a few feet of an island. But these are islands with a difference: they consist only of tree-tops showing above the flood and no land visible. The near bank on our left, which I can see across the gangway through the window beyond Arthur Helliwell's bush hat and neat grey moustache, the near bank at the moment is a detailed tracery of grey, sometimes almost white, tree boles with a continuous cover of green foliage. Very occasionally the patterned ribbon of trees is interrupted at its base by a thin strand of light-coloured beach. Closer, within ten feet of us, the top of an isolated tree breaking the river surface whips by. Ahead of our 'roaring turtle' (as the Indians came to call the hovercraft) the black Negro River is solid and smooth.

I had come aboard that morning unshaven, having spent half an hour in my hotel room trying to pack two bottles of Bacardi rum into my

personal gear (forty pounds only allowed) which already over-stuffed
my canvas hold-all, a haversack and a brief-case. After off-loading from
my taxi, I had picked my path among the Amazonas slipway rails,
sleepers and broken guaraná bottles like a tree walking. My umbrella
handle was hooked round my neck, my bursting haversack on a long
strap from my left shoulder was tangling with my camera, a bottle of
rum under my left arm needed a lot of pressure to hold it there, my
fat black plastic brief-case (donated by Jesco) was continually slipping
from under my right armpit: it was stuffed until the zip wouldn't close
with everything from personal papers to clothes pegs and a jumbo size
tin of Johnson's Baby Powder. Then, stuck in a pocket, was a spare
toilet roll – pink, supersoft, twopence off – yes, even here! I was wearing my army surplus canvas leggings because I'd nowhere else to put
them. On my grey head I had my Brazilian labourer's round-brimmed
straw hat with a speckle of blue decoration plaited in. On my feet, baseball boots. A red beach shirt (purchased in Henley by my wife) worn
outside almost white tropical pants. It seemed good gear for a day – or
even thirty days and 2000 miles – on the river.

Everything I was carrying I reckoned to be essential. In that climate
rum certainly was. It cheers you up when you are soaked with rain and
it keeps your stomach right – well, it does mine. Then the workman's
chapeau de palha – what the locals find serviceable is always a good indication of what's best for the circumstances: that hat was light, airy and
beat back the sun's rays from my silver hair (I've been grey since I was
twenty-five). As for wearing a shirt as pink as mine – my crew knew at
once where to find me; and as to wearing it outside my pants, previous
jungle experience had taught me the value of getting air to the body.
You keep cool; evaporating sweat does the job nature intended it for;
you don't get prickly-heat pimples and you don't get heat stroke.
Talcum powder, in spite of its large angular awkward tin, is, as they
say, a *sine-qua-non*. I proved that in the forests of India and Burma –
admittedly twenty-five years ago, but I remember vividly what happened to me without it. In jungle conditions hot sweat on the more
private parts of your person provides ideal forcing conditions for the
foulest growths. On one occasion in Burma I had five skin diseases
together: prickly heat, ring worm, impetigo, scabies and footrot. Whatever happened this time, I was determined that night and morning I
would powder and puff every sweaty wrinkle, every perspiring pore
of my body, even at the expense of a little fun-poking.

The hovercraft still charged on. Graham Clarke, the pilot, sat on a
single seat forward wearing khaki tropical kit with the addition of a

pair of driving gloves on hands which fluttered like weaving butterflies round the joystick. He was wearing laced-up top-boots on feet thrust firmly into the steel hoops of the rudder bar. All his attention at that time was on the craft, for it was early days, we were definitely over-loaded, the uneven distribution of weight was a worry and there were 2000 miles of the unknown ahead.

Squatting on a wooden packing case in the centre of the gangway next to Clarke, leaning forward gazing through the combined door and window was Captain Stuart Syrad of the Royal Marines – our second pilot. On his left, in the first double seat, sat our two Brazilian observers, middle-aged Colonel Igrejas and youngish naval Captain Perez. In the second seat slumped the Venezuelan river pilot Julio Castillo, whose launch had been hired for the second half of the expedition. Castillo had upset the delicate loading balance of the hovercraft by suddenly turning up one night in Manaus when he ought to have been waiting with his boat at the Brazilian border a thousand miles away.

The eighteen expedition members proper tended to fall into four groups whose interests were occasionally at loggerheads. The trip had been conceived by the editor of the British *Geographical Magazine* as a romantic, startling notion with a scientific base which would provide him with features for at least the first three monthly numbers of his magazine in its new format. Derek Weber, the *Geographical* editor, had cast around the globe for a little-explored region at the same time as he pondered on some modern, newsworthy means of transportation. Hence the wedding of the Amazon basin with the hovercraft. It was a brilliant idea and one which, to carry it off, would mean solving enor-mous and costly problems, such as how to get the hovercraft across the Atlantic and a thousand miles up the Amazon to Manaus, and then how to fuel it on a journey through some of the remotest, least civilised ter-rain on the face of God's earth. So the first group in the expedition could be said to represent the *Geographical Magazine*'s editor direct: its leader was the business manager, a journalist David Smithers, and with him were reporter Arthur Helliwell of the English Sunday newspaper the *People*, and Douglas Botting, writer and still-photographer working for the *Geographical*. The second group were the scientists, one of whom, Michael Eden, a geographer of Bedford College, London, had been appointed by Weber as overall expedition leader. With Eden were David Harris, geographer, John Thornes, geographer and Conrad Gorinsky, medical botanist.

The third group consisted of the hovercraft crew – its pilot Roland Graham Clarke, engineer John Hoyland (scarcely married before his employers whisked him away to South America), James Sweeney, electrician – and co-opted pilot, Captain Stuart Syrad, RM.

The BBC film crew formed the fourth group: cameraman Henry Farrar, sound recordist Peter Smith, production assistant Bob Saunders and myself, director and producer, all from London. In addition, on arrival in South America we had picked up our second cameraman Jesco von Puttkamer, a Brazilian and a very old friend.

A problem facing us film makers, was how to get hold of a light plane with which we could film the river journey from the air, and in which (if the worst came to the worst) we could carry the two members of our party who might be denied seats on the hovercraft. My colleague, Bob Saunders, had been working on the air-support problem for the previous six months, and (so we believed before we left London) had solved it. He had arranged with the Missionary Aviation Fellowship, an American organisation flying small aircraft in support of missionaries all over the world, to hire us the service of one of their Cessnas and a pilot. The flying of tiny single-engined planes over extensive jungle in countries like Brazil is hazardous. First, air-strips are few and far between; second, fuelling and oiling points are scarcer than the strips; third, there are practically no beacons or radio flight guides – as a result, each time a pilot takes off his life is really in his own hands, and if he crashes in jungle, even though not mortally injured, the canopy of leaves swallows him up – he disappears – and the tangled trunks, lianas and undergrowth hold him immobile like a fly trapped in a spider's web; if not attacked and killed by snakes, jaguars, wild pig, alligators, or Indians, then he dies of starvation. Just such an accident had befallen the Missionary Aviator flying the Venezuelan Amazonas beat. He had crashed in the forest in the upper reaches of the Orinoco River, and his body and those of his two missionary passengers had lain undiscovered for the last couple of months.

Hardly before we were settled into the cavernous rooms of the Lord Hotel, we had heard rumours of the accident and how because of a reshuffle in pilot's duties we were unlikely to get a plane from the Missionary Aviation Fellowship. It was a great blow: our film coverage would be crippled without air shots, and probably two of our team would be left behind in Manaus. There were ten days before hovercraft lift-off, ten days in which to crack these two very hard nuts.

We had gone about settling our difficulties at once. Bob Saunders telegraphed the nearest Missionary Aviation Pilot 600 miles north of us at Boa Vista. It was impossible to telephone. The chalked notice board at Manaus Post Office told anybody who could read Portuguese that the microwave link with Boa Vista (there are no lines or roads, of course) had gone out of action. Whether or how our telegram would get through, we didn't know – we suspected it wouldn't. We regarded the pilot from Boa Vista as a forlorn hope, so we cast about for help nearer home.

There is a once-weekly service by ancient high-wing Catalina from Manaus following the Negro River, to Waupés, the last settlement of any size before the Brazilian–Venezuelan frontier. This delightful flying orange-box of an aircraft can carry fifteen passengers only, so early bookings are inevitable if you don't want to wait a week for the next plane. Should we or shouldn't we? At least, here was a possible way of getting our two seatless team-mates as far as the Brazilian border.

I cast around in Manaus for some other – any other – form of air support.

By this time we had paid a visit to the hovercraft moored on the slummy Negro bank at the Amazonas Engineering Works slipway. The lofty brick-built sheds with their collection of nineteenth-century iron flywheels, pistons and pushrods, donkey engines, horizontal and vertical boilers symmetrically riveted in rows, reminded me of a Dickensian factory or one of Blake's dark, Satanic mills. Hauled up on the slips, two-thirds of it out of the water, was an old Mississippi-type stern-wheeler looming large as a street of houses.

But what was more important then than romantic comparisons with a past era was what I saw across the creek. Below some yellow stuccoed Portuguese-style houses set amid palm trees there floated – of all things – a small seaplane. Just the job! I asked Peter Eyre, the Engineering Works Manager, who owned it.

'Think it's a missionary fellow. Chap called Lyle Sharp. Lives across yonder somewhere with the New Tribes Missionaries – Americans.'

I got Lyle Sharp's address from a religious bookshop almost next door to our hotel. I jumped into a taxi and went to see him.

He and his family lived in a fairly spacious tropical bungalow with the usual mosquito netting on doors and windows. Lyle was a man of fifty or so, strong featured, grey clipped hair and a slow American drawl.

I asked if we could hire his seaplane and waited anxiously for his answer. He agreed, provided we could help to get his floats mended.

Next day (at my request) I was happy to see the seaplane had already been winched up on to a cradle at the yard and one of the hovercraft engineers was working on it.

David Smithers came back from Rio. Permission to leave had still not been formally granted. Anyway, said Smithers, he thought there was too much maintenance work on the hovercraft to allow the engineers to continue tinkering with Lyle Sharp's plane. Oh, and one more thing: in Rio he had received a copy of the BBC film contract, and we had definitely got only three certain seats on the hovercraft, with the other two only at his, the business manager's, discretion.

The BBC crew gathered in the room I was sharing with the two cameramen, Henry Farrar and Jesco, at the Lord Hotel. Burly, blond Jesco limped in and out of the bedroom fixing *pingas* for everybody. A couple of these incendiary bombs brewed from local rum, limes and sugar and you feel you could *push* the hovercraft to Venezuela.

We discussed our plight.

When the Expedition reached the Brazilian–Venezuelan border there would be waiting for it a large forty-foot boat with outboard engine which would carry two or three of the scientists who needed to work along the river banks divorced for a week or ten days from the hovercraft. There had always been the possibility that two of the BBC crew could travel on this boat. I personally disliked this idea. It meant splitting us up into two film crews which would be separated from each other and out of contact. I needed both crews to work in conjunction and under my control – for instance, one crew filming the hovercraft from the air or the river bank while the other filmed from the hovercraft itself. In this way one gets a complete picture.

Nevertheless, we had to face facts. At the worst, we should have to despatch a silent film crew (Bob Saunders, director, and Jesco von Puttkamer) by the weekly Catalina from Manaus to Waupés. And they would be forced by the aeroplane's schedule to leave at least three days before the hovercraft did. But if Lyle Sharp's seaplane could be made serviceable our second film crew could always be with us, leap frogging along to the Brazilian border.

That evening at our regular seven-o'clock meeting of the full expedition our position was unchanged. Graham Clarke, the pilot, was daily expected from England, and in spite of the fact that the substitute pilot Stuart Syrad had not been catered for in our contractual discussions in England, it seemed fairly clear to me that Smithers was set on keeping him. That meant one of our two possible seats definitely gone. When the regular pilot arrived by air next day the situation was settled. Clarke wanted Syrad's help. I sent Jesco at once to book himself a seat on the Catalina to Waupés while there was still a chance to get one. He got one.

It had been all go that ten days of preparation in Manaus. Most of the expedition stores, including hammocks, mosquito nets, hammock ropes, food and cooking utensils, had still to be bought. Conrad Gorinsky, ethno-botanist and cook, was in charge of all that. The BBC crew had to purchase stores and equipment for an expedition of our own which we intended to make away from the hovercraft during an enforced wait for the scientists working at a spot called Las Esmeraldas in Venezuela. We were going to try to contact wild Indians. Jesco had been doing contact work for ten years in the Matto Grosso and was, naturally, our expert. He scoured the market and shops of Manaus for the things he knew we would need, from hundreds of small fishhooks, scores of boxes of matches, beads and boiled sweets as gifts for the Indians, to a 16-bore shotgun and ammunition to supply the pot. Frequently I went with him, padding the hot dusty pavements by seven o'clock in the morning (Jesco never rose later than six a.m.) or dodging the tropical downpour which came like the turning on of a fire hose regularly about eleven thirty a.m. He was indefatigable in spite of his limp. This impediment was a legacy from the war. Jesco's full name is Baron Wolfgang Jesco von Puttkamer; his father, the old Baron, still lives in Southern Brazil at Goiania. Being a younger son, the old Baron left his princely German family fifty-odd years ago and wandered about South Africa gold and diamond prospecting. He landed up in Brazil, where he made his home and married the daughter of the Swedish Ambassador of the time in Rio. Jesco and his elder brother were born in Brazil. In spite of their top-drawer German and French connections (one of Jesco's great-aunts married Bismarck, the Iron Chancellor, while his paternal grandmother was La Duchesse de Braganza), Jesco and his brother regarded themselves as true Brazilians. So when the war broke out while the two boys were studying in Germany at Stuttgart University and the authorities demanded that two strapping chaps with a noble Teutonic name like von Puttkamer should join the Wehrmacht, they refused. 'We are Brazilians,' they said. 'Very well,' said the Germans, after Brazil declared war on the Nazis in 1942, 'you are therefore our enemies. Please to walk this way into our concentration camp.' Jesco and his brother were both imprisoned. They were accused of being spies. The brother disappeared. After the war Jesco found he had been tortured and shot. Jesco himself was tortured. He was condemned to death. While he was in prison an allied bomb came clean through the roof of his cell, killed two other inmates and shattered his leg. When he recovered (with a permanent limp) he was placed in the death cell with ten days to go before execution. On the ninth day (because of pressure brought by his mother's Swedish relations) he was reprieved. Eventually, the Americans freed him and he worked, ironically, as an official photographer at the Nuremberg Nazi Trials. Since returning to Brazil, Jesco has devoted most of his time, energy and money to helping the two famous Brazilian Indian Protection Service workers Orlando and Claudio Villas Boas. Jesco himself has spent most of the last ten years in the Amazon jungle along the banks of the Xingú River, at one time living alone with the Suyá tribe for a year, learning their language and nearly marrying the Chief's daughter.

I thought of all of these things on the frequent occasions in the hovercraft when his freckled hand pushed a mug of pungent pinga over my shoulder from the seat behind. Through the windows there was no indication of life, no birds, no animals, no fish. On the left, reflections of the forest tracery in a river of glass. Ahead, not a ripple on the mirror-like surface of the water: only the vast sky reflected there made you think you were flying at ten or fifteen thousand feet over an ocean of clouds. Through the near window by my right ear I could see first the wet squares of non-slip abrasive treads along the catwalk; then the oval side of a spare fuel tank above the ribbed plenum chamber; then the flapping scarf of spray. The river itself on this side was black against the east, against the rising sun, as was the distant ribbon of jungle. Inside the roaring hovercraft you felt strangely divorced from this extraordinary outside world, sheltered, cocooned; and the impression was strengthened by the Christmas aroma of rum rising to my nostrils from the mug in my hand. As I glance at Doug Botting and Arthur Helliwell across the gangway and we bump bus-like over the solid surface of the water I wonder what the creatures might be beneath us. Piranha, the cannibal fish with the underslung jaw, swimming in multitudinous shoals, each individual averaging only eight inches long, but with a V-shaped mouth, big out of all proportion to its body and spiked with teeth like flakes of flint. Their tiny maws smell blood. They are said to strip a forest pig or hairy capybara in five minutes and could shred a man's body similarly, turning him much, much faster than time into a skeleton. Then we have heard of the improbable candiru – a sliver of a creature, a swimming length of string; fish or eel or what? which tries to insinuate itself into the pipe of a man's penis and make its home in his bladder, or failing that, up his bottom. And once inside, this candiru erects a fin along its length, a saw of backward-pointing spikes which effectively prevents its being pulled out. Jesco once told me a story of his friend in the Xingú, the great Indian Protector Claudio Villas Boas, having to slit with a razor blade the urethra of a tribesman from foreskin to scrotum in order to extract this animal spiker. For once the fish is lodged there, what can a man do? The pain is really only the least of his worries. Far from hospital treatment, the passage from his bladder blocked, he is unable to pass water, and in a few days at most would die in pain poisoned by his own sewage.

We talk of the manatee, the fresh-water merman, now hunted almost to extinction in these waters. Cayman there are, but since our noise can be heard twenty minutes ahead of us, that's to say fifteen miles at our speed, what creature is going to wait in curiosity until we come? Only the fish who cannot swim quick enough before they are overwhelmed by this howling, churning monster, even big fish, huge by deep-sea standards like the tucunaré, whose collops and joints have appeared on Manaus hotel menus, or whom we have seen on slabs in the stinking tropical fish market with vultures swooping down for offal from the cast-iron beams of the roof.

Manaus and all our worries of the last ten days now seem behind us. I recall the evening Expedition meeting in the Amazonas hotel restaurant, where draped sweatily on wicker chairs we heard from Graham Clarke that the hovercraft engineers had been finally unable to repair the float plane. Our air support was out. We walked disconsolately back up the street past open warehouses rawly lit by naked bulbs where labourers were shovelling monstrous mounds of Brazil nuts into hessian sacks, back to our rooms in the Lord Hotel. Jesco had ordered pingas to be brought up from the bar while all of us grumbled, Peter Smith young and owl-like in large horn-rimmed spectacles; Henry Farrar dark-haired, dark-browed, protesting with a Yorkshire voice in sentences which usually began, 'What I can't understand, Brian . . .'; Bob Saunders, neat, groomed, with thin moustache; and myself muttering, 'We'll beat the buggers yet! Why should Syrad stay on – Graham Clarke's back now. Syrad's only coming for the ride. And what about Hanbury-Tenison? Camp master they call him. What do we want with a camp master? All we have to do is sling our hammocks from the nearest trees and help ourselves to a packet of Ryvitas and a tin of sardines. What a bloody fuss!'

Sunk in gloom and a bouquet of pingas and fresh limes, we felt as though we were defeated, that two of us would really be pushed off the hovercraft, and at first light next morning we'd have to try for another seat on the Catalina.

There was a knock at the door.

We thought it was a waiter; in fact, it was our salvation.

'Come in!' someone cried.

The door was pushed open and I was aware of the long peak of an American-type mechanic's cap, the bluest of blue eyes, a round raw face, rather creased jungle kit, calf-length boots and a bulging hold-all.

'Is this the BBC, gen'lmen? I been tol' to report to Mister Brian Branston. I'm your Missionary Aviation Pilot, seconded for dooty up to the Brazilian Frontier.' It was a voice and an entrance straight out of a Hollywood film.

I gulped my pinga in one burning swallow and leapt from my chair. 'My dear chap!' I said, holding out my hand, 'You really were sent from heaven. Have a drink?'

'No, sir, thanks. Don't take liquor.'

'We must get you something – a guaraná?'

'Sure – guaraná or coke.'

I introduced the BBC party and learned that our God-sent pilot was Elmer Reaser, a flying missionary who had set off in a single-engined Cessna at first light that morning and had landed at dusk at Manaus airport after a 900-mile flight over unbroken jungle. His flying feat didn't sink in as far as we were concerned for some days, and Elmer never drew attention to it. If anybody literally flies on a wing and a prayer it is these Missionary Aviation Fellowship pilots. All we were cock-a-hoop about, at that moment, was our having got the means to carry the rejects of our party from the hovercraft at least as far as the Brazilian Frontier; and we had also the means to film the hovercraft from the air.

Next day it was the expedition's business manager who was in trouble. The equipment now brought out of customs by the scientists weighed enough to sink a battleship. Graham Clarke, the pilot, was jibbing: he couldn't carry the weight. The business manager, David Smithers, had been as surprised as we were at the arrival of Elmer Reaser and his spick-and-span Cessna Skywagon; but he quickly seized on the possibilities.

'You could give two of our scientists a lift, Brian,' he said, 'on the first leg, and this would allow us to carry more equipment for their experiments.'

'Hold on a bit, David,' I said, 'the BBC is paying this aircraft to do a filming job. The passenger seats will be taken up by our cameraman and extra fuel containers – it's the only way Elmer can cover the distances.'

Smithers wheedled and argued – this time putting forward the scientific worth and public-relations value to Britain of the hovercraft journey. And I agreed with him about the second of these laudable objects; but I had a job to do myself, and I was prepared to be as tough as my hand and a reasonable amount of bluff would allow me.

'Tell you what, David: I'll still send Jesco by the Catalina to Waupés and I'll arrange for two of your scientists to be carried by Elmer from Manaus to Moura – in other words – our first day's journey. In return, I'll want *four* seats on the hovercraft for our team from Manaus to Waupés – and five seats – seats for all of us from Waupés on.'

Dark, slick-haired David's round eyes boggled behind his horn-rimmed glasses, but he knew I had him over a barrel, and he reluctantly agreed.

Our BBC party were jubilant as we saw Jesco off to Waupés on the Catalina. We urged him to get well in with the Catholic fathers at the mission there and arrange for comfortable quarters. His round blond face, like a buttery moon, smiled at us from the aircraft window. We should see him again in three or four days. His excess baggage on that flight cost more than his fare. As part of his impedimenta he had a kitbag as long as a man which we naturally called 'the sausage'. It was a sausage apparently stuffed with lead. We never did find out all that sausage's secrets until we were struggling in dugout canoes to the re-mote villages of naked Indians near the headwaters of the Orinoco. Of course, some of his luggage was sheer dead weight, such as the 16-bore shotgun and ammunition; while nothing anybody could do (for the moment) would lighten the plastic gallon containers of rum which years of jungle living had confirmed his faith in as food, medicine, prophylactic and encouragement in dire straits.

Elmer had moved into our hotel room and slept in Jesco's bed be-tween Henry Farrar and me. He showed no awkwardness in kneeling down at the bed-foot in his blue pyjamas and saying his prayers before stretching his well-padded length along the sheets. Overtly, we took no notice, though we certainly thought about it. It sent me back to my childhood. For a second or two the tarnished years of worldly living fell away and innocence filled their place.

As we roared northwards towards the equator on that first day there was a feeling of bonhomie and politeness as we settled down to getting to know each other in the cribbed confinement of the hovercraft cabin.

We had been travelling for an hour and a half, and had put some sixty miles between us and Manaus. It was a quarter past eight. The pilot shut off his engine and the hovercraft slowed, and with a gasping exudation of air from her skirts, squatted down on the river surface.

We were waiting for Elmer and his plane to buzz us.

Henry Farrar staggered up the centre aisle with his heavy Arriflex film camera; Jim Sweeney followed with the camera tripod and a couple of lifelines; Peter Smith joined them on the catwalk with his microphones and recording gear.

Three wooden blocks with holes large enough to take the tripod metal spikes had been fitted on both sides of the craft. Henry and Jim Sweeney fixed the tripod on the starboard side and then attached life-lines from the handrail outside the cabin roof to their own belts. They were ready for Elmer to put in an appearance.

Nobody else was allowed outside, and shortly after stopping we wallowed in sweat and gasped for air. With the engine switched off, the mechanism still buzzed lightly like a hive of bees, while underfoot there was a bubbling and rustling of water like an elephant's belly rolling. The legs of the tripod were at my eye-level a foot away through the near window. Across the other side of the cabin and through the port windows I could see a break in the jungle wall. It was a sandy red scar, a vertical cliff clear of trees except for a rubbish of shattered trunks and branches at water level. The rising flood had undermined the land, and a huge chunk had avalanched into the river.

Robin Hanbury-Tenison, our handsome young campmaster (he had wanted to bring his wife with him), handed out eight-foot lengths of harsh hammock rope. We were instructed rapidly in the art of splicing and producing a finished end which wouldn't unravel.

The hammock appears to be a South American Indian invention. It's ideal for hut and jungle life: you can sling it from two beams or from tree to tree. Nobody travels in Brazil without his hammock. Even in the modern hotels you find hammock rings cemented into bedroom walls, or a more sophisticated arrangement is a metal keyhole-shaped slot which takes the knot of the rope and holds it secure when the rope itself slides into the slot. Personally, I never got to like the hammock. I know they are cooler than beds in that muggy climate. I accept that they are easily portable and can be lumped into any kind of shape to store anywhere. I realise that they protect you from ground-crawling creatures, scorpions, ants, snakes and even jaguars (if you're under a mosquito net). But I could never lie half crosswise as the Indians do, with one leg drawn up at the knee. No matter how I started the night, I always finished up lying fore-and-aft, on my back, bottom sunk, almost in the shape of a horse-shoe. But what a boon this airy bed was to the early European conquerors of South America! The Elizabethan sailors in the Caribbean, Hawkins, Raleigh and Drake, were quick to seize on the hammock's possibilities for ship life – infinitely preferable to hard oak decks, taking up no permanent room like beds or bunks, and compensating for the unruly motion of the sea. The lower decks of the British Navy have been a-swing with hammocks ever since.

Elmer and his Cessna failed to put in an appearance until nearly nine o'clock. He glided from about 2000 feet until he was skimming the dark surface of the river, the trim red-and-white plane and its inverted image almost touching at the non-retractable wheels. We could see him plainly through his cockpit windows. He gave a thumbs-up signal and after a couple more passes rose and flew off northwards towards Moura, our first official staging point. In that desolate wilderness there was no fuel to waste on fun.

It was gratifying to be moving ourselves again. Because we travelled with the top half of the front door always wedged open an inch or two, a refreshing draught of air blew over us and kept us cool. But each time we stopped we all exuded a muck sweat and patches of dark perspiration mottled our shirts. In motion, we were pleasantly cool; and once you had adjusted to the noise level, the roar of the engine turned to a droning buzz and a slight flapping in the ears.

Henry the cameraman, dark haired, dark browed, had come inside after a short period filming tracking shots while we were in motion.

'There's not much use runnin' off a lot o' film,' said Henry as he rolled himself a cigarette having taken his seat next to me. He came from the West Riding of Yorkshire, as I did, and his flat Yorkshire vowels sent me home. 'Yo' see, Brian, there's nowt but river, jungle and sky. It's all t'same. Never changes.'

I asked him anxiously if the vibration tended to produce unsteady shots. No trouble, he said.

Of course, the monotony of the river scene was a problem; but I hoped to overcome it as far as our film was concerned by a variety of shots from Elmer's plane, from a camera on the bank sent ahead with Elmer to film us approaching and landing and by having a camera in a small boat tracking with us when the chance came.

We were forging over the dark surface of the Negro at forty-five knots. From the air, Elmer said later, he could pick us up fifteen or twenty miles away – the only moving object on the braided river. The wake left by the hovercraft appeared like a white tail firmly attached to its rear. There was practically no spreading of ruffled water in V-shaped fashion to the banks of the particular channel we happened to be in. We looked to be a monstrous tadpole or a gigantic spermatazoon surging up the secret passageways of a virgin continent to effect a magical fertilisation. This latter thought, my own, of course, after seeing the first film rushes. Such an idea would have been foreign to Elmer's innocent, accepting, missionary mind.

This white tail of our wake contrasted strangely with the black river. The name *Negro* means 'black', and nobody is quite sure why some of the rivers in Amazonas are 'black' and some are 'white'. The Amazon itself is a white river, and when it is joined by its tributary the Negro twelve miles below Manaus there is a distinct sharp edge which marks off the two. Some people say the darkness of the black river is caused by tannin, some by humic acid. What seems certain is that such waters tend to inhibit the multiplication of insects such as the malarial mosquito – in fact, most biting insects whose life cycle depends on water into which they can lay their eggs and their larvae can hatch out. The locals regard the black waters of the Negro almost as a powerful insecticide. Before we left Manaus the expedition manager asked me to get certain information from the Salesian Mission Fathers about the properties of the Negro River. Our ethno-botanist, Conrad Gorinsky, himself part Guayanian Indian, suspected there might be bilharzia germs present and was not looking forward, he said, to the prospect of not even being able to wash properly, never mind bathe for a month. When I had mentioned these doubts and fears to the Missionary Bishop, Dom Miguel, he and the German brother with him had laughed aloud. 'Malaria? No! Bilharzia? No! This river is a paradise – there won't even be mosquitoes to bite you! You should drink the water for your health!' Personally, I wasn't taking the latter injunction literally. I was still determined always to use my portable pocket filter. But I did find from experience that what the Fathers said about there being few or no biting insects by the Rio Negro was true. Once you moved a mile or two away from the bank (as was possible at Waupés – and nowhere else) the piums, the tiny black *jejene* flies, scourged you with skin punctures until you were distraught. It's the female *jejene* who is the bloodsucker, and after exposure to these clouds of midges any bare skin is sprinkled with tiny black spots which irritate and itch for two or three days before the pinhead scar rubs off. Of course, the Orinoco (like the Amazon) is a white river, and the natural channel which was supposed to link the two, the Casiquiare Canal, is also white. Both would be swarming with *jejenes*. If ever we managed to get to those waters we could expect to be eaten alive.

But for the present it was nearly noon on our first day, and a stir of excitement breathed among the passengers when the lookouts up front cried, 'Moura!'

We had reached our staging point on schedule. We were now 175 miles from Manaus; the easy journey with stops for filming had taken us about five hours. An outboard canoe would have taken two days at least; an Indian paddling – well, he could never have done it against the stream, but say sixteenth-century Conquistadors rowing – *they* would have taken a week.

We strained forward, looking over rows of heads through the square windows to see what Moura was like. Any change of scene in that vast monotony was a matter of vital concern and interest.

CHAPTER TWO

Bedding Down

THE only indications that the jungle bank was any different here from the last 175 miles were a square church tower seen through the trees and a couple of very imposing buildings with four or five tall arched doorways.

The church tower was whitewashed and embattled, half ecclesiastical building, half fort, no doubt a relic of the days when churches in these remote parts served as strongpoints and refuges for the tiny Caboclo populace against Indian attack or the depredations of river pirates and renegades. When Drake beset Nombre de Dios on the Isthmus of Panama the Spanish inhabitants barricaded themselves for safety in their church. In the church tower at Moura we later discovered a chime of bells useful as a tocsin as well as for summoning the converts. As for the two other stuccoed buildings seen dwarfing the riverside palms, they concealed a melancholy secret not apparent as we glided past them to an inlet farther on.

Our main concern at Moura was fuel; drums of kerosene laid in dumps months before against our coming. Brazilians as organisers (delightful though they are in other ways) are frequently more hopeful than effective. But if we found our forty-gallon drums clustered on end here we could be tolerably certain of the other dumps up to the frontier.

The hovercraft pilot and his lookouts – Julio Castillo, Stuart Syrad and Robin Tenison – had found a creek which looked like the village's landing. Of course, there was no sign of a jetty or even rudimentary planking, the ground simply shelved up to a little jungle beach surrounded by rock and tangled brushwood.

And there at the end, on plashy sand (for the river was rising daily), stood ten or a dozen ribbed kerosene drums each half a man's height.

The hovercraft's aero propeller had been idling for some time and the last of the air eructated from her skirts. She was like a relieved old lady easing herself of a vast accumulation of wind as she settled her bottom down. Inside, we were suffocating. The door was opened in two halves; the top half, glazed, sprang upwards; the bottom half, solid and treaded, opened down and outwards to form a miniature gangplank. We all trooped eagerly out.

Poor people in rags – but still European-type rags – watched us from the rocks. Their faces, too, were mainly European, but very brown, almost coppery, and with a dark slant-eyed suspicion here and there of Indian. These are the Caboclos, the poor people of Brazil, the people of mixed Portuguese and Indian ancestry.

The shock came almost at once.

David Smithers, through his round horn-rimmed glasses, eyes beginning to pop, was examining the caps on the fuel drums. 'These aren't ours!' he was saying. 'This lot is Esso. Ours are Shell.' But there were no other barrels about.

The situation was that the Esso Petroleum Company hold the oil concession along the Amazon. When Smithers had approached them months before to supply kerosene dumps up the Negro he had found their charges too high for his budget. He had therefore asked Shell, who had apparently agreed to supply kerosene free in return for publicity. The Esso concessionaires couldn't believe anyone else would go out of their way to bring oil into their vast and isolated terrain, and so they had laid dumps on the off chance.

But Smithers didn't want their kerosene. We hung about awkwardly. Our Brazilian observers, Colonel Igrejas and Captain Perez, were talking to the locals, and Smithers was urging them to find out if there were other drums near by. It seemed most unlikely.

The BBC film crew of four had by this time disembarked with camera, microphones and recorder in readiness to film. It was stiflingly hot, and the air felt to me so intractable and solid, hemmed in over the water by jungle vegetation, that you had almost to bite off lumps and gulp them forcibly into your lungs. No doubt we should get used to it before long. But this was our first real experience away from the refuge of our air-conditioned Manaus hotel rooms, those cool caves into which we had been able to escape every midday.

We hung about uncertainly, none of us quite knowing what to do, except perhaps Douglas Botting. He had his Pentax cameras dangling round his neck or up to his eye, and bounded from rock to rock searching for angles and snapping his shutter.

'There's another dump!' suddenly yelled Smithers. It was, it seemed, beyond a knobbly spit of land on our right as we stood with our backs to the river. The hovercraft crew set about backing their vessel gingerly out of the creek, and the rest of us followed some of the locals in Indian file through a jungle pathway.

The BBC crew were each carrying pieces of impedimenta – Henry had the heavy Arriflex sound camera, Peter Smith had his recorder and a huge grey Zeppelin-shaped microphone, Bob Saunders lugged clapper board and film magazines in a black changing bag, I carried Henry's still camera. I saw Peter Smith slip on a rocky slope and half sit down. He let out a yell. With his hands full, he was unable to break his fall or fend off obstacles. When I got to him I saw his left calf was like a pin cushion. The spines on the reverse side of an innocent-looking palm frond had brushed against his trousers, and a dozen or so spikes, like steel-grey darning needles, were sticking through the khaki drill into the muscle of his leg. He scrambled up, protesting to himself, but continued after Henry, for by this time we could hear the barking of the hovercraft engine and we had to reach the new shore line in order to film the craft's approach. In any case, Peter's tape-recorder was linked to Henry's camera by a short cable, and where Henry went, Peter had to follow.

I groaned for him as I saw the spines sticking through the cloth into his flesh.

In my experience, a wound of any kind in the jungle, no matter how slight, easily festers and takes long to heal. Here, right at the start, we stood the chance of having Peter out of action. I urged him to stop and pull the thorns out and disinfect the pricks. He said he was all right, and by this time we had burst on to a much rockier bay and another dump of kerosene drums.

Henry had his camera ready, but the hovercraft was still too far out for filming. Peter squatted on a rock and pulled the spines out of his calf one by one.

This landing by the craft was very slow and painstaking. The bank was a child's box of bricks of tumbled rocks which the rising river had half submerged. Some snags and jags were hardly below the surface, and we could see them through the clear water near the shore – and tiny fish were darting in among them. Candiru? Who could tell in these parts? In spite of the sweltering heat and the tempting clarity of the wine-coloured water, I had no intention of exposing my John Thomas to find out.

The hovercraft engine had been switched off some way out, and she floated deflated and log-like on the surface, slowly inching to the rocky shore. Graham Clarke was visible through the open doorway still sitting at the controls. John Hoyland, Stuart Syrad and Jim Sweeney stood on the catwalks holding coils of rope, fore and aft and centre.

John Hoyland jumped from the bows with a looped rope, leap-frogged from rock to rock over the shallows and found a suitable shrub clump to tie up. Jim Sweeney flung us another rope from aft, and the available expedition members ran it up the stony slope and slowly heaved the dead weight of the hovercraft in. She needed to be within ten feet of the kerosene drums on shore for the hose to reach her tanks (via the tiny pump motor permanently fixed astern). Captain Clarke anxiously peered over the edge of the plenum chamber into the river on the look out for pointed rocks. She came to rest and we all stopped heaving, our shirts black-patched with sweat. Jim Sweeney grabbed a petrol filler nozzle and hose, started the outboard-motor pump engine, while John Hoyland opened the first kerosene drum and inserted the pipe connection. Within a couple of minutes the fuel was being transferred. It was somehow satisfying and reassuring. Like reaching a filling station when your car petrol gauge has been registering zero for some miles.

Meanwhile, in a pattern we were to follow in the days to come, the cook (Conrad Gorinsky) and camp master (Robin Hanbury-Tenison) had organised the off-loading of a trunk-sized wooden food box, broken it open and begun dispensing the comestibles. It was pretty Spartan fare: two dry Ryvita biscuits in cellophane wrappings per man, tinned cheese or salmon or herring to spread on. Our parched throats revolted at first against those cardboard-like oblongs. We needed something wet; our dehydrated bodies cried out for it: we were almost in the situation of Coleridge's Ancient Mariner – 'water, water everywhere, nor any drop to drink' – almost but not quite. I watched with envy while Julio Castillo, the curly-headed, brown Venezuelan boatman, simply waded into the shallows and scooped river-water up to his mouth. If any of us Europeans had done that (especially so near a village), within a couple of days or less our intestines would have put in an uproarious complaint. Fortunately, the BBC party had come prepared. Each of us had brought from England a pint-sized plastic water filter. We had filled them that morning from the hotel taps in Manaus: we steadied them on convenient rocks and worked the piston pump. In principle, these filters are similar to a soda-water syphon. Pressure of air pumped into the plastic container forces the water through a filter-candle guaranteed to remove all impurities and microbes. The only drawback is the two or three minutes needed to produce a cupful of safe drinking water: your thirsting throat can scarcely contain its impatience.

The local inhabitants of Moura – all fifty of them – watched our every movement from the shade of the palms and brushwood. Our strange machine, our incomprehensible language, our curious eating habits fascinated the men, women and children, who gazed intently with un-selfconscious curiosity at any of us who, for the moment, caught their fancy. For them, we were creatures of another world, almost as strange as Martians, and for an hour or two their drab lives (so glamorous to us) were coloured with excitement and they were taken out of themselves like people at play.

I tried a little of my rudimentary Portuguese on some of them and found that they believed we were 'Americanos'. When told we were 'Ingles' they were visibly surprised. 'What?' they said, 'with a machine like that? Did the Americanos make it?'

'No,' I said, 'the Ingles.'

'My, my!' they said – or its equivalent – too polite to state unequivocally that they found it hard to believe me.

I asked where the air-strip was, and one of them pointed with his elbow (the heat was too crushing for any but minimal movements) along a jungle path.

Elmer Reaser and his plane ought to be there by this time – he had, of course, had to make two journeys that morning from Manaus to Moura – one to carry extra fuel, the other to lift two of the scientists.

Together with Bob Saunders, my usually dapper colleague now a little wilted, I set off for the strip. The path led by a couple of palm-thatched shelters open at the sides, past a cluster of meek and friendly dogs, spotted black and brown and white, with stumpy tails and re-sembling smooth-haired terriers. They wagged their stumps, but didn't care for the exertion of a closer inspection, which would have meant leaving their cool shade. Well, one calls it cool; it was probably ninety degrees in the shade, and anything you like to mention out of it. I know the back of my neck and my shoulders were beginning to feel horribly scorched.

The path led immediately in front of the two imposing stuccoed buildings we had seen from the river. I call it path, but it was really a slide of sandy yellow goo, the result of the previous day's torrential rains. As for the buildings, they were a hollow sham, merely a frontage with nothing behind but palms and tangled jungle, a sort of Hollywood set suitable for *Lord Jim*. They held secrets we weren't in a position then to uncover – very early attempts at colonisation? A mission building whose European Fathers had fallen victims to yellow fever? A rubber baron's palace tumbled to ruin after 1911, when the bottom dropped out of the market?

It was really too stifling to think about it.

Then the church – a primitive affair standing next door to the false fronts. Whitewashed inside and out, it was the essence of simplicity – the sort of building the founding fathers of Christianity have set up from Ethiopia to Greenland: a single room with pitched roof, embrasured windows in the thick walls and a dozen rough wooden benches. This did have its embattled tower, four-square and sturdy, with ropes for bells hanging just inside the door. We pushed our noses for a second or two into the comparative cool and then walked on.

The path was narrow, bordered with tall grass up to shoulder height so that you felt enclosed, uncomfortable. Large moths and strange stick insects, disturbed by our passing, flitted out from the matting of dry stalks. It was all so silent and faintly hostile, sinister even. Just the two of us with the river on our left somewhere, and a thousand miles of jungle wilderness on our right. At least, that's how I felt. It was a relief to come out into the cleared space of the air-strip. It was simply hard-packed sand, cleared of jungle, with a couple of serviceable huts for a tiny radio station and generator. In a nearby corner of the forest, quietly rotting away, squatted an abandoned Catalina flying-boat. She had at one time been converted for ground landing and had a pair of fat-tyred wheels and telescopic legs protruding down the side of her belly. Strips of her fabric hung off like old wall-paper.

There was nothing else and nobody.

At least that's what we thought for a minute until we rounded the corner of the radio hut, and (welcome sight) there stood Elmer by the side of his trim red-and-white monoplane. He was stooping over a large square plastic container, into which he was draining gasoline from an auxiliary tank in the wing of his aircraft. He had already completed his two trips from Manaus and seemed surprised we had not encountered his pair of passengers, the scientists David Harris and John Thornes. They had gone off believing the river bank and hovercraft were near by, not realising they had a two-kilometre walk.

Elmer's preparations were against his return. By the time he had finished his mission for us and was backtracking from the Venezuelan border to Manaus his fuel tanks would just about be dry at Moura. This little dump of three ten-gallon containers would see him safely back to the jungle city.

His round pink face glowed even brighter as he stooped over his task. He was wearing a red-and-white square-checked folksy shirt and his usual skull cap with an exaggerated peak. We chatted about his background. He came from Jersey Shore, Pennsylvania, he was thirty-three, married and had two boys and two girls. He had been flying for twelve years and had left his family a thousand miles away in Southern Brazil to help us out. I was curious to know what made him tick and while we waited for the last of the petrol to drain into the container I asked, 'Why do you fly for the missionaries?'

'Well, because I feel that's what the Lord wants me to do.'

Nothing could be more quietly certain than this straightforward declaration of faith. He went on, 'Not all of us are preachers. Some of us like to be mechanics, and we have a natural ability towards those things, and the Lord wants to use that kind of people too, so that's why I'm doing it.'

By this time Elmer had completed his petrol syphoning. He dragged the containers, helped by Bob and me, to the shelter of the bushes, then locked the doors of his plane and left the key in the boot like a housewife leaving the door-key under the mat.

We set off back to the hovercraft, crossing a concrete path leading to the radio-beacon building. Had we been able to see six months into the future, at that moment we should have shivered. For eight or nine piles of human bones, the last remains of an expedition into nearby Indian territory, were going to be heaped along that path.

The sky had clouded over with a high ruckled lid of leaden vapour; sweat stood on us in beads and the air tasted hot. It was nearly three o'clock.

The hovercraft swam in the haze, and the expedition members wilted in the shade near by, drooped over rocks like melted candle-grease men. Some of them had succumbed earlier to the attraction of the river, or rather the steamy heat of the atmosphere had driven them (despite the hazards) into the water. They had dived off the plenum chamber of the hovercraft wearing their underpants, scattering the tiny fish like glittering sparks. Nobody had been 'spiked' by candiru or nibbled by piranha.

It was difficult to discover how real the natural hazards were. I personally was determined not to learn by bitter experience, if possible; and so

I accepted the travellers' tales, until they were proved untrue – even the candiru story told by the French explorer Marcroy a hundred years ago. Marcroy said the Caboclos along the Amazon would whisper in his ear not to stand on the bank and piddle in the river because the candiru had the skill and agility of the salmon and the trout in surmounting waterfalls.

While Bob Saunders and I had gone in search of Elmer, the leaders of the expedition had been persuaded by one of our Brazilians, Colonel Igrejas, that Moura was too unpleasant a spot for a night camp. The Colonel (who had been born in Manaus) knew of a good camp site some six miles farther up the Negro. Now that Elmer and the two scientists were here, it was decided to move at once. Their extra weight was acceptable for such a short distance. Next morning the hovercraft would return to Moura carrying Elmer, Bob Saunders and Henry Farrar our cameraman, who would fly an aerial filming stint as far as our next refuelling point, Barcelos.

So at three p.m. in the afternoon we buzzed noisily away from sleepy Moura, those of its drowsy inhabitants who were still awake rising sluggishly on an elbow to watch us go. Not one yawning dog achieved a bark.

After about five minutes we caught sight of a break in the green jungle wall, a white sandy beach which rose fairly steeply up to three huts on stilts. Jungle began immediately behind the huts, and the ridge on which they stood hung about a hundred feet above the then height of the river. The craft slid on to the sand.

First, we off-loaded our personal packs, using the time-honoured device of the fireman's chain, whereby buckets of water were passed from hand to hand before the days of pumps and hoses. After the packs came the individual plastic sacks holding each man's hammock, ropes, blanket and transparent vinyl sheet for protection against downpours. Mosquito nets had not yet been issued – an oversight which caused one or two murmurs of protest. Lastly came the large wooden chests holding food and pots and pans – since now we were going to have to cook.

We began to lug our private gear up the hot powdery sand towards the huts. The BBC crew had been assigned the one to our left as we struggled away from the river. Bob Saunders dragged his pack alongside me. We both smelt the putrid stench at the same time. 'What is it, Brian?'

'Smells like something dead.'

'Where's it coming from?'

'Up near that bush.'

The musty odour of death was drifting from the carcass of a dog. We finished hauling our baggage to the foot of a flight of wooden steps leading into the end of the hut. Bob said, 'I'm going to get a shovel.' He retraced his steps to the river, slithering down the loose sand, ankle deep, leaving shapeless blobs of foot marks till he reached the hard-packed beach. The others of the twenty were fanning out from the craft up towards the huts, lugging their loads and sweating profusely. At each landing every man in the chain had to catch, snatch and lift forward twenty forty-pound packs, followed by twenty thirty-pound bed rolls, plus any number of assorted parcels. I calculated the handled weight at well over half a ton per man within a period of about ten minutes. In that heat and that humidity it was punishing.

Bob returned with a shovel and quickly covered the maggot-creeping carcass of the dog. The stink rapidly died away.

Henry Farrar, Peter Smith and the *People* reporter Arthur Helliwell joined us. Elmer the pilot came too. Up the steps, the end room of the hut had enough space to sling three hammocks. Inside, in spite of half the walls from the eaves down to waist height consisting only of wire mosquito netting, the atmosphere was muggy. I didn't like the underside of the dry, dusty banana-leaf thatch either, with its promise of animal life from ants to spiders. It's true the floor was five feet off the ground, and that, together with the mosquito-netted door closed, offered protection from snakes and the larger animals such as jaguar. And, of course, there was the weather to consider – the sky had been overcast all day, and a thunderstorm could not be dismissed lightly. However, I myself preferred to sleep outside, slinging my hammock be-tween a couple of trees near the bottom of the steps, for the jungle grew right up to the backs of the huts. Peter Smith joined me. Bob, Henry and Arthur Helliwell elected to sleep in the hut. Elmer had decided to sling his hammock elsewhere – partly, I suspected, not to embarrass us when he said his prayers.

Grey-haired, grey-moustached Arthur Helliwell had been assigned with me (the other grey head) to help our cook, Conrad Gorinsky, with the evening meal and with breakfast the following morning.

So that evening Arthur and I filled large dixies with chopped onions, carrots, potatoes and corned beef to produce a straightforward hash. There was also curry and, afterwards, coffee available.

Then, in the dark, by the help of lantern-light we went to bed. I normally slept without a stitch of clothing on during my month in Amazonas. Pyjamas or night shirts stifle me, cook me alive. So I swung

into my hammock starkers, like any Indian, merely using my blanket
as a pillow and draping a towel over my middle to prevent catching
a chill in the small hours when the temperature usually drops. The sky
had cleared overhead, and as I gazed straight up at it between the
branches I saw a deep, deep blue, almost black, like velvet thickly spat-
tered with fairy frost – the stars. There were so many stars that in places
they seemed to run together in brilliant blobs. In other places individuals flashed and sparked.

I dropped off to sleep registering three things: no mosquitoes; none
of that wild cacophony of jungle noise at night the books all tell about;
and (positively) a far-away rumble of thunder and distant flashes of
lightning. Somebody was having a storm.

When I woke in the grey light of morning I could have been sleeping
out at the bottom of the garden in Henley. There were the beginnings
of the same sort of dawn chorus from the birds that I would have expected at home: first a twitter from an early riser; then an answer; then
two or three getting in on the act, and finally a full continuous burst of
song. It was just as musical too. Obviously, the stories of the Amazon
jungle being denizened by gaudily plumaged birds, brilliant splashes of
red, blue, green and yellow with voices like fog-horns or football-
rattles were not entirely true.

Something was stirring – not in the forest but up the steps in the hut.
It was Arthur Helliwell. During the whole of that trip nobody rose
earlier, washed and shaved sooner, nor presented himself more quietly
ready for duty than Arthur. As the days went on I gradually got to know
him, and the more I knew him, the greater grew my admiration. He
was fifty-nine years old (five years older than me – and in those conditions and that climate five years is a tidy stretch) and perhaps, because of
his age, felt a responsibility to do just that little bit more when it came to
camp chores, lifting and heaving, volunteering for sudden extra duties.
In the worst conditions he always looked spick and span, his wide-
brimmed hat, grey moustache and (as we got farther from barber-
shops) his grey hair beginning to curl in the nape of his neck, all
giving him the look of a benign Southern States colonel. It came as
a shock when later we began to realise that something was wrong
with his health, for stripped to the waist, brown chested, freckle-
armed and with white lather round his chin he looked the picture of
fitness.

He was shaving with his mirror and a mug of water on the third
wooden step from the top. It was cold in my hammock, so I pulled the
soft blanket from under my head and spread it over my naked body. My

battery razor was a-top of my pack, and I reached over the boat-like
side of the hammock to unzip it from its case and begin shaving in
bed.

Ten minutes later I plunged through the warm sand down to the
river to wash.

The water was luke-warm and soft to the touch. The hovercraft lay
quietly half in, half out of the river. I stood on a convenient smooth
stone, soaped myself all over and swilled down with cupped hands. I
still didn't feel like total immersion. Afterwards, on the ridge behind the
dilapidated huts, Arthur and I got the Primus stoves going and cooked
(of all things) porridge, and heated a large dixie of water and powdered
milk to make coffee. Before long people were standing around eating
their Quaker Oats out of tin plates and supping coffee from tin
mugs.

In the half-light Arthur saw something moving in the sand at his feet
and drew attention to it. Elmer, standing next to us, at once lifted his
foot and brought his boot down with a crunch

Startled, those near by turned their heads.

'Tarantula,' said Elmer.

He lifted his heavy jungle boot, and the bunch of angular hairy legs
skittered away – the soft sand had saved it.

'Sure wouldn't love to be bitten by one o' them,' said Elmer.

After breakfast the plan was that the two scientists lifted by Elmer
from Manaus would have seats on the hovercraft, while Bob Saunders
and Henry Farrar, as director and cameraman, would fly with Elmer to
take the first aerial shots of our journey. So Elmer, Bob and Henry
quickly finished their meal, unslung their hammocks, packed their gear
and went aboard. We listened to the roar of the engine and watched
them skim away down river towards Moura and Elmer's plane waiting
quietly on the air-strip. It would take an hour before Graham Clarke
returned with his craft and we had loaded up with our fireman's chain
and Elmer had got his plane overhead in position to photograph our
lift-off. The sight of a hovercraft on shore suddenly rising four or five
feet on its bulging skirt, swinging round and gliding on to the surface
of the water never failed to surprise. It was like a house miraculously
deciding to move; or, in fairly tight shot from the air, as if the
whole landscape of sand, trees and river had begun to slip from
under.

By nine o'clock the hovercraft had reappeared and we were in our
cramped seats again, knees rubbing against the backs of those in front.
Above us, God's representative, Elmer, was in his heaven and, as far as

one could see, all was right with the world. A strange world, certainly, but we were rapidly coming to terms with it. We sped up the black deserted Negro on the second leg of our 2000-mile journey; Barcelos (said to be in the grip of a hepatitis epidemic) our next stop.

Interlude for Death

DURING the past week, while I have been writing the previous account, I have received almost daily letters from Jesco in Brazil with cuttings from the newspapers there reporting the tragic end of a pacification expedition to Indians in the Amazon forest some 180 miles from our starting point, Manaus.

Jesco's first reference was in a letter posted in Brasília on 22nd November 1968 which said, 'I had just sent you a letter, when on the next day the paper brought the news that probably Padre João Calleri and all his companions (twelve, among them two women) were massacred by the Atroari Indians. Now the air force and paratroopers will look for them. But probably will discover just that they have *desaparecido* (disappeared).'

The headline in the enclosed cutting from O *Globo* ran:

INDIOS ATROARIS MASSACRARAM EXPEDIÇÃO DO PADRE CALLERI
(Atroari Indians Massacred Father Calleri's Expedition.)

Previous to this, Jesco had sent me a list of current pacification attempts among Indians in the Amazon forest in areas sometimes a thousand miles apart. Calleri's expedition had been one; another was listed as follows, 'RONDÔNIA [the most westerly province of Brazil]: Francisco Meireles is trying to contact the wild Cintas-Largas Indians, not far from Porto Velho. Also the explorer João Americo Peret is trying to contact in the same region (close to Vilhena) big groups of hostile Indians, probably Cintas-Largas. The reason here is the hostilities between gold and diamond prospectors and the Indians.' In a note, Jesco

added, 'All these efforts are being made simultaneously because the
Indian Service has been re-organised. These contacts are necessary to
protect the tribes from being killed by progressing civilisation (rubber
tappers, gold and diamond hunters, skin hunters and because of some
major road projects the Government needs to build through Indian
lands).'

The situation in Brazil today, as far as the expansion west is concerned, is exactly parallel to that in the United States one hundred and
fifty years ago. In both extensive countries a European population established itself in a comparatively narrow strip the length of the eastern
seaboard. After many years a time comes when circumstances force the
population (expanding in numbers, ideas and desires) to burst its bounds.
Beyond the only bounds it *can* break – its western borders – lie vast
lands full of promise. Unfortunately, these lands are the homeland, the
only land, of the indigenous population of the Americas – wild Indians.
The gulf between the two cultures is unbridgeable. On the one hand,
you have an organised agricultural, industrial, technological business
people whose production of the basic needs of food and clothing has,
through the discovery and practice of agriculture, been relegated to a
tiny minority of their number; such peoples inevitably clump together
in towns and cities, and (as we see in England) the cities inexorably
spread outwards until the logical development will be that they cover
all the available land. On the other hand, there is a people, the wild
Indians, who from time immemorial have been hunters and gatherers,
nomadic, wandering over the face of the earth – needing wide expanses
of prairie and forest to support themselves. True, they go in for a rudimentary agriculture, but this work is not delegated to a section of the
population. The women of the family may do the growing, but in
practice each family provides its own food and clothing, whether from
agriculture, hunting, fishing or gathering.

Everybody knows what happened to the North American Indian.
Fighting a rearguard action, hounded, cheated, shot up, they retaliated
against the 'white-eyes' with barbarous cruelties. Their remnants were
eventually herded into reservations, stoutly refusing to be integrated.

A similar cycle of events appears to be in motion in Amazonia. The
move westwards of the Brazilian *civilisados* got spectacular impetus with
the shifting of the capital in 1957 from Rio de Janeiro to Brasília six
hundred miles to the west. Brasília is not a state capital like São Paulo,
Manaus or even Rio: it is a national capital whose main function is to
act as a hub from which roads will spring like spokes to stretch to every
point on the rim and perimeter of the land. This road building is hap-

pening *now*. Highways are being driven willy-nilly with no permission asked through forests which from time immemorial have belonged to the Indians. The Indian retaliates in the only way known to him: he kills. The Indian knows that in the jungle the law is kill or be killed. He also knows that the most dangerous animal in the jungle is Man. He therefore kills and carves up intruders as savagely as he knows how in order to deter other men. So from *our* side, identifying ourselves, as we do, with 'civilisation', when we hear of Father Calleri's pacification expedition (including a number of women) being 'massacred' and mutilated we are shocked: we forget that such expeditions are the spearhead of an attack by 'civilisation' on the Indians which can only result in their destruction.

'Pacification' of the South American Indians has been going on since Europeans first stepped off the Old World on to the New. In the beginning, the wild children of nature were fleeced of their possessions, especially gold and land, and then they were tortured and enslaved. Those who escaped retreated to the fastnesses of the forest, or, if they were already there, pushed farther into inaccessibility. It is only within the last hundred years that an onslaught is being made by 'civilisation' towards the heartland of the Brazilian and Venezuelan Indians. Rubber-tappers, gold and diamond prospectors, skin hunters, missionaries, pioneers and renegades of every kind have left civilisation to exploit or help or to winkle a living, and if possible a fortune, out of the fringes and now the depths of the forest. To most of these intruders (as in the days of the Indian Wars in North America) the only good Indian is a dead Indian, and many shoot on sight. The forest Indians have retaliated in exactly the same way. Governments have stepped into the conflict out of shame. Just as the American Congress did, they have organised Indian protection services. In the wrong hands an Indian protection service becomes a quick Indian destruction service: even in the best of hands it seems inevitable that the destruction can only be slowed down. This very year, 1968, the main branch of the Brazilian Indian Protection Service was disbanded after a scandal. It appeared that an organised extermination of Indians had been perpetrated. As a result of the recent rehabilitation of the Service, at least half a dozen different pacification attempts are being made at once. Father Calleri's ill-fated expedition is but one. Another, which I have also mentioned, is that led by Francisco Meireles far west into the territory of the Cintas-Largas. The *Journal do Brasil* on Tuesday 26th November 1968 reported on the heels of the news of Father Calleri's death that 'the jungle expert Francisco Meireles with forty men appears to have been lost in the Amazon forest.

The last news was when he was 120 miles from Vilhena outpost and about to approach the Cinta-Larga tribe. According to the Inspector of the National Foundation for the Indians in Rondônia "the possibility that Francisco Meireles' expedition has foundered is a very grave one".

Reading these reports, I have felt myself personally involved for a number of reasons. First, Calleri was slaughtered only 180 miles from our base at Manaus; and if we returned from our hovercraft trip there had been talk that we might join him to film his 'pacification'. Then, Francisco Meireles was one of the last Indian Protection Service men we met in Brazil before returning to England. I quote from my diary dated 22 May 1968: 'Today we had a chance of seeing Goiania, founded only 33 years ago and growing like mad – skyscrapers pushing up in the city centre like mushrooms. Much more peopled than Brasília, human, alive.

'In the morning we met an old friend of Jesco's from the recently discredited Indian Protection Service, now disbanded after proven charges of exterminating Indians by shooting and dynamiting and infecting with white man's diseases such as measles. This friend, Francisco Meireles, is a dedicated man of about 50, bony, dark-complexioned, black, greying hair and Latin moustache – very sad at what has befallen the Protection Service but not himself connected with the genocide – quite the reverse.

'Meireles was the man who pacified the Xavante Indians and who has given his life to bettering the Indian condition. He told me (Jesco acting as interpreter) what happened to Richard Mason, the young English student killed by Indians in 1961. Mason had come into my office – the Travel and Exploration office of the BBC at Ealing Film Studios – before leaving for Brazil. He had asked me for an advance of money on film he was hoping to shoot; but having no previous knowledge of his filming capabilities, I had to decline, simply offering to view his film when he returned to Britain. Of course, Mason never did return. The Indians killed him. Meireles said that Mason had contacted him in Brazil and asked for advice which had been freely given but unfortunately not taken. Mason (according to Meireles) and his party took as guides and helpers people with little or no experience of wild Indians. They flew to Cachimbo and went forward to contact Indians. They made a base camp and were watched for some days in secret by a band of Kreen Akorore Indians. Meireles knew this because the day after it was learnt that Mason had been killed he flew into the jungle to retrieve the body. Meireles spoke to the locals, who had acted as guides and who protested that there were no Indians about. The experienced backwoodsman Meireles said there were plenty of signs betraying the presence of many Indians in that part of the forest. He found the camping place of the hunting party who had spied on Mason and his friends without their knowledge, and he deduced from the semi-decayed state and number of piles of human excreta that the Kreen Akorore had been watching for some days.

'These Indians are still unpacified and tomorrow evening, Adrian Cowell and Claudio Villas Boas are beginning yet another attempt to make a first successful contact with them to turn them into friends. Even their real name – what they call themselves – is not known. The Kreen Akorore has been given to them by other Indians and means "the men who wear their hair cropped".

'The Kreen Akorore clearly thought Mason's party were *garimpeiros* or *seringueiros*, prospectors and rubber-tappers, who regard Indians as natural enemies to be hunted and killed – a sentiment reciprocated by the Indians. They would hesitate to attack the party congregated together, but when Mason left camp on his own to fetch further supplies they simply padded after him silently, barefoot, through the forest and at a convenient distance from his friends, shot arrows into his body. After that they clubbed him and broke his limbs. Meireles told me that Mason received three arrow wounds any one of which would have proved fatal. They shot other arrows into his flesh and left their weapons by his corpse – to take the blame of the killing.

'A tragic affair, and Meireles was as much moved by the telling of it as we were listening to it. Both for the Indians and for Mason since it need never have happened. . . . '

So reads my diary. For the last ten years I have had contacts at one remove with the problem of the South American Indians who don't, won't, can't fit into the city life, the *civilisado* life of modern Brazil. My first contacts came through Adrian Cowell, a young film maker just out of University, who together with Jesco filmed stories on the Indians of the Xingú River, a southern tributary of the Amazon. Along the Xingú, the brothers Villas Boas have created a huge natural reservation into which, over a period of twenty years, they have attracted complete tribes of Indians whom they first had to 'pacify'. 'Whole tribes' sounds formidable, but many tribes had been reduced to a handful by fierce fighting with others, by the harsh conditions of jungle life, by wife-stealing and child kidnapping, by being killed by white intruders, by white man's diseases – childish things like measles, influenza – contracted from the intruders and against which they had no natural immunity. One such tribe, the Suyá, with whom Jesco lived alone for two years, had been reduced to sixty-five survivors. Another tribe, like the Caiabi, Jesco rescued in three canoes from slavery among *garimpeiros* and *seringueiros* in a nightmare journey lasting a week down the Manitsaua-Missu river – a story we told in the film *Incident in the Matto Grosso*.

But before such rescues can be brought about, the wild tribes have first to be 'pacified', they have to be contacted and made to believe that *these* contacting white men do not wish to steal their women and shoot their men; that the presents of sugar have not been laced with arsenic nor the food with typhoid; that, in fact, these white men are their one hope of protection, of survival – at least for a time. We told the story of one pacification in a unique film shot by Jesco which we called *Contact with a Hostile Tribe*. It showed, just as it happened, exactly how the two Villas Boas brothers, Orlando and Claudio, made their attempts to pacify the savage Txicão – savage in the respect that they had previously killed and mutilated all intruders who fell into their hands – just as the Atroaris and Cintas-Largas have done in these past weeks to Padre Calleri and possibly Francisco Meireles and their helpers.

A pacification takes months, often years, to bring about. Take, as an example, the Txicão. For months the Villas Boas brothers had known roughly of their whereabouts from reports of killings and women-stealing the Txicão had practised on two tribes, the Aura and Yaualapiti, already pacified by the brothers. Things got so bad the Brazilians could wait no longer. They made a reconnaissance over the jungle in a light plane from their airstrip at Diauarum, an outpost they themselves had rooted up from the forest. Quartering the monotonous expanse of leafy green, near tree-top height, below them their plane's shadow roller-coasting over the uneven jungle cover, they at last found a cluster of broken patches – the Txicão village and its gardens.

They saw tiny figures of people round the single large *maloca* or communal hut with its curious new-moon-shaped roof-ridge.

They dropped presents from the open window of the plane – fish-hooks, beads, knives.

The Txicão were running this way and that like ants in the open space round their *maloca*, seeming to be picking the presents up.

From a couple of hundred feet the observers could see a clearing in the forest which appeared free of tree stubs, fallen trunks and branches; it was grassy and tolerably smooth; they reckoned that it would be possible to land a plane there – at risk, certainly, but a risk they were willing to take – later, not this time; they would let the presents work first.

So they came back in a couple of weeks with two light planes and eight helpers, including Indians already becoming *civilisados* and Jesco with his cameras to film the actual contact.

Burly, moustached Orlando Villas Boas, stripped to the waist, ordered everyone to keep inside the planes after landing until he himself had tested the situation.

Both planes touched down safely. But the Txicão were nowhere to be seen.

The propellers ceased turning and silence fell over the clearing, broken only by the occasional creak of a leather seat as the occupants of the aeroplanes craned this way and that. It was hot and sweaty inside the cramped cabins. A sharp metallic echoing clang startled everyone. Nerves were edgy. It was Orlando opening one of the plane doors. He carefully got out and stood in the shadow of the wing.

His brother Claudio, bearded and moustached, wearing surprised horn-rimmed spectacles under a panama hat, followed him.

Although they could see no one, they knew they were being watched.

The cooling aeroplane engines ticked now and then as the metal shrank, and wafts of sickly sweet high-octane fuel puffed in through the open windows.

God, it was hot! Shirts and pants were darkening with sweat.

Orlando held up an arm calling for attention, for caution, for no noise. He had seen movement in the edge of the trees. Then the others saw. A glint of sunlight on the smooth bamboo shaft of a spear, pale yellow-brown bodies standing out from the shadow and the green. The Indians were armed.

Orlando walked from the planes towards the wall of trees. Under his arm he had a bundle of knives, machetes. This was the moment of truth. Would he be met with a shower of arrows and spears? His companions waited with breath held tight in.

Slowly Orlando walked on. He was wearing only a pair of bulky shorts and a floppy forage hat. His friends could see his broad freckled back and his stout bare calves. But the Indians were interested in his bundle. He stopped and held up a machete towards the line of trees. He stooped and deliberately laid down one knife after another, then he backed away until he was half-way to the planes again.

Like rabbits timidly leaving the shelter of their burrows, two men and then a third of the Txicão slowly edged away from the forest towards the knives. All the time they kept a sharp eye on Orlando. Sometimes they looked back over their shoulders and beckoned to others to follow.

Orlando stood still as a stone.

The first Txicão man, completely naked, small in comparison with the Brazilians, but armed with a bow and arrows taller than himself, reached the machetes. He transferred the bow to his left hand and the arrows under his left armpit. He bent to pick up a knife with his right hand. He saw it was in a sheath. He glanced at Orlando. He put down his bow and arrows on the grassy tumps by his bare toes. Near. Ready to take up swiftly. He drew the machete from its broad leather scabbard and held the blade in the air so that the sun flashed from it – a sign which his companions behind him could not resist. Two other young men followed until the little bundle had been claimed. Those with nothing stood looking expectantly towards the planes.

Orlando and Claudio quickly unloaded more presents, and soon the area around the two flying machines was milling with Txicão. They were still timid, snatching presents like zoo monkeys snatch nuts proffered by spectators and then darting back to examine what they had got.

The Brazilians, by signs, asked for bows and arrows in return. Once the Txicão could be persuaded to make such gifts, the contact could be regarded as successful. But they were reluctant, afraid, and they refused.

Two pretty girls, mothers already with babies slung under their arms and sucked on to their breasts, were chattering loudly to each other and pointing to Orlando. Their black hair was cut short in a round bob, their dark eyes had an eastern slant, and their light-brown shapely bodies were without a stitch of clothing. They couldn't have been much more than thirteen years of age. One of them pulled Orlando by the elbow and gazing up into his face kept repeating, 'Aura! Aura!'

He was puzzled. These were Txicão, not Aura. Then he noticed a tiny scar on the smooth skin of the girl's upper arm. It was a vaccination mark. A vaccination against smallpox which could only have been given at the Villas Boas' post at Diauarum. This girl was an Aura – as she kept reiterating. Then Orlando remembered her face. She and her companion had been kidnapped by Txicão warriors some years before and were now wives and mothers in their adoptive tribe. Orlando put his arms round both mother and baby. They stood hugging and laughing together in the middle of that strange tableau – the first successful contact of white men with the fierce Txicão Indians. For now the warriors were prepared to make presents in return of their spears, bows and arrows. As always, it had been touch and go at first, but the machetes and then the two young wives who recognised Orlando and Claudio had done the trick.

Of course, the successful contact was only the first step towards pacification. The two planes flew off after a few hours, and it was almost a

year later that the second contact was made by a larger expedition in
canoes with outboard motors.

Now, two years later, the Txicão have been gathered into the fold
at Diauarum and are living fairly peaceably with their former mortal
foes the Aura and Yaualapiti. For a time they will be protected from
outsiders and from each other in the extensive Xingú 'Parque' or reserve. But what is sacrosanct about a reserve, whether it is for animals or
men, when the pressure of rapidly changing events associated with so-
called 'civilisation' begins to crowd the barriers? Unless the Indians can
assimilate themselves into the culture of the whites they will be wiped
out as their forest is cleared away. In any case, even if they do assimilate,
they will become but a strain in the new population of Brazil and Venezuela: it is inevitable that, in time, the way of life of the jungle Indians
of South America must be lost for ever.

Because of my interest in these events, satisfied up to now only at one
remove, I had determined when I heard of the hovercraft expedition to
make use of it to see and film the forest Indian. Just how I should be able
to bring this about I did not know at that time. But I did realise there
was danger in it.

NOTE

Further news of the Meireles' and Calleri's expeditions continued to
arrive with each post. *O Globo* and *O Jornal* reported on 2nd December
that Meireles' disappearance had only been reported and not real: his
radio had broken down and taken five days to mend. As for Father
Calleri, *O Globo* had a full page of the most tragic and horrifying
photographs I have ever seen. The first showed a pile of bones on the
leafy forest floor with a human skull resting on top. This was all the
physical remains of one of the party. It seems that the Atroari Indians
strip the entire fleshy covering from their victims and burn it; but how
they could have produced, in so short a time, a broken skeleton of polished bones and shining skull was to me a puzzle. Not a shred of skin or
tissue or muscle and hardly a hair remained and the bones looked at if
they had lain a thousand years to be burnished by nature and time. Why
the Atroaris do this is another puzzle. My guess would be to lay the
spirit of the dead man and prevent his haunting them by walking again
in the flesh.

The second photograph showed two paratroopers of the rescue
group about to stow the bones and skull in a sack.

The third picture was a large close-up of Father Calleri's own skull
held to the chest of an Air Force man. High domed and with tremen-

dous dark eye-sockets, the head had been identified as the priest's by the particular conformation of certain gold teeth.

Other of O Globo's photographs showed two paratroopers carrying a sack slung from a pole between their shoulders as they walked by an Indian hut to their helicopter; but most chilling and macabre of all was that depicting eight heaps of higgledy-piggledy bones surmounted each by an upright skull arranged neatly at intervals on a concrete path. In this way had eight members of Father Calleri's pacification expedition been carefully accounted for. And the concrete path led on to an air-strip hacked from the jungle, while in the background was the long ragged wing of a Catalina. It was the air-strip at Moura where we had helped Elmer to syphon his petrol. Of the two women there was no sign.

The headlines suggested that the attack had been made with the sole purpose of capturing the women. Local *garimpeiros* and *seringueiros* who know that part of the jungle are reported as saying that a great scarcity of women among the Atroaris and Waimeris forces the men into continual wife-stealing and into marrying little girls of nine and ten years old. An even more startling rumour from the same source says that the Atroari tribe has split into two parts and that the Chief of each of these groups is a white man.

How this will all turn out remains to be seen. Jesco is asking the BBC to commission him to film the next attempt (which must be soon if the women are to be rescued) to contact the Atroaris. The new expedition will be led by another Brazilian explorer mentioned in Jesco's first letter to me, namely João Americo Peret.

CHAPTER THREE

Lost

WE heard the hovercraft a long way off as it returned from Moura to pick us up. It buzzed in the distance like a persistent bee, and when we first saw it, a black speck on the sharp horizon of the slate-blue river, it was no bigger than a bee. Apart from the craft, the blank expanse of the Negro was empty, void: since we had left Manaus no boat had passed us, we had overtaken no boat – for all we knew we were alone on that wilderness of water. That morning there wasn't even a bird in the sky or a ring made by a pouting fish on the glassy surface of the river to suggest life other than our own in this sequestered backland.

It was seven twenty a.m. and our sandy beach with the loaded and waiting hovercraft suddenly exploded into life.

Elmer rocketed from the jungle at tree-top height, his red-and-white Cessna a contrast of colour and noise in that grey-green silent world.

Two of the BBC film crew were up there with him shooting our departure. Elmer had removed the door from the port side of his plane and I could clearly see Henry Farrar with the movie-camera up to his head.

For the next half hour as we travelled the aeroplane made runs and passes at various heights and in various directions to enable Henry to film. Some of the most effective shots (as we found later) were those

where the plane would track low over the jungle canopy and unexpec-
tedly approach the river, with the hovercraft suddenly revealed, speed-
ing along its dark shiny surface; always surprising, too, were the high
shots from three or four thousand feet which showed the forest stretching
from horizon to horizon with the braided river looping in curlicues
across it, and at first no hovercraft to be seen. Then you would become
aware of a speck with a white tail (as I say) a spermatozoon seeking to
fertilise the secret passageways of a continent.

I could imagine Henry in the plane with his black hair whipped back
and forth in the fierce wind as he leaned against his safety straps to hold
a steady shot on the river. No doubt it was cold up there with the slip-
stream of the whirling propeller pressing his shirt and trousers round
his limbs and body like the wet clothes of a man fished out of the sea.
Bob Saunders was with him, a brave fellow whose nervous disposition
gave him little liking for heights, but who was prepared to spur himself into any risky situation for the good of the cause.

The two expedition members who had joined us in the hovercraft
(taking over Henry and Bob's seats) were David Harris and John
Thornes, geographers. David Harris was dark and handsome, quietly
spoken, fluent and expressive, betraying (I would guess) Welsh ancestry.
John Thornes, on the other hand, had one of the most penetrating West
Riding voices I have ever heard (and I've heard a lot – being born and
bred there and speaking that way myself). In any group, at any time,
you had no difficulty in knowing at once that John was there – it was
simply the presence or absence of the Ilkley Moor sound which told
you. He was, in fact, from Wakefield.

After half an hour of passes, Elmer rose in front of us like a swan
taking off and headed north-west above the river. He had used as much
fuel as he deemed wise and was making for Barcelos with its landing
strip, our fuel dump (we trusted) and its hepatitis epidemic.

News of this outbreak of yellow jaundice had been cabled to London
by David Smithers a week before we were due to set out. His wire also
contained a plea for inoculation. This particular injection is a massive
one (as injections go) and left a lump the size of an egg on my left arm.
Hepatitis was the sixth disease we had been jabbed or dosed against,
the others being smallpox, typhoid, tetanus, yellow fever and malaria.
Dysentery there appeared to be nothing we could do about, except take
specifics when we had contracted it. Of course, we were lucky. Amazonian travellers in the past have died from disease like flies. Think, for
instance, of what happened to the hundreds of engineers and navvies
lured into the Amazon jungles by the fanatical enthusiasm of that

American Civil War veteran, Colonel George Earl Church. As we scooted along that early morning in April, one island after another passing our windows, some near, some far, some only a dark grey distant line, some glowing green as the sun hit them almost horizontally – as we bounded forward I thought of restless Colonel Church. He was an enthusiast in the seventeenth-century meaning of that word – a fanatic that you damned well needed to watch; and about 1870 he focussed his fanaticism on Bolivia. He told anyone interested enough to listen that Bolivia was potentially the richest country in South America, nay, in the whole wide world; and that Bolivia, rendered practically incommunicado by the Andes in the west and two thousand miles of jungle to the east, only needed a railway as an 'open sesame' to a far richer Ali Baba's cave than ever appeared in the Arabian Nights. Now, the shrewd businessmen of this world, who are always looking for a fast buck and are therefore at the mercy of a convincing enthusiast and more than willing to put their trust in his magic password or rub-of-the-lamp, poured money ($6,000,000 as a matter of fact) into the Colonel's scheme to drive a railroad – the Madeira–Marmoré railroad – through the jungle barrier between Bolivia and that part of Brazil towards which we were now heading. This God-forsaken back-of-beyond, which a Brazilian author christened *o inferno verde*, 'the green hell', had always been notorious for fever. That didn't daunt an English engineering company from undertaking to run his railway line wherever the Colonel wanted – provided they saw the colour of his cash; and in 1872 they sent the first materials up the Amazon to San Antonio by the small schooner *Silver Spray*.

Her captain and some of her officers died on the way.

They were merely the first casualties.

Within a twelvemonth the English surrendered to the jungle, the company having accepted the fact that 'the country was a charnel-house, their men dying like flies, that the road ran through an inhospitable wilderness of alternating swamp and porphyry ridges, and that with the command of all the capital in the world, and half its population, it would be impossible to build the (rail) road'.

Colonel George Church was a New Englander, and the word 'impossible' was not included in his vocabulary. He himself had cut the first sod of the Madeira–Marmoré railway on 1st November 1871 while wondering Indians watched. For him, this represented Progress; for them, if it came off, eventual destruction – not yet, in 1968, utterly achieved. Even after the engineering company threw in the sponge, there was still money in the kitty, still enough of the original $6,000,000 left, and a new contract was awarded, this time to an American firm, Messrs P. and T. Collins of Philadelphia. There was no nonsense here. Collins undertook to build a metre-gauge railway within three years, a pledge which sent their local Press into euphoric delirium, the *Eagle* asserting that 'two Philadelphians are to overcome the Madeira rapids, and open up to the world a land as fair as the Garden of the Lord'. And when the steamer *Mercedita* with fifty-four engineers and material left for San Antonio on 2nd January 1878 the morning papers in Philadelphia proudly drew attention to the fact that strong men, as well as women and children, sobbed aloud on the steamship's departure. Nor was their weeping premature, though it arose from proud emotion and not (if they could have seen into the future) from grief. Of the 941 men who left for San Antonio at different times, 221 lost their lives, a far higher mortality rate than that of the American Civil War in which Church had won his colonelcy. To the English graves already smothered over by the forest there was added a large complement of American ones. The region was so difficult of access that supplies were slow in getting through. The Company doctors made their daily forlorn rounds pretending to give quinine when all they had to offer was a deception concocted from flour and water. The situation was parlous and was further worsened when a supply ship was completely lost: starvation followed sickness. Once again, the primitive jungle defeated the civilised men, and the railway undertaking collapsed. The huts, workshops and short length of metre-gauge line laboriously laid were quietly strangled by the creepers and vines. And along with the abandoned men and material, the Company also left behind in San Antonio a pathetic little coffee-pot locomotive called Baldwin. The contractors, Collins, had in fact used Baldwin to inaugurate the six kilometres – four miles – of laid line on 4th July 1879 when, puffing jubilant smoke, he did a spectacular leap from the rails. He was left to lie, poor Baldwin, for twenty-eight years until 1907, when yet another US railroad company arrived and found him practically creeper-covered, doing service as a hencoop, his water-tender being used as a slipper bath. The loving American engineers took him to their repair shop at Porto Velho, where they replaced his stolen whistle, bell and numerous other missing parts. By 1912 Baldwin was as good as new, and they reckoned he was due for a new name, so they rechristened him 'Colonel Church' – though that restless spirit had himself steamed into his terminus at No. 216 Cromwell Road, London, England, two years before on 4th January 1910.

A rapid change in the noise of the hovercraft engine brought me back to the present. The bull-like roar had suddenly stopped, and we were slowly coming to a halt and sinking to the river's surface, our deflated skirt rumpling round us.

'What's up, then?' people were saying.

'Nothing to be alarmed about, gentlemen,' said the captain, looking round over his shoulder from the driving seat. 'Just stopping to check our bearings.'

There was a rustle of maps and charts up front among the guides and helpers – Stuart Syrad, Robin Tenison and the two Brazilian observers Captain Perez and Colonel Igrejas.

The fact is, we were lost.

I had previously noted in my diary that the river banks appeared to be closing in on us. No more did we have those vistas between islands of hooded shores obviously miles and miles away. Now the jungle walls were pressing close, rather like the story of the terrible bed – where the walls move in and the bed top comes down on the trapped traveller at the inn. I had written in my diary, 'Much tangled jungle, not very high but with a scribble of lianas. River narrowed by nine a.m. to perhaps half a mile.'

You'd hardly think it possible to be able to get lost while travelling along a river. But this river is no ordinary one. As I have said, round about here it is twelve miles across, and the rising waters had made the banks change daily, while the numerous islands in the middle never stayed the same from one year end to another. If you could film a time-lapse sequence of the Amazon and her tributaries over a five-year period, that great river system would seem to thrash wildly backwards and forwards, looping and leaping over half a continent like a colossal cat-o'-nine-tails. Seen from the air by Elmer, Bob and Henry, the Negro looked like a gargantuan maze, a colossal skein of blue-black wool flung higgledy-piggledy over the jungle by a Fate grown tired of knitting: and crawling up one of the strands a helpless flea – the tiny hovercraft.

We couldn't afford to get lost: or if we did, we couldn't afford to charge backwards and forwards for any length of time finding our way. We just didn't have the fuel for it. I believe that on average, for any leg of the run between dumps we had a safety margin of about one hour's fuel.

I quote again from my diary, scribbled on my knee as events unfolded: '9.05 a.m. saw four parrots – two and two flying fairly high over jungle on left. Took a wrong turning and retraced our path from a dead end. Forest with water all round us at about 400 yards in what appears to be every direction – as though we are in a lake. Trees standing with water over their boots.

'9.30 a.m. Still lost. Lianas drooping into river like cables anchoring the floating trees.

'10.15 a.m. Still lost. Stopped to pump fuel from port tanks (which are full) to starboard tanks (just about empty) in order to trim the craft's balance. Sombody suggested that Elmer (long since flown ahead) might be anxious that we hadn't shown up at Barcelos. Douglas Botting corrected this to "curious", Elmer being a man least likely to become anxious.'

We really were in something of a pickle. Anybody who has got thoroughly lost in Hampton Court Maze will know the frustrated coming-to-the-boil feeling. I felt for Graham Clarke, whose isolation in responsibility became apparent for the first time. When we stopped, everybody at once broke out into beads of sweat; when we ran, we were fruitlessly wasting fuel. Occasionally, at a stop, Graham gave permission for the expedition members to scramble outside on to the catwalks. The air was clammy and the water slapped against the buoyancy tanks underneath with an oily noise. The curved metal roof of the cabin burnt your bare elbows if you leaned too far back.

At ten-thirty a.m. I reported again in my diary 'still lost'; a few minutes afterwards somebody called attention to a movement about a mile away where the river and jungle met. Those who were still outside the stationary hovercraft were called in, and Graham Clarke swung the huge machine towards the tiny something that moved. As we came near enough to recognise it for what it was, it moved quicker and jinked away from us: it was, in fact, a dugout canoe with the usual banana-leaf canopy and outboard motor. The three young Caboclos aboard that canoe must have had the fright of their lives. The noisy monster roaring down at them was something out of a nightmare or another, to them, more frightening world than the Amazon – for all its deadly creatures. So the canoe took avoiding action, but we skidded round, and after a zig-zag or two the occupants gave in.

What an anti-climax for the three coppery-skinned men in tattered khaki pants and frayed straw hats when one of our Brazilian observers stepped through the open hatch and asked, 'Which is the way to Barcelos, please?'

Imagine a flying saucer landing beside a remote Yorkshire road up Blubberhouses way where a solitary shepherd is tending his sheep: the hatch opens and one of the crew calls, 'Can you tell me the way to Halifax, please?'

This was the comparable situation the three boatmen found themselves in. What made them even more surprised and mystified was the knowledge they had that Barcelos was only just round the corner, so to speak. They all pointed at once and watched us sheer away with evident relief.

By eleven a.m. we had reached what was once the capital of Brazilian Amazonas. Some periwigged bureaucrat in eighteenth-century Portugal had stuck a pin in a map and decreed that a city should be built here in the middle of nowhere. In two hundred years it had spread no farther into the jungle than the width of two streets. The houses stood some thirty feet above the river along the top of a steep clayey bank. The most imposing edifice was the mission, whose church had a tall tower with a pyramid top. The other buildings were mainly single-storey dwellings of concrete with corrugated tin roofs.

A large trading launch, a sort of house-boat, was already half aground, and people were buying supplies from a balcony at the stern. Some had paddled there in canoes, others were tightrope-walking along dog-legged gangplanks set up for the purpose. Everybody turned their heads and stared. In a couple of minutes crowds of children began to run down some wide concrete steps towards the water's edge and the hovercraft. We got out and patted their heads like benign Stanleys on our way to discover Livingstone.

A little olive-skinned boy with black straight hair and slant eyes was wearing a once white T-shirt with across his chest a British Lion in top-hat confronting a Brazilian footballer. The caption under the picture said in Portuguese, 'In London the Brazilian team will knock 'em cold.'

We were desperately thirsty, and Stuart Syrad and Robin Tenison split the ends off green coconuts with their machetes and handed them round. The milk was cool, delicious and thirst quenching – it was also, if you drank too much, mildly aperient.

Elmer, our missionary pilot, turned up, pink and baby-faced, together with Henry Farrar and Bob Saunders. Elmer's next flight would take him to Waupés almost at the Brazilian border, for there was no air-strip at the next hovercraft stop, Taparucuará, where we were due to spend the night.

We knew there were rapids at Waupés, and I wanted Henry the cameraman aboard the hovercraft to film our passage over them. Peter Smith, our sound recordist, volunteered to take Henry's place on the plane. He unshipped his hold-all and bedding and prepared to join Elmer and Bob Saunders for a night at the mission.

The fuel had been pumped from the drums into the hovercraft's tanks, and after only ninety minutes we were sheering off from the bank and waving goodbye. For most of us, it had been simply a case of 'hail and farewell' at Barcelos. Whether there was really a hepatitis epidemic there we never found out.

CHAPTER FOUR

Taparucuará

I⊤ had begun to rain just before we zoomed away from Barcelos. The jumbo windscreen wipers on all three large front windows were kept at it swishing the tropical-size raindrops away. We had reached Barcelos at noon and stayed only an hour and a half – time to eat the usual snack of dry biscuits piled with tinned salmon, herring and cheese plus a handful of fruity raisins. I forgot to mention that into my own green coconut I had poured a large glug of Barcardi rum. My nearest lunch companions needed no persuasion to join me: the heady mixture of coconut milk and cane alcohol was delicious and inspiriting. I looked forward to what lay ahead and I didn't even mind the rain. Anyway, by two o'clock the rain had stopped and the clouds dispersed.

We were skittering along near fifty miles an hour, and on our right we began to pass extensive strands of yellow-white sand. Apart from this, the jungle and river never changed: we never saw sign of human or animal along the banks, and we never passed a boat – we could have been the first explorers on a deserted planet.

Because the long yellow sand beaches continued to flash by I was reminded of the Vikings who first discovered and sailed down the coast of North America. It's told in the Saga of Thorfinn Karlsefni how, round about A.D. 1,000, two open boats with square sails crept south along a coast with such endless shores of yellow sand that the crews nicknamed that region *Furthurstrandar* – 'Wonder Beaches'.

I noted in my diary: '3.15. Rode up on to an extensive sandbank and stopped to transfer fuel and stretch legs. Sand blazing white and large grained. One single small shrub-like tree in an area the size and shape of a race track. Various prints including turtle and alligator. Graham Clarke, the captain, said such sandbanks in mid-stream ought by now to be covered with water and he had some doubt whether we should be able to negotiate all the rapids. We need more water to cover the rocks or at least to reduce obstacles to below 4′ 6″. A house-size rock with flood markings painted on in metres at our last overnight stop (Moura) was still completely out of the water.'

Everybody wandered away from the craft singly or in groups. The sandbank was egg-shaped and almost as smooth as an egg. From end to end it measured perhaps three-quarters of a mile. I walked slowly towards the down-river tip, where a channel of water eighty feet wide separated the island from the jungle of the river bank – or maybe just another tree-covered island, it was impossible to tell at water level. Looking back, in the distance I saw the sharp shapes of the craft, an open black umbrella and scattered expedition members etched against the brilliant blank expanse. At my feet, a line of turtle marks ran like the imprints of a tractor-tyre into the dark pellucid water. The air was oven-hot. Suddenly I felt an overwhelming sense of loneliness, of hostility in that strange exotic scene. How did I know whether or not a snouting cayman, reptilian, saurian, dragging with it echoes of a pre-historic, extinct world would crawl from the depths and pull me down? A quarter of a mile away someone was now strolling with his umbrella up to ward off the brazen blows of the sun. I turned to join my companions. When I reached them there was a sense of comradeship and common purpose, of refuge.

'Right, gentlemen!' called the pilot in a sort of 'any more for the Skylark?' voice: 'Will you take your seats please? It's getting on and we have to reach Taparucuará before nightfall!' We obediently trooped back up the landing-craft style gangway into our Ark, journalists, geographers, soldiers, film makers, a botanist, a river-pilot, an electrician, an engineer and a farmer. It was perhaps a quarter to four in the afternoon and we had some seventy-five miles still to go. Graham waited for Stuart Syrad to pull up the gangway and shut down the hatch with a two-inch space for the breeze to enter by, then he started the engine. The 'roaring turtle' gathered a gigantic bellyful of wind under her carapace, rose smartly from the sand and in a billow of swirling yellow dust moved off this Never-Never-Land of a beach on to the brown bosom of the Negro. I settled myself into my cramped bus-seat three down on the starboard side behind the pilot. There was little room for my feet, for I had my bulging haversack on the floor with immediate daily requirements, such as changes of underwear, spare shirt, socks, razor, soap, toilet roll, brush and comb, vitamin pills, salt tablets, insect repellant, the long Medieval English poem *Sir Gawayne and the Grene Knyghte*, a navy blue lightweight nylon rain anorak and over-pants to match, two tins of sardines, Dickens' novel *Barnaby Rudge*, a tightly rolled bright yellow oilskin cyclist's cape and sou'wester, a rubber-covered waterproof torch, some boxes of matches, spare rolls of colour and black-and-white film for my still camera, knife, fork and spoon, an aluminium plate and mug. On the seat beside me I had my two bottles of Bacardi rum, neither of them full any longer, and my Minolta camera borrowed for the purpose from my married son John. Hooked on the back of the seat in front of me was my umbrella. This really was packing everything but the kitchen stove. Nevertheless, I regretted none of these articles; they were all not only useful but essential. My diary on my knee, I scribbled with my ballpoint pen, '4.45 p.m. Whichever way I look there is a blank wall of jungle, a solid mass of trees: it varies only in height – the farther away, the narrower the band separating the monotonous river from the almost as monotonous sky. Here, the part of the river we are in is still over a mile wide.

'5.15 p.m. arrived at Taparucuará: mission buildings dominate the usual palm or banana-thatched huts and shelters. Landed on a sandy beach on the north bank of the river from which a rutty sort of sunken road gently slopes upwards to the mean level of the surrounding open ground. There is coarse grass, a few coconut palm trees, a rudimentary hut village through which the track wanders in the direction of a large group of solid, even imposing, mission buildings, white with red tiled roofs, covering several acres.

'We formed our usual fireman's chain and off-loaded our gear from hand to hand under the steadfast, unblinking gaze of two to three hundred people in what appeared to be their Sunday best. The majority of them were children, which prompted Stuart Syrad to comment that in these remote parts whatever they did, they certainly did one thing. The bright reds and blues of the women's and girl's frocks, their coppery skins and dark eyes, their shapely bare legs and feet splashed with sand splodges after rain contrasted warmly with the green of the woods and the grey of the sky. Before we left the beach, crowded as a bank holiday at Blackpool, we encountered two or three of the locals quite "market fresh" with drink on account of Good Friday, I suppose. One of them very volubly expressed his opinion (in Portuguese plain enough for us to understand) that the rapids ahead were "very hot, very strong" and that the hovercraft stood no chance at all of getting over them and we were all mad.

'We trooped up to the mission of Santa Izabel carrying our hold-alls rather like resigned holiday-makers plodding from the railway station to their lodgings. The mission at Taparucuará is a vast complex – the walk through the mission buildings to the hospital where we were to sleep being almost as lengthy as the walk from the beach to the mission. Everything spotlessly clean. A middle-aged nun, originally from Italy, lighted a brass lamp (given to her as a personal present, she said, once long ago) and showed us typical hospital iron beds in rows – sheets clean, cool and snowy – beds beautifully made – lavatories – showers. She said there would be roast pork for dinner and they are anxiously waiting for us.'

The hospital dormitory was about forty feet long and fifteen feet high to the white ceiling. The walls were white, too, above a five-foot-high buff-coloured dado. At the far end there were two windows stretching from the dado up to the ceiling, the bottom half with a wooden venetian-type shutter, the top half with glass doors and blue curtains. Similar windows were set in the long side of the outer wall, five of them, one behind each bed. The room had no decoration apart from one religious picture of the Virgin hanging high in the middle of the opposite long blank side. A table in the aisle between the two rows of beds was covered with a newly laundered cloth on which stood a fat brown earthenware carafe of cool water and glasses. You could tell there were women about because of the neat linen tablecloth, the way the sheets were folded back and the towels neatly hung over each bed-rail foot.

It was a wonderful release to peel off our clammy clothes and plop along the shadowy cloisters in sandals and a towel to the showers. Night had fallen, and we borrowed lanterns to move about the passages. Each shower room had a simple rose to dispense cold water, though one (I found) also had a short chunky porcelain bath. There were flush closets of the continental type, a ground-level porcelain pan with raised foot rests and a four-inch-diameter hole in between. It was a never-failing source of wonderment to me how accurately placed those holes are, seeing they're comparatively narrow. Once on the foot rests you didn't even need to aim. A Brazilian lavatory custom I could never get used to was that of screwing up your used sheet of toilet paper and dropping it – not down the lavatory – but into a wooden box provided at your side. Presumably this unsavoury mode of procedure has been instituted after continual and irritating experience of blocked drains. Paper in the jungle is, of course, rarer than diamonds, but I could hardly believe they would want to reclaim it and use it again.

At seven thirty I was summoned from my shower by Conrad Gorinsky with a panic call to dinner. As expedition cook, I suppose Conrad felt responsible for our meals, although he had no active hand in the preparation of this one. Back in the dormitory next to Arthur Helliwell, we could hear the fluty chanting of the nuns at vespers. Arthur (who is a Catholic) said to me, 'There's no reason for this fuss. We shall get nothing until this singing stops,' and he was right. In the refectory two tables had been beautifully laid out in a T-shape: soup plates, dinner plates, solid shining cutlery, crisply folded table napkins. We believed at that time that they had had warning of our coming by short-wave radio from the bishop of Manaus. Later we found they had not, that our arrival was completely unexpected. Nevertheless, in true Christian fashion, in the tradition of the great religious houses of the Middle Ages, they had taken us twenty secular pilgrims in without question and proceeded to shelter and feed us. Two young women, one definitely Indian as you could tell by the typical thickset square body and bandy legs, and the other of European extraction, served dinner under the direction of two nuns in starched and shining habits of white cotton. One nun was short, stout and dark with glasses and spoke Italian; the other, slightly taller, with skin the texture and colour of a fine wax candle, spoke German. The main dish was indeed roast pork, sweet and succulent. After dinner, on the way back to our bedroom, I stopped in the moonlit cloister with Douglas Botting to chat with the first nun who had showed us to our dormitory. She was sitting in the shadows in a low chair. She spoke in Portuguese, most of which I could follow, for she expressed herself simply, saying she had left Italy over thirty years ago from her home at 'Vincenza, Veneto', where her mother and father had ten children. She had been at several mission stations in Brazil – at São Paulo and at Waupés, where we were going the next day and which, she said, was *muita olinda* (very beautiful). She was a dedicated, simple soul, and several times repeated the word *sacrifiça* (her sacrifice) – this life was her offering to God. Her robe and wimple glimmered in the moonlight reflected from the tessellated marble floor of the cloisters, and the face which looked calmly up at us was the colour of smooth parchment. Behind us, in the quadrangle formed by the buildings, crowded a luxuriantly foliaged mob of spear-branched coconut palms. Only ten feet or so high, each tree had green coconuts, scores of them, fatly clustered round its trunk like a gigantic bunch of grapes.

Next morning, as I passed those palms on my way to the showers, I noticed a tame parrot perched on a low frond. A beautiful gaudy green, he didn't even open one eye when I stopped. It was six a.m. and the parrot was still sleepy. He merely changed feet like a sleep walker and resumed his slumbers.

It was Saturday 13th April and we were due to leave Taparucuará at nine o' clock. Henry Farrar and I carried the heavy tripod (all awkward legs and knobs) and the Arriflex camera down to the river to film the loading and departure of the hovercraft. Before we did leave we also filmed shots of the distant mission, pulling back on the long lens from the modern mission to the river bank to show the Indian shelters with their banana-leaf thatch. The Indians who live here have been thrust into skirts and trousers by the priests and nuns, but they have clung to three of their traditional items of culture. A woodcut from a book published 400 years ago depicts exactly what we saw at Taparucuará: the banana-leaf thatched shelter, the cooking hearth and the hammock.

These changed riverside Indians represent the only inroads made by a Western style civilisation on Brazilian and Venezuelan Amazonas. The Church ardently desires to save souls, while the State intends to stake its political claim to bodies and land; but the jungle resists both Church and State. As a result, after 400 years of trying, the main impact of civilisation in Amazonas is an attenuated string of settlements like isolated beads strung along the river banks, outposts maintained by missionaries and soldiers. Even at these posts, two miles back from the river bank, the forest is as it was since the last Ice Age, the gloomy home of jaguars, snakes, peccary, tapir, ant-eaters, myriads of insects, monkeys and some primitive men. Apart from a few missionaries, the only intruders into the *interior* of this vast 'land all covered with trees' are gold and diamond prospectors, rubber tappers, renegades and fugitives from justice or from political and social systems they detest.

Our own presence (made possible solely by the hovercraft) also concealed menace for the primitive Indians we were likely to encounter once we got beyond the mysterious Casiquiare Channel. Technological Man has surmounted or swept aside, one by one, the barricades which in the past have protected the Indians of Amazonas. Modern prophylactic medicine has enabled Europeans to enter the Green Hell armed against malaria, yellow fever, dysentery and other killing diseases; modern means of transport such as the hovercraft (surmounting formerly blocking obstacles like rapids) will henceforth shrink distance and time on the river from months to minutes. These forest Indians are people with an infinitely long past, no present and a finite future: their future is rushing upon them with the speed and deadly import of an intercontinental ballistic missile armed with an atomic warhead. At least, this is what I was thinking as we roared away from Taparucuará for our first trial against real rapids. For 40,000 years they have lived literally from hand to mouth picking berries, fruits, grubbing roots, even earth, and eating all on the spot. It was a development when they saved something for the next meal, when they carried something 'home'. It was an even greater development when they learned a simple form of farming with the digging stick. But beyond this their past progressed not at all. Such a vegetative development seems to us to take an infinitely long time; compared with it, they have no present to speak of. Their present consists largely of hand-outs from missionaries or Indian Protection Service men. In return for the hand-outs they are told to forget their tribal customs, and particularly their tribal religious beliefs. Clap a hat on the head of the Noble Savage and at once you make him realise he is naked – with nothing to temper the cold wind of change, for in compensation he is offered by the missionaries something called 'salvation'. Is it any wonder that from a strong community life where one individual is bound firmly to another by links which, though sometimes irksome, nevertheless give life a purpose, many Indians find themselves isolated, disorientated and with no real reason to continue living? And, very sensibly, they sit down and die.

Such a present is bleak. Their future is bleaker, for it surely entails the destruction not simply of individuals but of whole tribes. Destruction comes in many forms, the simplest and most direct being murder – white men killing Indians. Then there is destruction by disease. Intruders bring in measles, influenza and other common ailments of the whites, against which the Indians can only put 40,000 years of non-immunity: whole congeries of them die like flies. A white man sneezes (they say) and an Indian village dies. Then there is destruction by civilisation when an Indian finds himself caught in the outer cogs of a capitalist society based on the power of money and who has got it and who can make it; a society where 'mine' and 'thine' are strictly demarcated. Dispossessed of his lands, the Indian no longer has anything to call his own but his labour. Behind him, again, are 40,000 years of being unaccustomed to the capitalist idea of 'work'. In Indian society it is the women who 'work' – digging, delving, fetching, carrying: men hunt and fight. In the process of adjustment he falls by the wayside – or what is worse, finishes up in a slum of Caracas or a *favella* of Rio.

CHAPTER FIVE

The First Rapids

So far we had been going two days since leaving Manaus and had passed two nights ashore. In distance we had covered over 400 miles, and the next step of the journey was roughly 150 miles to Waupés – a mere morning's run.

Provided, of course, we weren't held up by the 'very hot, very strong' rapids.

It was nine a.m. when we left Taparucuará, and by ten we were skimming past the first high ground since Manaus. On our left there were three or four cone-shaped hills clad with blue-green jungle from top to bottom; on our right, the flat slab of compressed trees stretched (as far as we knew) from here to eternity.

Henry filmed inside the hovercraft. He had removed the big drum-shaped ten-to-one zoom lens from the camera and replaced it with a snub bull's-eye, almost fish-eye, 5·7 wide-angle lens. The advantage of such a lens is its chameleon-like coverage. It's the sort of lens house agents want photographers to use when preparing selling brochures so that a pokey living room takes on the dimensions of a fashionable salon; it's the lens which will turn the interior of a cramped river cruiser into the spaciousness of the *Queen Mary*. We needed the 5·7 so as to include as many of the hovercraft passengers as possible in any one shot. Of course, the wide-angle lens has its disadvantages: if you pan your camera – move it sideways – parts of what appear in the edges of your picture seem to stretch like a drawing on a balloon which is being blown up. Jesco's pink and globular head (the Indians of the Xingú call him 'Moon Face') was particularly prone to such elastic plasticity. And as for Mike Eden (our leader), a vertical tilt with the 5·7 lens on the camera produced the living spit of an Easter Island head. The moral was, of course, not to move the camera when the 5·7 was in use for close subjects. So, with a little caution, we got pictures of Graham Clarke hunched over his joystick and Stuart Syrad sitting alongside him on a wooden box in the gangway. In the first double seat on the left sat a river pilot, Francisco Gomez, taken on at Taparucuará to help us through the rapids. With him was Captain Manoel Perez, one of the two Brazilian observers who were due to leave at our next stop and return to Manaus. Behind these two were Julio Castillo, the Venezuelan river man who had joined the expedition in Manaus, and the other Brazilian observer Colonel Igrejas (he was to prove helpful). The other members of the party sat in seats allotted to them – the two crew members John Hoyland and Jim Sweeney, by the radio set; Robin Tenison talking to Mike Eden; Conrad Gorinsky chatting with Arthur Helliwell and David Smithers; while at the back, lolloped over the uncomfortable luggage, lay John Thornes, David Harris and Douglas Botting. Three of the BBC camera crew had flown already to Waupés – Jesco on the once-weekly Catalina flight from Manaus; and Bob Saunders and Peter Smith with our Missionary Aviation Pilot, Elmer, from Moura.

Before Elmer left us we had arranged for him to fly back from Waupés with Jesco and his camera to meet us over the rapids at eleven a.m. that Saturday morning. If necessary, Elmer could direct the hovercraft by radio through what appeared to be the least dangerous passages, and Jesco would film the operation.

If you live in a land quietly threaded by gentle-flowing rivers, a country like England, whose sweet Thames runs softly, then it is difficult to understand what harsh cataracts mean to people of fiercer and more embattled lands. To those who live along its brink, a dangerous rapid is first and foremost a menace to life and limb. Fall in the river there, or out of foolhardiness or by ill-luck allow your boat to be drawn into its sucking maw, and the chances are that you will not live to tell the tale. And when they fish your body out (if they do) it will be a bag of broken bones, for a rapid has grinding teeth – the rocks round which and over which the gurgling waters flow. Then a cataract is a formidable barrier to your material prosperity. If your land is rich in minerals, whether they be gold, silver, copper or iron, or if it has the wealth of Croesus in its woods, then that richness and that wealth will remain locked up as safely as if it were in the Bank of England or Fort Knox unless you can somehow circumvent that cataract. People who have known cataracts from experience all their lives don't need to be told this: in spite of the danger, intrepid characters will sometimes shoot the rapids to bring down a meagre boat-load of costly cargo. And frequently they lose both cargo and their lives. When our Brazilian companion, Colonel Igrejas, first heard of the hovercraft journey he offered to eat his staff officer's dress cap, scrambled egg and all, if the hovercraft succeeded in surmounting the Waupés rapids. We natives of the Old World thought this was merely a bit of New World exaggeration – or a joke. Actually, he was deadly serious. We Europeans really had no conception of the danger inches below the surface in a rapid, and in our ignorance we were blissful.

At eleven a.m. we saw ahead on our left a large half-moon of sandy beach: Graham Clarke decided to stop to pump part of the fuel from one set of full emergency tanks to the empty ones on the other side in order to balance and trim the craft before attempting the rapids.

As we were completing our shots of the operation, David Harris, one of the geographers, called from the bush that he'd found leaf-ants. Henry Farrar and I pushed carefully through the foliage, spines and brittle branches to a tiny clearing and saw a wonderful sight – a beautiful sight. A flotilla of leaf-cutting ants busily carrying triangular sails of fresh-snipped leaf, ten and a dozen abreast, jiggled over the forest floor. The leaf-sails bobbed and waved in a non-existent breeze as the ants forged steadily through the spear grass and tangled roots – a yacht race with all canvas crowded on. Or perhaps they more resembled (on second thoughts) an army marching with banners flying – Conquistadors of a peaceful conquest, the reduction of leaves to food or a food-growing mulch – part of the continuous cycle of growth and decay which is the jungle. The whole impression at the time was one of delicacy, quiet industry and dedicated purpose. Looking back, I detect something a little more sinister: a blind mechanical motivation.

These ants of the genus *Atta* are a mystery wrapped up in an enigma. They do not delicately snip the leaves they carry away to their nests in order to eat them. They use them for a much more wonderful purpose.

These ants are farmers.

They appear to have discovered agriculture some 40,000,000 years before the first men even appeared on earth. Ants set in amber since the Oligocene age of geological time are hardly distinguishable from the living species, and if their appearance is so similar it is logical to suppose that their habits were also similar. The plants whose leaves they so single-mindedly scissor may have changed: nowadays, the leaf ants make do with the foliage of the numerous lianas, wild figs, hibiscus, bougain-villaea, *hevea Brasiliensis* – the Brazilian rubber tree.

What *do* they do with the leaves?

In the dark chambers of their nests they set aside special cellars in which they lay down a compost formed of the mulched leaves; and on this compost they force mushrooms. Well, you could call them mush-rooms – at any rate, a fungus which is their daily bread.

Another extraordinary fact is that a special caste of tiny worker ants called *minims*, much smaller than the collectors, tend the subterranean gardens and keep them free from weeds. But what is most extraordin-ary is that these unique fungus species, on which the ants depend im-plicitly for their food, are found nowhere else except in company with the leaf-ants: so the fungi in turn are dependent on the ants. The associa-tion of the ants and the fungus is a classic case of what the biologists call *mutual symbiosis* – a beneficial interdependence of two species without which both would fail and die out.

When new queen ants leave old nests on their nuptial flights they carry with them, as a vital wedding present to the yet unborn colony, fragments of the fungus in their cheek pouches.

Thus is the food supply of the descendants assured – as long as the forest bears leaves.

At a quarter past noon the river was still as smooth as glass, still nearly a mile wide, and the hovercraft speed had never dropped less than fifty knots since we left the sandbank. Waupés was about three-quarters of an hour away, and where were the rapids?

I glanced at the grizzled bristle-head and red leathery face of Francisco Gomez the local pilot we had picked up at Taparucuará. He was fidget-ing as he gazed from side to side through the front windows. Plainly, he was uncomfortable, even agitated. Occasionally, he would raise his right or left hand and slice the air with a gesture which meant 'Go right!' or 'Go left!' But the hovercraft pilot took no notice. Such gestures I was later to become very familiar with when we went off on an expedition in dugout canoes. They were urgent and (as the Road Code says) mandatory. If the steersman at the stern of the canoe failed to obey such a peremptory sign, which meant 'There are rocks ahead: go right (or left) if you want to miss 'em', then the craft would finish upside down with its cargo lost and the crew struggling to save their skulls from being stoved in and their lungs from invasion by the boiling waters.

But the hovercraft charged on.

Francisco Gomez was nonplussed.

Obviously, we were going through rapids. I could see broken water splashing and coiling past the window on my right. I could see occasional clutters of rocks protruding from the eddying river – rocks normally a whale-grey colour, now turned black on their leading edges by drenching waves.

And all the hovercraft did was to pitch slightly, once or twice a minute. This passage of the Joana Boni cataract, of the two-mile stretch of the Cachoeira Taubi followed by the Cachoeira Cocal was unique. Never before had they been shot upwards with such expedition and contempt for their dangers.

Francisco Gomez looked at the pilot and then dropped his gnarled and useless hands on to his knees. He knew that if a boat steersman had ignored his signs by now we should have been a heap of wreckage tumbling downstream with the tossing current. But this was something different, something new, something extraordinary – a craft with no keel, with nothing to speak of below the surface of the water – and so a magic carpet which made a nonsense of rapids.

This is how we ourselves felt, certainly how I felt at that time – though my confidence was to be shaken before long.

And so we came through the rapids before Waupés with less disturbance than we would have done riding in a horse-drawn trap down a rough country lane at home. It was an experience which lulled some people (me, I'm a sucker that way) into a false sense of security.

CHAPTER SIX

Intrigue at Waupés

WE came ashore at Waupés, that *muita olinda* mission of the Taparucuará nun, an hour after midday. The wide expanse of yellow strand, as empty as the Sahara desert, was easily a mile long. The hovercraft glided straight off the surface of the black Negro on to the billiardtable beach without the slightest sign of a hesitation or jolt.

Henry Farrar and I jumped out first to film the disembarkation. We were entirely alone on that splendid shore.

And no wonder. At one o'clock the sun was vertically overhead (the equator being a mere cock-stride away) and the heat was fiery. I felt like Shadrak, Mishak and Abednego – or as though I was inside a sandwich of fire, what with the sun above and the scorching sand below. A quarter of a mile back from the water's edge the feather brushes of a thin line of palms cogged the skyline. The ground rose in gentle slopes, and half a mile away to our left on a little hill we could see the tall spire of the mission church.

One or two Caboclos (wakened by the hovercraft noise from their siesta) began to leave the shelter of the trees and wander towards us across the sand.

Graham Clarke started up his engine again when he saw our tripod in position ready to film, and he drove the hovercraft well clear of the water and waltzed her along the beach. The straggly line of sightseers a quarter of a mile away halted uncertainly at this strange sight. A boat, even a noisy one, they could understand. A something which walked up out of the river was another kettle of fish: a monstrous cayman, a mutated turtle or a machine from Mars? They didn't wait to be investigated – they ran like rabbits for the shelter of the trees.

The expeditionaries staggered a little stiffly down the lowered gangway and stood about in self-conscious clumps, uncertain what to do.

They watched their feet as if wondering where their shadows had gone.

Those, like me, who wore baseball boots with rubber soles moved from one foot to the other to gain a few seconds relief from the scorching heat of that oven-bottom beach.

In spite of this discomfort, Waupés *was* a 'very beautiful' place. Downstream, the river rolled wide and restful to eyes set free at last from confining jungle banks. In the far distance a wedge of three sharp-toothed mountains slanted up the horizon like a blued-steel segment of saw – a living justification of the first Spanish Conquistadors who called the New World ranges *sierras*. The sky was high and wide, blue and cloudless. Green grass clothed the nearer slopes leading up to the mission buildings. On this side, the jungle seemed to have retreated, and the trees beyond the sandy beach were mainly palms with a low bush linking the bases of their slender trunks. All was still – except one thing. All was silence – except one thing.

And that one thing gave everybody cause for concern.

It was the Waupés rapids.

The broken water we had just come through was really of little consequence. The *real* Waupés rapids (as I discovered for the first time) were above the beach on which we had landed. They rushed and rolled at something like twenty-five miles an hour, angry and irritated, constricted by a bouldered, rocky shore, the same on either bank: a burst of broken water lasting perhaps three-quarters of a mile from where we stood to way beyond the mission buildings. Later, the Fathers told us that the locals called these cataracts the *Cachoeiras do Morte*, 'the Rapids of Death', because scarcely a month passed by without a life being claimed. Only recently, an American lady, they said, had slipped on the rocks by the bank and immediately been carried away. Nothing could save her – she had been battered and drowned.

And so, for ten minutes at least, we continued to stand about uncertainly. Douglas Botting, hatless, sweating, his straight hair in a limp lock over his forehead, grumbled to me that somebody had pinched his hat and his brains were frying. He knew who it was, but was too English to approach the purloiner direct. It was, in fact, Dr John Thornes – he of the penetrating West Riding voice. And because he had taken his spectacles off and had that vague and unfocussed look of short-sighted folk without their glasses, and because the wide-brimmed school-girl-type hat was too big for him anyway, he reminded me irresistibly of that one of Walt Disney's seven dwarfs who's always last.

Some small boys ventured from the shelter of the distant palms, pushed on by curiosity, to see who and what we were.

Two or three timid dogs accompanied the boys.

Then their fathers and mothers and sisters came; and soon there was a crowd of a couple of hundred people milling round the hovercraft. They all had black straight hair, they all had copper skins and they all (both male and female) wore brightly coloured shirts or frocks. Few, if any, had shoes, and the finely powdered sand seeped in between their toes.

A procession of Fathers and nuns had wended its way down the zig-zag path leading from the white and buff Salesian mission buildings. At the head strode the bishop, Dom Miguel, a small-boned, round-headed, neatly built Italian with short dark hair in a natural tonsure and horn-rimmed spectacles. His long priest's cassock dropped straight from neck to heels – a very light khaki in colour. Beside him, in pure white habit and black shining boots (but sheltering from the sun beneath a black umbrella), walked Sister Bernadette, the Mother Superior. She, too, wore largish horn-rimmed glasses, the dark frames of which served to emphasise her pale and waxy face. She was a Brazilian from São Paulo who later helped us with filming and served at table – 'A young very nice person,' Jesco told us later, 'always smiling.'

Our Brazilian observers, Colonel Igrejas and Captain Perez, introduced the bishop to our leaders. Afterwards, when he saw me standing with Henry by the camera, Dom Miguel came with right hand outstretched to shake while he patted me on the back with the other in that welcoming embrace typical of Brazil. When I had first seen him in Manaus (he had recently flown to Waupés on the weekly Catalina to conduct the Easter weekend services) he had inquired if I could sell him the hovercraft. It was my first insight into the wealth of the Salesian Mission. Of course, I told him through Jesco, who was acting as interpreter, that at that particular moment in time I didn't even own a car never mind a hovercraft.

Well, would the captain sell it? Or whoever did own it? And how much would they want?

I said I believed the original cost had been £125,000.

Very well, he would pay £75,000, cash. Wasn't that fair – seeing it was second-hand?

I had said I would pass on his inquiries to Captain Clarke. The bishop had been serious, though nobody believed it.

But now a general movement, a drift towards the tree line, shelter and eventually the Mission, asserted itself. A truck was waiting to carry the expeditionaries and their gear to quarters. Willing hands helped us to hump our packs, and in ten minutes we were bumping up a deep-rutted track eroded by fierce, intemperate tropical rainstorms, the chassis and springs of the lorry twisting and squeaking as one road wheel plunged and another was forced up into the belly of the vehicle like the feet of some unnaturally goose-stepping soldier.

Although the date over the mission entrance was 1925, the buff and white buildings reminded me of colonial forts of a hundred and fifty years ago such as I had seen in India – Wellington's fort in Madras, for instance. The walls were so thick, the ceilings so high and the windows embrasured. Most had shutters and bars and looked out on to internal courtyards or cloistered walks.

Jesco, round-faced and smiling, met us as we turned into one of the cloisters all staggering like a crowd of Christmas shoppers under the various items of our impedimenta. He was dressed in trousers and rolled shirt sleeves, and he broke into a hasty limp to relieve me of my largest hold-all.

'Welcome, Brian!' he said, 'Welcome Henry, welcome Arthur! This way please. You'll find the nuns are very good, very kind. Mother Superior has asked me to show you the rooms.' In fact, Jesco had organised the guest-rooms according to his own ideas. Always a re-specter of authority (not from subservience, but because he could mani-pulate it better by a show of respect), Jesco had seen to it that the two Brazilian officers had a pleasant little room nearest the showers and a private lavatory. Next door, he'd placed the hovercraft captain Graham Clarke and Stuart Syrad. A small dormitory with three iron beds he reckoned was best for Arthur Helliwell, Bob Saunders and me. Each apartment had a placard pinned to its thick wooden door. Ours had a drawing of a camera on its tripod and the letters 'BBC'. On the door of a large hospital ward Jesco had pinned a notice in block capitals written on white card with that cameraman's friend his 'magic marker' – THE YOUNG EXPEDITION MEMBERS, SCIENTISTS AND FRIENDS. It was his way of softening the blow or soothing the pique of anyone who might feel put out at not getting exactly the treatment he felt he merited.

In spite of his evident pleasure at meeting up with us again, I could see from his behaviour that Jesco was uneasy. Something was worrying him.

After we'd chosen our beds and had a wash he drew me on one side in a conspiratorial sort of way.

He cleared his throat. 'Brian?'

'Yes, Jesco; what's up?'

'Very nice here. You like your bed?'

'Yes, thanks. You're a clever old sod. What's the matter?'

'Brian, there's been a bad telegram.'

For a few seconds my heart stood still.

'Is it Dodo – is it my wife?'

'No, Brian. It's not for you.'

'For the Expedition leader – for David Smithers or Captain Clarke?'

'No.' Here he became more conspiratorial than ever, looking aslant over his shoulder and screwing up his eye as he whispered into my ear, 'For the Brazilian officer, for Captain Perez. It comes from the Ministry of the Interior. It says the Expedition *can't go on!*' He looked up at the white walls of the room as if exploring the possibility of their having ears. Deciding that nobody else was paying attention, he told me the whole story.

Wherever he goes, Jesco has what I believe must be a Brazilian characteristic, the urge to make influential friends. One of the friends he had made at Waupés was the Air Force sergeant in charge of the landing strip some six kilometres away in the jungle. This young man had received a radio signal for Captain Perez. He knew Jesco was part of the hovercraft expedition, as was Perez, and needed little persuasion to show Jesco the telegram. It did indeed contain an order to hold the hovercraft at Waupés.

At first it was difficult to see how we could make use of the information. It was obvious that if we told Captain Perez we knew of the existence and contents of his signal, then the Air Force sergeant would be for the chop. Jesco was adamant that nothing should be done which would hurt his informant.

I told Bob Saunders and Arthur Helliwell the news, and they both tended to laugh a little cynically. It was difficult to take Brazilian bureaucracy seriously; and I am bound to admit that after our own struggles with the hovercraft expedition organisers, the BBC party was inclined to be amused at organisational setbacks. Not that we didn't all come together in an emergency. It's just that we had our share of human frailty.

However, we had a film to make, and the foundering of the expedition at the Venezuelan frontier with an ignominious return to Manaus was the last thing we wanted.

I found a sleek and polished David Smithers (he had just showered and changed) and told him of the telegram.

His eyes popped roundly behind his hornrims.

'Wha – what?'

I told him again. 'Let's go and see Graham,' he said.

We walked along the cloister to Graham Clarke's cell and told him. 'Hm. Rather expected something like this,' he said quietly.

Jesco was fetched and asked to repeat his story.

David Smithers came to the conclusion that Captain Perez would keep the contents of the telegram to himself until Monday morning (it was now Saturday) just before we were due to lift off. Then he would relieve himself of responsibility and reproaches by flying back to Manaus later that day on the weekly Catalina. The length of our delay would then be anybody's guess, for because it was Easter Week, it was unlikely that any of the functionaries in Rio would be at their office desks to be contacted and argued with by wire or by our helpers at the British Embassy into lifting the ban.

We had to force Perez' hand, and a way occurred to me of doing it. 'David,' I said, 'You've got to tell Captain Perez that the arrangements have been altered. Say the hovercraft is leaving tomorrow, Sunday – not Monday as planned. He'll then have to come out into the open and tell you about the telegram.'

We left it at that.

By this time a meal was ready, and we ambled in twos and threes along the cloisters, through the mission hospital building and across a courtyard to the refectory. That late lunch was the first of a number of meals distinguished not only for the assiduous, kindly service but also for the tasty variety and startling profusion of courses. Here we were at the back of beyond being treated to the most exotic and sumptuous banquets. The whole situation reminded me of some medieval traveller's tale plus a touch of the bizarre when stocky Indian girls served shoulder to shoulder with white-habited nuns. It brought to my mind descriptions of feasts in King Arthur's castle or Chaucer's of the Franklin's hall – 'it snowéd in his house of meat and drink'. To quench our parching throats, brown fingers offered us cordials of crushed fresh lemons mixed with bottles of cool water from a spring in the rocks. As always, the water in this region ran delightfully over the tongue, silky to the touch with not a shade of harsh lime in it. The food ranged over soup, chicken, pork, cassava, palmetto hearts, rice, black beans, a type of piquant cornish pasty (asked the name, the Indian serving girl put me in my place by saying 'paasti'), bananas (long and flaky or chubby and winey), syrupy almost transparent jellified fruits deliciously smooth and sweet. Some twenty of us all sat down to table with great enjoyment and amicability. The only snag was that after dark those sitting under the electric bulb were dive-bombed by daddy-long-legs-type flies and tiny insects attracted by the light. I found myself in such a position the first night at dinner, and Mother Superior (she was younger than I was) finally covered my drinking glass with the plastic saucer on which it was designed to stand.

After dinner, Bishop Dom Miguel came in and sat at table. He would very much like us to film the solemn midnight mass he was to conduct that night (said Jesco). The main trouble, as far as we were concerned, would be insufficient light for colour filming. But the bishop was eager, and so Henry allowed himself to be persuaded into having a go. At least he was prepared to examine the possibility by taking light readings in the church.

At all these isolated knots of civilisation we usually found electric light. It would be supplied by a petrol generator started at dusk and turned off at ten o'clock – the main circuit-breaker having been thrown out a couple of times ten minutes before the lights would finally be extinguished as a warning for all and sundry to jump into bed. It was like that at Waupés, the Mission's own generator producing alternating electric current at 220 volts.

Henry's light meter wouldn't even give a reading in that vast whale's belly of gloom which was the church's nave. We asked to see the generator, for Henry thought it might not be turning to capacity. A priest took us to the shed at the back of the museum. The engine was in fact running to produce a steady 220 volts, but the obliging electrician in charge pushed the throttle until the whirring armature and sparking brushes were forcing out 245 volts. His only observation was that if he kept that speed up too long he would blow every bulb on the mission station. Nevertheless, back in church we found this acceleration was producing appreciably more light, and in addition I asked Jesco to inquire if the bishop would mind my circling his head with a halo from my powerful electric torch. He was completely agreeable. So the filming of the midnight mass was on.

We walked through the velvet dark back to our quarters and were there told by Graham Clarke that our two Brazilian observers had been informed of a change of plan – that the hovercraft would move off next morning. Such a start was a practical impossibility, because the engineers John Hoyland and Jim Sweeney were already stripping the engine down and had at least a day's maintenance ahead of them.

In addition, there was a formidable obstacle: the hovercraft had still to surmount the *Cachoeiras do Morte* – the Rapids of Death.

Nevertheless, the 'try-on' did succeed, and Captain Perez' hand had been forced. After a couple of hours contemplation he revealed the existence and contents of his telegram.

'You cannot go,' he said to Smithers. 'The Ministry of the Interior forbids it.'

So that Saturday evening our leaders David Smithers, Graham Clarke and Mike Eden discussed ways and means with a fair amount of gloom. There was mention of ignoring the Brazilian order (Perez would return to Manaus on Monday anyway) and simply driving on to the border. This was swashbuckling talk, in the best traditions of gunboat diplomacy, but it had its snags. In the first place, there was a strong military post at Cucui, the Brazilian frontier station, with at least a company of well-armed and tough jungle troops – quite capable of machine-gunning us to a stop; then, even if we were successful in running the gauntlet, I myself could only be a party to offending the Brazilian authorities by accepting that the BBC team would not be allowed back into the country to finish two other films we had to make, and that the BBC would lose £10,000, being the value of the bond put up to the Brazilian Customs to ensure proper re-exportation of our camera gear, a deal of which we had had to leave in Manaus.

Still, it is not my habit to worry unduly, and I went off at midnight with Henry Farrar, Peter Smith and Jesco to film the mass in the belief that somehow the good Lord would extricate us from our difficulties.

The main impression that Easter mass made on me was that the Indians, or near Indians, who formed ninety-nine per cent of Bishop Dom Miguel's congregation must have found the transition from their own and their forebears' forest rituals to the rituals of Catholic Christianity a fairly easy matter. All the basic ingredients were there in this mass – fire, water, pungent vapours, chanting, ritual vestments, processions marching and counter-marching, a sense of religious awe.

A crowd had collected on the steps of the church, their solemn bronze-Buddha faces glowing from the tongues of flame lapping the smoke rising from a brazier of burning wood. The fire was occasionally encouraged by an Indian who cranked a mechanical blower, such as a blacksmith uses, the fan whizzing the coals white hot and feathering sparks into the air as a reminder of what man is born to.

A procession led by the bishop in his gold-and-crimson cope swayed down the nave of the church from the high altar out through the Gothic arch of the main door and stopped by the brazier. An acolyte handed the bishop a pair of tweezers to tweak a bright coal from the fire for his brass censer. But the fire was too fierce for those white fingers, and the hand drew back to be replaced by a hornier, browner one as a by-stander simply plucked a golden gleed and popped it into the basin of the censer. The bishop sprinkled incense powder on to the brand and proceeded to swing the censer smoke towards the watchers before handing the chains to a helper. One of the priests at the bishop's side carried a candle six inches thick and two feet high. It was a shaft of coloured and ornately sculptured baroque. A cross of Christ engraved in the wax of the candle had the individual numbers of the year 1968 fitted into the four angles of the cross. The bishop took a pointed knife and scored marks along the cross and traced the outline of the figures. Next, he thrust five large pins with bulbous heads into the cross – one in the middle, the others at the ends of the limbs.

I realise, of course, that the symbolism represented the five nails and wounds of Christ; for me, the bishop might have been sticking pins into a wax doll. But for the Indians I have no doubt that here was a mystery, and as long as these rites are the latest in a series carrying on from where their shamans, medicine men, witch doctors left off, so long will the Indians come into contact with the numinous – a thing most of us city men have forgotten how to do.

After this ceremony the intoning and chanting resumed and the bishop's procession went back into the church with ten small boys wearing crimson shoulder capes over their white cassocks and each carrying a lighted candle in a long holder. With the motion of the measured tread, ten flames floated back and forth on their tiny baths of melted wax, illuminating ten innocent Indian faces.

We followed them in, camera, zeppelin microphone and outsize torch in action. We were bringing an air of the ridiculous to a solemn occasion – like a rehearsal for a wedding.

A beautiful image of the Virgin and Child, life-size, was set high in an arched alcove of the wall behind the altar. I shot a shaft of light from my electric torch on to the head and shoulders while Henry filmed and then panned his camera slanting down to the bishop and priests at their symbolism with chalices, and the pyx, and the wafer which becomes flesh on the altar table. 'Their god turns into a biscuit and they eat him!'

It was two hours after midnight before we stepped out of the church into a night black as the inside of a lady's jewel casket. It was cold enough to make you shiver, though the temperature was well up in the seventies; but that represented a drop of twenty-five degrees from the day's heat, and the stark contrast made you feel you were freezing.

The cool night air was filled, too, with a continuous bumble of rumbling sound. At first I didn't recognise it, and then the penny dropped: it was the Rapids of Death insensately roaring by in the gorge below the church.

Arthur and Bob were fast asleep in the room I shared with them – Bob motionless and soundless, Arthur occasionally giving a gasp and a snore. In five minutes I had joined them.

Next morning, as usual, Jesco was pottering about shortly after six a.m., and I got up and joined him and Elmer in the refectory for breakfast. Elmer was flying back to Manaus within the hour, and we arranged to go with him to the jungle air-strip to wave him off.

The news was, according to Jesco, that Graham Clarke had decided to take the hovercraft up the rapids in the afternoon about three o'clock – or, at least, to try. (Jesco was sleeping in the large dormitory with the main body of expedition members, and so had access to the latest goings-on.) According to the gossip, said Jesco, our two Brazilian observers didn't see eye to eye over the fateful telegram. Colonel Igrejas was on our side. He had told Jesco that the signal was intended to delay, but it really couldn't stop us. He himself (the Colonel went on) had a letter from the Ministry of the Interior permitting us to go on. Like Captain Perez, Colonel Igrejas had to take the Catalina back to Manaus next day, otherwise (he said) he would have come with us to the border and seen us safely across.

We passed on this information to David Smithers, who reported that Captain Perez was still opposing our leaving.

Nevertheless, an attempt would be made that Sunday afternoon to drive the hovercraft up the rapids. All the expedition stores and cargo would be taken out and ferried on the loop road round the rapids and, apart from the crew, only two other men would be allowed aboard to make the trial of the rapids, namely Robin Hanbury-Tenison (who had shot this cataract in a rubber boat some years before – coming down) and a local river pilot who had acted as Tenison's guide. From my point of view, it would have been a good thing to have had one of the cameramen aboard, but Graham Clarke and David Smithers had decided otherwise, and on this occasion I came to the conclusion that this was one time I didn't need to argue. Here we had a splendid chance to get both long and close external shots as the craft battled with the rumbustious water. So I climbed with Jesco and Henry up the wooden stairs and ladders leading to the top of Waupés church spire – an obvious camera position. The topmost ladders were rickety, crumbly, their inner strength consumed by white ants, termites, and the three of us scrambled warily like apprehensive monkeys from rung to rung and beam to beam until we reached an airy window giving a field of view thirty miles downstream from the saw-tooth mountains to the smooth water way up above the rapids.

While Jesco was shooting from the top of the spire, Henry and I would be down on the rocks shooting from the very edge of the snarling waters.

The lorry was now waiting to take Elmer to the airfield, and the BBC crew piled in the back with him. It was six kilometres of petty hell through an airless canyon whose walls were trees and whose bottom was like a dry river bed – all rocks and gullies. It was hell not only because of wrenched muscles as you stood on the swaying deck; not only because of the choking golden dust; but also because you actually burnt your fingers and elbows when they came into contact with the metal hood and sides and bottom of the truck.

At the lonely strip Elmer tossed his bedroll into the cabin of his red-and-white gleaming Cessna, shook hands all round, stepped in and closed the door. We looked at his shiny, chubby, baby's bottom of a face for the last time. He was one of the quietest, most dedicated, bravest men I have ever met, and we watched him buzz into the sky, knowing that we should probably never meet again.

Because we felt depressed when we got back to the mission (or for any other reason) Jesco fixed us a round of pingas guaranteed to give even a nun ideas about dancing on the table. As a matter of fact, these lively young nuns *had* been having ideas (according to Jesco). He said Sister Bernadette, the Mother Superior, wanted me to ask Graham Clarke to give six of the nuns a joy-ride on the hovercraft.

At lunch I pleaded with Graham to give the nuns a flip, and he agreed to do so just before he made his attempt to shoot up the rapids that afternoon.

Meanwhile, Captain Perez had shifted his ground a little. He had told David Smithers and Graham Clarke he would allow the hovercraft to leave Waupés provided they were willing to give a lift to Sister Hilda Tissot, a nun who had to go to the border post at Cucui. They refused on the grounds of the extra weight jeopardising the hovercraft's efficiency to the point of failure.

So we were neither out of the wood nor up the rapids.

By half past two that afternoon all the inhabitants of Waupés who could walk or, if they couldn't, who could persuade somebody to carry them, were on their way to the beach or to other vantage points on rocks overlooking the length of the rapids. Six nuns in chaste white habits led by Bishop Dom Miguel in his khaki cassock filed down the zig-zag path from the Mission to the beached hovercraft. Jesco was already perched up the spire under the bell with his camera. Peter Smith, Bob Saunders, Henry Farrar and I lugged our own filming gear down to a rocky cove about two hundred yards upstream of the craft. A puff of smoke and a bubble of noise belched from the hovercraft engine and the prop began to rotate. Graham, John Hoyland and Jim Sweeney were getting ready for their first seriously testing time so far.

Slowly the hovercraft slid off the sand on to the surface of the Negro River. The familiar nimbus of spray enveloped the moving machine as Graham quickly beat up the revs until SRN6 was skating at forty-five knots at right angles across the river directly below the rapids. Henry panned his camera right, following the machine, which sped like a demented water-beetle across the bottom of a backcloth of the distant blue mountains and dollop on dollop of white cumulus clouds flung up the wall of that wide sky. Before the hovercraft turned to come back to disembark the joy-riding nuns and bishop it had diminished in Henry's viewfinder to the size of a flea.

He took his eye from the camera and looked quizzically over his shoulder to me standing behind him.

'Got it?'

He nodded.

'Let's go, then.'

He unscrewed the camera from the tripod and began to scramble across the rocks upstream. The rest of us followed with tripod, spare magazines, camera box and microphone. We intended to take up a second position two-thirds of the way up the rapids to get one continuous shot of the hovercraft's approach to the cataract, its performance in the ragged, leaping, exploding waves at the bottom of the rapid, after which (if it got so far) we should have it filling the frame as it passed within twenty yards of us, finally (we hoped) to surge away from us upriver, having surmounted the *Cachoeiras do Morte*, its one great obstacle before leaving Brazil.

By the time we reached our camera set-up position on a slanting rock half the size of a tennis court we were all blistered with beads of sweat and hurking our hearts out.

The hovercraft had returned to the beach, the nuns and bishop had stepped ashore, and she was heading out again on the same line as she had taken before. To the naked eye she almost disappeared, then she

turned and gradually began to head towards us upriver. Graham Clarke
was pushing her along at something under fifty miles an hour. In the
smooth water before she reached the foot of the rapids she was steadily
drifting sideways, almost as though an invisible hand were shoving her
in towards the beach.

I called Bob Saunders' attention to this accelerating skid. It was so
marked that the saw-toothed mountains and cumulus cloud appeared
to be sliding behind her from left to right on rollers.

Then, above the roar of the waters, we heard the banshee wail of the
900-h.p. engine as Graham Clarke gave her the gun and pointed her
nose at the eddying, whirling waves at the bottom of the rapids. She
rocked back and forth, her dips scooping up clouds of spray which
enveloped her cabin and trailed in tatters behind her, giving her the look
of an intermittent meteor.

She grew fatter and fatter as she appeared to drive at us head on. At
our feet the river was racing past our rock with the speed, force and
weight of a stream of lava new-burst from a volcano.

In true terms, I suppose, the river speed was about twenty-five knots,
and as the waves charged against her this would reduce the hovercraft's
forward speed to about twenty knots.

The greatest danger, and the thing he feared most when he thought
about it, Graham had told me, was an engine failure.

Such a failure was unpredictable.

If it happened there would be no compressed-air cushion to raise the
craft within its crinoline, and no propeller turning to drive it forward.
It would flop belly flat on the billows and be borne backwards up and
down, willy-nilly like a drunk on a cake-walk. If there were rocks just
below the surface or protruding slightly and she bashed into them or
tore her tanks open she would become water-logged. Nothing the
pilot could do would have the slightest effect. We hoped it wouldn't
come to that.

I could see the giant windscreen wipers thrashing from side to side
clearing away the wet.

Behind them, Graham Clarke was crouched with both hands at the
controls gazing straight ahead, dwarfed, like a jockey faced for the first
time by the Grand National course.

It was frightening. I mean it was frightening for me, and I was only
standing on the rocks watching.

About two hundred yards below us there was a maelstrom of struggling billows caused by a marching together of rocks against which a
number of separate currents were repeatedly charging. The hovercraft

drove at the whirlpool. Her front went down, and two wings of water were flung fifty yards out to the right and left. She nuzzled into tons of river.

She shuddered and seemed to stop.

My heart missed a beat.

Then her nose came up and she leapt through the cataract like a salmon at a weir. It was thrilling to watch.

The din of her engine had now completely obliterated the noise of the rapids. I could see Robin Hanbury-Tenison through the rain-grazed windows. Like Graham, he was looking straight before him, motionless, tense.

Now she was alongside us, roaring by with the speed and power of an express train and, for me at least, creating just that mild exhilaration and joyful fear one experiences standing on the edge of a railway-station platform as the non-stop rockets through.

And so at last the realisation came to us that the Rapids of Death were no obstacle at all to SRN6. Before we could fully collect ourselves she had shot past, our heads and the camera following to the right, and we were looking up her disappearing bottom as we watched her square-cut stern fins directing her into smooth water.

For the first time I became conscious of Bishop Dom Miguel and six nuns standing behind us on the boulders. They were bubbling like silver kettles in that strangely hissy language Portuguese, where every other word sounds like 'goloshes'. This was for them the experience of a lifetime. *They* knew the Negro. *They* knew the rapids. They'd just watched the impossible.

Clearly, Colonel Igrejas would have to eat his hat.

Or perhaps, if we let him off the hook, he would finally persuade Captain Perez to let us depart in peace.

Interlude for Mystery

THE Father Calleri massacre promises to become as much of a mystery as the disappearance of Colonel Fawcett.

Fawcett was searching in that vast tract of swamp and scrub, the Matto Grosso, for – of all things – the Lost Cities of Atlantis. For forty years his quest fired the imagination of newspaper readers all over the world in much the same way as the search for El Dorado excited the European adventurers of the first Elizabethan Age. And there was just about as much (or as little) substance in the objects of the two quests.

El Dorado (translated it means *the Gilded Man*) began from an exotic rite performed in the Lake of Guatavita in the Andes near Bogotá in Bolivia, a rite which had in fact died out forty years before the Spanish Conquistadors savaged Peru. According to hearsay, an Indian prince of those parts, at an annual fertility festival, anointed his naked body from top to toe with aromatic turpentine oil and then rolled in gold dust to turn himself into a living, life-size statue of the precious metal. He was afterwards rowed with great ceremony to the middle of Lake Guatavita, where offerings of priceless jewels were dropped to the deity of the waters, then the prince himself dived in and washed the gold dust into the depths, where, for a few moments, the darkness was luminous with the shimmering, glittering particles as they sank.

A dozen expeditions braved the terrors of the Amazon rain forest drawn on by that will-o'-the-wisp El Dorado. Sir Walter Raleigh caught the most famous seeker of them all, the Spaniard de Berrio, just when the grey-bearded old searcher believed himself to be within a stone's throw of El Dorado and Manoa the city of gold. Poor Raleigh was himself infected with the fever: he never found his El Dorado and, because he failed, King James I (in true fairy-tale tradition) had his head chopped off.

As for Colonel Fawcett, part of the bait which drew him on was a strange region in Brazil known as Sete Cidades – Seven Cities. This area of the backlands has been eroded by dust devil and rainstorm and by the brick-baking sun into a semblance of ruined streets and houses, of halls and palaces long since brought low by some cataclysm of earth and sea – the very catastrophe which to a romantic soul might have swallowed up Atlantis. At least, this was Fawcett's way of thinking, and as a result, the Matto Grosso swallowed him up.

Colonel Percy Fawcett disappeared on 29th May 1925 together with his son Jack, and his son's friend Raleigh Rimmel. For forty years the English newspapers have speculated on what could have happened. Had Fawcett found his lost cities? It was a stirring thought. Had he become an Indian prince and together with his companions fathered a new race of fair-haired, white-skinned children of nature? The most extraordinary eye-witness accounts of chance meetings with the lost colonel or his supposed progeny appeared at odd intervals and were forgotten in the British Embassy pigeonholes in Rio de Janeiro. A celebrated automatic-writing medium, Miss Geraldine Cummins, wrote a lively account at the dictation of the colonel's spirit of what had really happened.

But in sober truth, Colonel Fawcett never found his lost cities and never became an Indian prince. Far from it: the shy forest Indians, apprehensive for their very existence, knocked him and his two companions on the head. They had done it before, and they will do it again.

In fact, they have just done it (as we know) to Father Calleri. But how and why is fast becoming a strange puzzle.

Jesco has been keeping me posted of developments in the Calleri story with cuttings from Brazilian magazines and newspapers where a baffled argument is raging. Sides are being taken either for or against Alvaro Paulo da Silva, the one person on the expedition who escaped the massacre. [Why was Alvaro able to escape? Did he suspect there was going to be a massacre?]

Those who side with Alvaro are accepting his story, which goes like this. Alvaro Paulo da Silva is a true *sertanista*, a dyed-in-the-wool backwoodsman with a profound knowledge of life in the jungle and of Indian ways of thought. At the funeral mass in Manaus chanted over the recovered bones of seven men and two women of Calleri's expedition, Alvaro is described as a man of rough appearance, like a true backwoodsman, unshaven, calm, tranquil. You feel he knows what he is talking about. And the interpretation put on what Alvaro says by João Americo Peret, an acknowledged expert of the Indian Foundation, leads to the blame for the massacre being laid on Father Calleri himself. Apparently the Calleri expedition started off on the wrong foot: the project as approved by the Indian Foundation (FUNAI) was to establish a base *outside* the territory of the Atroari Indians from which the first contacts would be made. But Father Calleri, by his own account, decided to disobey this.

The Atroari Indian village consisted of one huge cone-shaped *maloca*, or communal hut, and a second one near by in course of construction like a mushroom of scaffolding.

The Padre ordered his expedition's encampment to be built a mere 200 metres from the village, and the Indians helped enthusiastically, including raising the expedition's wireless transmitter aerials. During this work another group of Atroaris arrived with various articles which they wished to barter. Father Calleri 'rejected this offer derisively'. He distributed presents to those Indians who had helped in the work, only. 'For him,' says the Indian Foundation expert Peret, 'that represented a kind of wage, an obligatory salary for hire of labour, as might be understood in the terms of the civilised world.' When an Indian showed disgruntlement with the two boxes of matches wages which he had been given – he wanted more – Father Calleri deprived him even of these two and scolded him for being 'unsubmissive'.

Alvaro, who understands Indians, disapproved of Father Calleri's apparent tight-fistedness, because he felt it would lead to trouble. The Father appears to have gone out of his way to upset the Atroari: on one occasion he tried to get into the *maloca*, although two warriors positioned themselves before the door with outstretched arms; on another occasion he did get in and counted those inside – 103 in all. This intrusion, in the opinion of Peret, 'was really invading their homes. And this act of counting heads must have been interpreted by the warriors as a hostile act, as something done by an enemy force.'

Nevertheless, the Indians continued to visit the expedition's encampment, bringing drink to exchange for presents; but the Father gave nothing in exchange. By this behaviour, in the opinion of Peret, Father Calleri 'wished to demonstrate clearly the superiority of the white man to whom the Indians must submit respectfully'. On one occasion the Padre caught an Indian in the expedition's canoe and drove him out, pushing him like an unwanted animal.

While Alvaro became more and more upset and apprehensive, Padre

Calleri became more and more complacent. 'They are already learning obedience,' he is reported as saying to Alvaro, 'I never thought it would be so easy to bring discipline to these Indians. We must go on like this for several days without let up, and they will be completely under our control, under our feet.'

But Alvaro didn't want to be part of this 'we'. He warned Calleri that the situation didn't look good, but the priest laughed it off, saying, 'We've seen this sort of disgruntlement before, but nothing ever comes of it.' The other expedition members were said not to have been as experienced as Alvaro and didn't have his intimate knowledge of Indian psychology. It seems that Calleri's methods had previously been effective with the Yanamani Indians, but, says Peret, 'the Yanamanis were Indians already pacified, and all the Father did was to organise a system of labour'. With the Atroaris, Father Calleri was doing more harm than good when, having noticed some expedition property missing, 'he reacted in his usual way by grabbing a shotgun and yelling, "If Indian steal – Father *bang, bang, bang*, kill Indian!"' Afraid he was going to be killed, one of the Atroari ran to his chief, who shouted at the Father, 'Cachorro brabo!' (literally 'You ill-tempered animal!').

It was obvious to Alvaro that things were going from bad to worse, but nothing he said seemed to influence Padre Calleri.

The account of the tragedy is confused. For the first time there is mention of a 'burnt-out compound'. In Portuguese the phrase is *a maloca queimada*, indicating that the compound was an Indian village and not an expedition camp. But at some point Padre Calleri had hidden weapons and ammunition in this compound, and he decided to return there to pick up the gear, possibly because he himself suspected hostility.

The burnt-out compound was twenty-five kilometres (fifteen miles) from the Atroari village and the expedition camp. Calleri seems to have been unsure of the way through the dense jungle, and the Atroari chief ordered eighteen of his warriors to accompany the pacifiers. These Indians were said to be 'very unsure of themselves and withdrawn'. They began to slide off into the forest, and the Padre, extremely annoyed, chased them, shouting. The FUNAI expert Peret interpreted the Indian behaviour as that of men who feared 'they were going to be killed when they got to the burnt-out compound'. Four of the Atroari did in fact refuse to continue, but the other fourteen stayed with Calleri. At last the party arrived at their destination. Some one-sided bartering appears to have taken place which left the Indians dissatisfied. Father Calleri is said to have acquired a jaguar pelt of immense value in return for a piece of cloth. Alvaro 'sensed an imminent and inevitable catastrophe'. For the last time Alvaro Paulo da Silva warned Padre Calleri, saying, 'Father, things are going very badly. These Indians are going to kill us. Let's go back to their village, give out the presents, say a nice goodbye and make a quick getaway.'

Calleri refused.

Alvaro decided there was only one course left open to him: to abandon the expedition. And he did so. His defection appears to have been on 31st October 1968. Exactly what did happen is uncertain. It seems that Alvaro stayed at the 'burnt-out compound' while Calleri's party retraced their steps through the forest, presumably with their guns and ammunition, back to their camp at the Atroari village.

Alvaro claims that his first move was to build a small canoe for his escape. Since there were only eighteen native canoes around there, he did not want to take one of these, for fear that afterwards he would be accused of having caused the massacre of his companions because of theft. He did not sleep that night. His conscience began to trouble him. 'What if my companions are killed?' he asked himself. In repentance he got to his feet and decided to go back to the village. It took him seven hours to travel the twenty-five kilometres which separated the destroyed compound from the village. When he got to the vicinity of the *maloca* he hid himself behind a tree and watched in silence.

There was no sound or any other sign of activity.

Not a noise, not a person to be seen.

He breathed more easily and thought, 'It's possible that the Father has gone off with the Atroaris'.

He stepped forward several paces and then saw, half-hidden, the first body lying to one side of a fallen tree. A little farther on, a second corpse. Shocked almost to death, he ran away from the murder. He lay hidden until nightfall and then made his way back to the burnt-out compound. This time he did the journey in three and a half hours. There he gathered together several objects which would be useful for the journey and got into his boat. When day broke he was already far away from that region, and safe. Two days afterwards he met a hunting party who gave him provisions, and a little farther on a settlement of geologists. From there he set off for Itacoatiara on board a safe, secure boat. Those who saw him said that this hunter seemed very nervous. He wasn't able to bear the memory of such a spectacle – the revenge of the Atroaris against the White Father and Authority.

This, then, as far as one can piece it together, is the story from Alvaro's side. But before the scent was completely cold at least two other sets of witnesses have brought stories from the kill which in their implications make the blood run cold. These witnesses are, on the one hand, the parachutists of the Brazilian Air Force (the Parasar) who finally collected the bones, and a cattleman or *gaúcho* called Ernani Renon Barros, who made a statement to the Chief of Police at Manaus.

When the Parasar dropped in with helicopters on the Atroari village they found that the Indians had fled. Rooting about, the airmen discovered a large sack of mineral samples collected from the surrounding region. A significant find. The lust of gold, or what can be turned into gold, of El Dorado, is still driving men into the forest.

The officers of the Parasar force, Major Gil Lessa, Captain Guaranis and Lieutenant Magalhães, commented significantly that there was every appearance of a kind of military know-how at work behind the Atroari Indians. It seems that the first member of Calleri's expedition to be killed was the radio operator, thus destroying the priest's communications link with Boa Vista and effectively preventing news of the massacre getting back to base. Then the exits from the Atroari village, which the expeditionaries might have fled down, had been blocked. Such strategies are white man's thinking, not Indians'. The arrows used in the killing had metal tips – not points of bone or other jungle materials commonly employed by isolated forest tribes. The obvious, blood-chilling conclusion, according to the Parasar officers, is that white men instigated and directed the murder of Father Calleri and his band.

Who could they be, and what were their motives?

Another slightly sinister fact has come to light. It seems that Padre Calleri's expedition, directed from the bishopric at Boa Vista, was not interested only in Indian pacification. Such pacification expeditions are very expensive, and there is reason to suppose that Calleri was at least partly subsidised by a group of businessmen interested in prospecting for minerals. But it is believed that rival parties were also prospecting in the Atroari tribal lands, and the sack of mineral samples found near or in the village may well have belonged to one of them. There is a strong suspicion that Father Calleri with his seven men and two women was massacred not primarily because he may have treated the Indians badly nor because the Indians of their own volition wanted to destroy his party: the wiping out of Calleri's group was at the instigation of ruthless white businessmen who were determined that no one else should horn in on territory they have marked down for exploitation. In this way the hapless forest Indians have themselves once more been exploited by the new conquistadors – the oil tycoons, the bauxite grabbers, the laterite ladroons.

The statement by the *gaúcho* Barros to Senhor João Valente, Chief of Police in Manaus, bears out the above interpretation. Barros reported how he was in the Atroari lands after the massacre. At the deserted Atroari village he found Padre Calleri's tent intact, but no sign of generators or radio-telephone. He found nothing more valuable than an old white shirt. He formed the opinion that Father Calleri's encampment was looted by employees of the large landowners (*fazendeiros*) of the region after the Indians had been incited to massacre the expedition.

The Parasar force which recovered the remains of the pacifiers returned to the area to observe the behaviour of the Atroaris. Captain Guaranis said the Indians had made a temporary village of seven shelters in a circle about twelve kilometres from the abandoned village and six from the burnt-out compound. In a few days they had cleared an area of huge jungle trees nearly a mile in circumference, in the middle of which were set the seven huts. No new gardens were being laid out, and they continued to support themselves from the fields near the old village. There, descending by helicopter, the officers were impressed by the cleanliness and the care with which the Indians looked after their farms. They were growing sugar cane, manioc, pineapple and beans, all in abundance and very well cultivated.

When the helicopter flew low over the new settlement the cacique or chief of the Atroaris, called Xamaroaga, brandished his bow to the skies, which the paratroopers took to indicate his determination to oppose intruders.

But for Xamaroaga and all other Indians, the writing is in the skies.

Note: The material for this chapter was taken from Brazilian national newspapers and magazines, including 'A Morte Do Índio' from *O Cruzeiro* of 20th February 1969.

CHAPTER SEVEN

Venezuela and Spanish Gold

IT was six fifty-five a.m. by my wrist watch – a Japanese imitation of the Rolex Oyster bought in Manaus for two pounds ten. By equator time it was probably half past six.

Outside my window, seen from my usual seat in the hovercraft (half-way down the right-hand side looking forrard), all was grey. Dove-grey skies, slate-grey jungle, mud-grey river. If the sun was standing at the portals of the east, then the gates were shut fast and not the slightest effulgence forced its way through the cracks. It was a pastel world desaturated of colour, cool, quiet.

Quiet, except for the hum of the hovercraft, which to the adaptable human ear was now as noiseless as silence.

Graham Clarke in the pilot's seat turned his head over his left shoulder, cleared his throat and called:

'Gentlemen! We have just crossed the equator – for the first time in the history of mankind in a hovercraft!'

One hardly knows how to react or reply to such news. I felt at a loss and a bit dissatisfied with myself for not being able to show elation or excitement. Somehow, one is deprived. Surely there ought to have been a bump as the craft crossed this imaginary line marking the world's waist.

Nothing.

Stuart Syrad swivelled round on his box seat in the gangway at the front. His leathery face had a portentous look. Feeling the occasion, he stood up and delivered himself in his best Army-cum-Public-School voice, 'In the circumstances, we have decided to push on. At a convenient beach there will be a little ceremony. Thank you.'

Blond Jesco was sitting beside me. Pink morning face, new shaven, blue-eyed. Through the spray-splashed window we both caught sight of a palm-thatched hut in a clearing wheeling by. Jesco said, 'A man lives right on the equator and he doesn't even know it.'

Other voices cried facetiously, 'Where's the line?' and received equally schoolboyish replies – 'Whitewashed on that tree!'

I noted in my diary on my knee, 'Light increasing. Craft travelling at forty-five m.p.h. River black and silver now. Sky completely overcast. Jungle on far bank (across the cabin past Mike Eden's Easter Island silhouette through the line of square windows) a distant black ribbon and almost featureless – on near bank a suspicion of green – the usual snarled wool skein of silvery trunks, branches, hanging lianas and cauliflower greenery – a few yards in from the bank any interstices simply black shadow.

'An air of expectancy. Besides passing the equator we are also nearing the frontier. Our progress has been overshadowed by Brazilian suspicions. David Smithers, our business manager, told me on the walk down to the craft from the Waupés mission that intrigue and opposition to our going forward had continued up to the last moment. The previous night Captain Perez had told him, "You can't proceed without an official representative of the Brazilian government aboard and neither I nor Colonel Igrejas can come – we have to fly back to Manaus. But if you will take a nun who has to go to the frontier post at Cucui we will name her the Brazilian representative."

'You could only call this a piece of blackmail. For Perez had already asked Smithers and Graham Clarke to take Sister Hilda and had been refused. As a matter of fact, when I was walking across to the refectory for our last dinner Captain Perez had drawn me aside and, speaking to me for the first time, said in halting English, "You are BBC boss – no?"

'I said, "Yes." He then went on to ask me to intervene with Graham Clarke. At that time I had not heard of the previous attempt to find Sister Hilda Tissot a seat and so I agreed to try. After dinner I spoke to Graham and in his quiet, reasonable way, he told me the answer was no. It was a reluctant no, especially after all the friendliness and kindness to us of the missionaries and nuns, but the hovercraft was up to weight and the only other alternatives were to leave behind another expedition member or off-load supplies.

'Captain Perez' next move was to demand unconditionally that the nun be given a lift. Our leaders suspected that he had already told the bishop Dom Miguel that he would fix it and he couldn't bear to lose face and be embarrassed by a refusal. David Smithers (a fairly ruthless negotiator in spite of his beaming bonhomie) had still refused and in the end said he would postpone our departure and signal what had happened to the British Embassy in Rio and the Foreign Office in London.

'Perez then gave way over the nun but said nastily, "You will, of course, be stopped at the frontier, anyway, because one of your passengers has no passport [this was Julio Castillo the Venezuelan boatman] and at least one of your expedition members is carrying a bird or animal as a specimen." It was true that one of the conditions of our free passage through Brazil was that no scientific work was to be done on the way and no specimens collected; it was also true that Robin Hanbury-Tenison had the day before bought a rare bird, the orange-crimson cock-of-the-rock and was hoping to carry it back to England in a wicker skep as a pet.

'Smithers in the end decided that the way out of the impasse was to take Sister Hilda as a gesture and not on order (and risk overloading) and to ask her to carry the caged bird at the frontier.'

As we continued our journey, because no convenient sandbank showed up nor a break in the palisade of jungle bank, Graham Clarke decided to stop the hovercraft in mid-river and hold his 'little ceremony'. It was ten minutes to eight and beginning to warm up. Graham left the pilot's seat, opened the top half of the door and facing his seated passengers including a rather wide-eyed, white-habited Sister Hilda Tissot (surely the first nun ever to hitch-hike by hovercraft?) said, 'Stuart, have you got those things?'

Stuart Syrad handed him a sheaf of papers from a folder.

'Gentlemen,' Graham went on, 'this is the first time in the history of mankind that the hovercraft has been crossed in an equator – ' He corrected himself, 'that the equator has been crossed in a hovercraft. If you'll step this way I have a document for each one of you!' Turning to Syrad, he asked, 'Have you got the coconuts, Stuart?' The Commando Captain pushed out past him with a machete under one arm and a couple of green coconuts and proceeded to hack the ends off on the narrow decking at the nose of the craft. 'Since this is a dry ship,' said Graham, 'we shall celebrate on coconut milk.'

This last remark puzzled me at the time and has puzzled me since, for I know the leaders had a case of whisky hidden away somewhere, and as for the BBC party, as I have already described, we were well supplied by Jesco with native rum, and I still had a little of my Bacardi left. However, the 'dry ship' remark may well have been intended for outsiders who would see the ceremony on film (Henry was busy turning his camera, and Peter Smith was pushing his zeppelin mike into the most unlikely places). It was a part of the Englishness of the occasion, doing the right thing and making sure that the right thing was seen to be done.

We all bundled out (including Sister Hilda) and like scholars at a prize-giving shook hands with the Captain and received a certificate. Stuart Syrad then passed us a holed coconut apiece and we edged carefully round the catwalks slobbering deliciously sweet milk down our chins from the jagged holes and reading our awards. Mine went:

KNOW ALL MEN BY THESE PRESENTS
that our Right Trusty and Worthy

BRIAN BRANSTON

Distinguished Member of this EXPEDITION this Day being the FIFTEENTH DAY OF APRIL in the Year of Our Lord NINETEEN HUNDRED AND SIXTY-EIGHT did make memorable History

FOR UPON THIS DAY being by the CALENDAR OF THE CHURCH EASTER MONDAY the said EXPEDITIONARY did CROSS THE EQUATOR in HOVERCRAFT S.R.N.6 the craft being named and numbered 026 of the class called WINCHESTER and under the Command of Captain ROLAND GRAHAM CLARKE

AND WHEREAS this was the FIRST OCCASION in the History of Mankind that a Hovercraft of the design of S.R.N.6 or of any mark Hovercraft whatsoever has CROSSED THE LINE under its own power the same NOBLE EXPEDITIONARY shall be REMEMBERED and VENERATED for all time as a TRUE and COURAGEOUS PIONEER of Science and Progress.

Signed and Certified under our hands this day
MICHAEL JOHN EDEN – Leader
ROLAND GRAHAM CLARKE – Captain
DAVID CARLETON SMITHERS – Manager

The British – or should I say 'English'? – are a funny peculiar lot: in spite of everything – Arthur Helliwell wrinkling his trim grey moustache at me and sending an imploring glance up to heaven as much as to say 'Good God! What next?' – there was a certain half-serious, half-debunking sense of occasion as far as I was concerned. There we were, nineteen hundred miles from the mouth of the Amazon, approaching a frontier beyond which stretched a wilderness of jungle unknown to men, a matted mass of tangled plant life lush and leathery, dark and wet, by whose rotting roots stagnated a little known channel, the Casiquiare Canal, leading, we fervently hoped, to the headwaters of the Orinoco – and we were behaving like Lords of the Earth receiving our prizes simply for being superior. Well, perhaps not entirely. We laughed at ourselves as well and made a bit of a mock of our leaders – but if anybody else, any outsider, had mocked we'd have been up in arms. I don't know what Sister Hilda Tissot made of it at all.

This little bit of grave fun-making took place just short of the mouth of the Rio Dimití, a comparatively tiny tributary or igarapé of the Negro coming in from the north. I didn't know it at the time, but a few miles up the Dimití in the year 1939 there had taken place an astonishing encounter between primitive Indians of the Waika group and a poor peasant white family.

Carlos Valero was paddling up the Dimití with his wife, his eleven-year-old daughter Helena and two younger sons, Luis, who was seven, and Anisio, a baby. They were journeying to two huts and a clearing in the forest left by the mother's brother and given to the family as a present. Early in the morning of the second day's rowing up the igarapé they caught sight of the two huts, but, rather strangely, a layer of low smoke appeared to be drifting from them and mixing with the mist on the river.

Since nobody ought to be there, the father prudently drove his dug-out into the bank and instructed his family to wait quietly while he, with machete in hand, crept up to the huts to investigate.

Shortly after, those left with the canoe saw Carlos Valero come running back from the huts with blood trickling down one arm. An Indian arrow had hit him, but he had pulled it out. His wife was standing on the bank asking, 'Carlos, what's the matter?' but he bundled her into the boat and pushed it off with his foot. He jumped in and began paddling downstream for dear life. He stopped only to rub salt into his wound, for he feared the arrow was poisoned.

They appeared to be getting away when a shower of arrows rained round the canoe, and the father called to his family to lie down in the bottom. Young Helena was hit almost immediately: an arrow ran under the skin of her belly and skewered it to her left thigh. Her mother gripped the arrow shaft, drew it out and threw it into the water. But the point remained stuck in Helena's leg as well as a piece in her belly. The mother managed to extract the belly bit, but the other was so deep in the thigh she could only see the wound. With her mouth and lips she nuzzled into it, trying to grip the arrow point with her teeth. Frantically, she worried it until at last she did grip the head in her teeth and then spat it into the river.

Running along the river bank, the Indians reached some rocks below the boat and shot off many arrows. Carlos, the father, was hit in arm and legs eight times. He pulled all the arrows out. He and his family threw themselves into the river and struggled to the bank. Carlos picked up his wounded daughter Helena and tried to carry her into the forest. She remembers saying to him, 'Father, leave me, I'm dying.'

Demented, the father rushed back to pick up little Luis, his son, while the mother ran off carrying the baby Anisio. As they got deeper into the jungle the father and mother lost each other. After two days they found each other again. But of Helena there was no sign. She had been carried off by a clan of Indians calling themselves the Kohoroshiwetari.

Helena Valero recovered from her wound and was taken to wife by an Indian chief. For twenty-two years she endured the life of a primitive forest Indian, working, bearing children, gathering berries, tending plantations, harvesting manioc roots and preparing flour; like many others, she was beaten casually by her current husband and suffered broken limbs; twice she was stolen and taken by new husbands. She is said to have had four children. Her wanderings took her through the still unexplored jungle north of the Negro behind Tapacucuará to the upper Orinoco. Then in 1961, after many unsuccessful attempts, she managed to escape from her Stone Age captivity, reaching first Tama Tama, and then San Fernando de Atabapo. Now, she lives on the Negro again, a sad woman, disillusioned with the world of white men and unable to regret the life she led with the Indians.

The hovercraft charged on for another hour and a half, when a stir up front drew our attention to the fact that we must now be nearing the frontier post. Stuart Syrad was driving while Graham Clarke was threading his Captain's gold bars of rank on the epaulettes of his khaki shirt. At the same time, Jim Sweeney (naked to the waist as ever) was brushing the gold-braid badge of Graham's naval officer's cap with the back of his hairy forearm.

Robin Hanbury-Tenison, a lock of damp hair curled over his forehead, pointed straight ahead along the river. I couldn't see what it was he was drawing attention to.

A smell of Christmas pervaded the rear of the cabin. Jesco was mixing 'BBC water'. There was, of course, no water at all in the tin mugs he began to hand round – only raw *cachaças* and the juice squeezed from fresh limes. The limes he carried like yellow snooker balls in a capacious string bag; the rum he was glugging from a plastic gallon container. That jungle-juice certainly put fire in your belly.

I struggled from the gummidge round my feet and into the gangway up front to see what was attracting Robin Tenison's attention. The silver-grey river stretched away from the hovercraft like a flat arrow-head, broad at the base, and at the narrow tip I saw a small mountain, small as mountains go, a mere dumpling of granite. But in that feature-less terrain the *Piedra do Cucui*, the Rock of Cucui, stood out like a boil on a bald head. The *Piedra* is a mountain whose grey granite flanks are bare of vegetation, smooth and weather-streaked with black. On top there are two knobs of rock, the one on the left, as we approached, rather larger than the other. If there'd been only one knob the rock would have looked for all the world like a nippled breast. At the base, on the right bank of the river, lay the buildings of Cucui, from one of which protruded a flag pole flying the Brazilian flag.

It was just ten o'clock when our forward lines were flung to the bank by Jim Sweeney and caught by a Brazilian soldier wearing a bush hat and having a little trouble with a slung rifle which inclined to get be-tween his knees and trip him as he staggered along the eroded bank trying to keep up with the slowing-down hovercraft. A procession of three officers, one in formal dress, the other two in bulgy battle dress, a civilian wearing a miniature sombrero-type straw hat and a mixed crowd of school children, the boys in short pants and the girls in gym-slips, crocodiled after the private soldier now trying to secure our line.

We came to a halt at the bottom of a ten-foot baked-mud bank, and a couple of planks were balanced from shore to craft and Sister Hilda Tissot handed across by the soldier and one of the officers. She dis-appeared in the centre of a swarm of twittering schoolgirls, never to be seen by us again. Her lift had accomplished in three hours a journey which by outboard canoe would have taken the best part of a week. No wonder the missionaries had been so eager for her to come with us. We intruders had still not come to recognise the difficulties and hazards facing ordinary travellers in these regions.

Captain Clarke with some formality was saluting the officer in charge of the post and asking hopefully, 'Do you speak English?'

Our leader, Mike Eden, was talking to the sombrero-ed civilian. They seemed to recognise each other and were immediately mentioning place names where they had worked together on a previous visit to South America by Mike. This young, darkly handsome chap was a botanist and lecturer at Caracas University. The two battle-dressed soldiers in jungle-green were Colonel Evilio Colmenares Leal and Captain Yepez of the Venezuelan National Guard. Both were scientists as well as soldiers. Colonel Leal was a graduate in geography of Wisconsin University. All three had flown from Caracas to the remote jungle air-strip at San Carlos, the Venezuelan frontier outpost corresponding to Cucui. They had then come down the Negro to Cucui in an outboard canoe. They would stay with us for the rest of the journey, which would be as new to them as to us: none of them could tell us anything about the Casiquiare Canal.

David Smithers had collected our passports before the craft came to land, and we all trooped behind him to the solid two-storeyed H.Q. While David was having our passports examined and stamped, the rest of us hung about the first-floor verandah overlooking the river, with the *Piedra do Cucui* almost at the bottom of the garden.

A romantic kind of character came up the steps on to the verandah and began speaking in Spanish to the Venezuelan pilot Julio Castillo. Jesco listened and occasionally chipped in. The character, who was a burly fellow of about thirty, wore a wide-brimmed felt hat, a sort of trilby or fedora such as American gangsters of prohibition days used to affect, and is still worn by most Indians in the high Andes. His belly bulged over his waistband and was covered by a wide expanse of blue cotton shirt. His ruckled pants were rolled at the bottom and his feet were bare. Altogether there was a swashbuckling, buccaneerish look about him.

He was a Colombian.

The Colombian frontier ran along the opposite bank of the Negro a little farther north of Cucui, and the buccaneer (whose name I never did discover) had come downstream from his home on the other side from San Carlos bringing the Venezuelan observers.

Jesco translated what the buccaneer was saying and, looking back, I'm ashamed to think how we pricked up our ears.

It was nothing less than rumours of gold. Spanish gold. Shades of El Dorado! We at once began bombarding Jesco with questions.

It seems the buccaneer had found gold coins, gold rings, jewels even, and other things on the Colombian side of the river opposite our next stop, San Carlos.

We were due to spend two nights at San Carlos, because the whole of our next day would be taken up with meeting a party of Venezuelan journalists and TV men who were flying in to this jungle air-strip – the very end of the line – from Caracas the capital on the northern coast. Bob Saunders said to me, 'Can't we do something about this, Brian?'

'How do you mean?'

'Well, I've got my pendulum with me – and we're stopping for a day at San Carlos – we could do a bit of divining for gold.'

Bob was referring to the metal-detecting properties of a small wooden ball on the end of a cord into whose mysteries we had been initiated a year or so before by Tom Lethbridge. Tom used to be a well-known Cambridge archaeologist, a participant in many a celebrated dig, including the Sutton Hoo treasure. For a long time Tom Lethbridge has been interested in dowsing, divining, call it what you will, and has worked out a method with the pendulum which (no matter how much one scoffs) appears to give results. According to Tom, a relationship exists between the length of the cord from the ball to the hand and any substance you care to mention. So if you want to prospect for gold you measure twenty-nine inches on the cord, swing the bob backwards and forwards with your right hand and with your left arm outstretched horizontal slowly describe an arc. If there is gold within the arc the pendulum, instead of swinging, will rotate when the left arm points towards gold. Having achieved a rotation of the ball, you move away from your original spot and repeat the operation. You should then have a second line intersecting your first. At the point of intersection, dig for gold!

'O.K.,' I said, 'If we get any chance at San Carlos we'll give it a go.'

By this time our passports had been stamped, and with them bundled under his arm David Smithers walked out of the office and strode briskly down to the hovercraft. In five minutes we had taken our seats and were roaring upriver with our three new passengers. The two officers sat up front with expressions of interest, even amazement, on their faces. Ernesto Medina, the young university lecturer, sat half-way down, still swapping stories with Mike Eden.

Once past the Rock of Cucui we encountered the same monotonous level jungle landscape as before. At eleven fifty we landed for a few minutes for the first time on Venezuelan soil. It was San Rosa, a huddle of huts atop grassy clay banks. An old, old lady, wrinkled and sun-baked, was doing her washing at the river's brink, bashing hell out of a shapeless something on the rocks. She didn't even raise her eyes to look.

It was twenty minutes after noon when we departed San Rosa, and within five more minutes we came to a stop in midstream. One of the dials showed overheating of oil in the engine, and Graham switched off the motor to allow cooling down. He was uncertain whether the dial was faulty or whether the engine lubricant was actually overheating. It was really not the time to take chances. We were now some 800 miles from our start and nearing the point of no return.

Belly-flat on the broad river in the middle of the day with the equator only just behind our backs, the hovercraft began quickly to resemble a bake-oven inside – and we were the loaves.

'Gentlemen,' said Graham, 'please step outside if you want to, but go carefully. Don't put your feet through the plenum chamber.'

A few decided they would have a swim. This didn't appeal to me, partly because of what might be in the water from snakes and caymen to microbes; and partly because when one returns to the furnace of the cabin the discomfort, the prickling heat and the pouring sweat are only intensified after the dip. I know all this from experience: as a young chap in Southern India I used to swim in a deep, tank-like well until one day I found I was sharing the amenity with a couple of poisonous water snakes. If ever anybody dived *out* of a well, I did on that occasion. I came up like a submarine missile. Then once in Freetown harbour I left a troopship cabin at midnight to frolic naked on deck in a tropical thunderstorm. In those great gouts of cool rain I felt like a trout under a waterfall. It was delicious, refreshing, the first time I'd been cold for weeks; but when I had to return to my cabin for the rest of the night I endured such parboiling agony that I've never forgotten it.

However, our recordist Peter Smith, Robin Tenison, Douglas Botting and our manager David Smithers stripped off to their under-pants and dived in. The rest of us watched rather enviously from the decking. Colonel Leal looked particularly hot in his jungle-green battle-dress complete with wide webbing belt supporting a large automatic pistol, a conspicuous jungle knife which appeared to be a combination miniature machete and saw and a large felt-covered water-bottle. Nor did he discard his combat cap – a sort of kepi with a jutting neb. He looked down at the swimmers with a certain disapproval and muttered that the piranha in Venezuelan rivers were especially savage and would strip a man clean 'to leave nothing but white bones'. He was supported by Julio Castillo, the river pilot, who described in Spanish huge fish capable of eating two men at once.

Still, our friends enjoyed their swim none the less for that, darting here and there like silver fish in the dark waters of the Rio Negro. Dark waters which in a couple of days we should be leaving for the ominous white water of the Casiquiare Canal: for the really troublesome part of our trip lay before us. In five days we had covered almost half the distance of our journey in miles. But from now on our progress would be much slower. The scientists had their work to do. The BBC party intended to hive off and find primitive Indians. And then would come the climax of the celebrated forty-five-mile stretch of Maipures and Atures rapids – so celebrated that in Caracas 800 miles away they are simply referred to (and have been for four hundred years) as *Raudales – the* Rapids.

Graham Clarke called the swimmers aboard, Stuart Syrad closed the hatch and we were off once more.

At two o'clock in the afternoon we reached San Carlos with Colombia on the opposite bank. Colombia, where at that very moment in the dark woods guerillas were being hunted to their death – though unknown to us. Colombia, where the buccaneer had found his Spanish gold. Colombia – the home of El Dorado – still luring men on to destruction.

CHAPTER EIGHT

The Secrets of San Carlos

THE detainees of San Carlos will forgive me if I call their village a dump.

They'll forgive me, I hope, for calling them *detainees*, but for the ordinary folk who live here, San Carlos must appear as remote and prison-like as any camp in Siberia. For them, I am sure it *is* a dump, a few rows of mud-brick huts, adobe one-room hovels with the shameful letters DDT and a date daubed on the buff-coloured walls by the shrunken wood doorposts (the latest date of disinfestation by Government order). San Carlos – a higgledy-piggledy collection of human kennels, windowless, or if there were any windows I don't remember them, blindly facing earth streets savagely rutted and gouged by tropical rains. But there were street lights, electric lamps in curved conduit pipe atop wooden poles, lamps which looked defiantly ancient and frontier-like as though they had been there since Edison first made electric bulbs. Two or three pigs aimlessly rooting across the road made San Carlos for me redolent of a Donegal or Connemara village, lost, forgotten, at the edge of the world, especially with the river at the end of the street creating the illusion of a sea horizon.

No roads lead into or away from San Carlos to anywhere else on earth.

There is one surprising thing about San Carlos: it has a plaza.

The Spanish, someone has said, never forgot that they are an urban people, and wherever they settled away from Spain they laid out the foundations of the church, the town hall and the gaol – probably in that order – and built them round the all-important plaza.

The plaza at San Carlos, no bigger than a respectable garden, has an unfinished air. Paved paths run – in that heat 'dawdle' would be a better word – round the four sides of the square and cross from corner to corner. Where the diagonals intersect stands the phallic symbol of Venezuela, the invariable centre of any Venezuelan plaza whatsoever, a concrete column topped by a bust of the country's eagle-nosed liberator, Simon Bolívar. The column, called the *rollo*, is an ancient institution with very sinister associations which, at that time, I was unaware of.

At two o'clock in the breathless afternoon the plaza was empty, not even a dog – at least, that's what it seemed like as we entered; but there *was* a dog, one dog, a poor bony pariah disturbed by our dry footsteps from the shade at the far side of Bolívar's column. He struggled arthritically to his feet and cocked a leg absent-mindedly against Bolívar's support. But nothing came and he staggered away, leaving the great man unsullied. You could almost hear his desiccated joints rasping together in the heat.

The BBC party had walked up from the river in the company of Arthur Helliwell, Douglas Botting, Conrad Gorinsky and Colonel Colmenares Leal. We were in our normal state in that humid clime – pouring sweat, panting a little for breath, lumbered as we were with our forty-pound hold-alls, our hammocks and mosquito nets. The campmaster had instructed Arthur and Douglas to take up quarters at the mission for our two nights' stop. The mission was a single-storey building on one side of the plaza, unpretentious, uninviting, gloomy and (as they later complained) clouded with mosquitoes. Colonel Leal and Conrad Gorinsky came on with us BBC men past the square to a bit of rising ground where stood the most imposing block in the village, the military post. We had been allotted hanging space for our hammocks on the open verandah of the substantial building which housed officers' quarters, quartermasters' stores, guard room, barracks for ten or a dozen men – even showers.

In front of the barracks and separated from the verandah by a drop of two feet was an overgrown garden, chock-a-block with fleshy-leaved shrubs and cachou-nut bushes.

This military post must surely have been regarded as a punishment station by the youthful soldiers who welcomed us so amicably. It really was the end of the line, its only effective communication with the populated coast and Caracas being by air over endless miles of savannah, mountain and jungle to the tiny scar of an air-strip a quarter of a mile beyond the back of the barracks.

And yet, dump as it was, to me San Carlos became an exciting spot – a romantic oasis in the middle of that dreadful wilderness of trees. It was exciting and romantic for three reasons: one was at the bottom of the garden, one on a huge rock down by the water's edge and a third across the river on the Colombian shore.

But at two ten in the afternoon none of these reasons for romance had been made apparent and we flopped limply into wicker chairs on the verandah, still gasping a little for breath.

It was here that we first began to get acquainted with Colonel Leal. He was a small, fine-boned man, very dark, with a round head and black eyes: his beard showed blue under the skin. He spoke English with a soft American accent.

Colonel Leal's first move was to unbutton his tunic, unclasp his webbing equipment and begin nosing round for drinking water. Two large earthenware filters (like jars from the story of Ali Baba) stood on either side of a man-sized refrigerator. Water from the filters was drawn off as needed into hip-flask-type whisky bottles, which were then stacked in the ice-box. A young soldier, with rifle slung over his left shoulder, opened the fridge at Colonel Leal's bidding and poured deliciously cold water into the tin mugs each of us always carried about our persons.

Lying in a cane chair, I needed nothing more at that moment; but young Peter Smith, Henry the cameraman, Jesco and Bob Saunders began to perk up and become conscious of the next appetite needing assuasion.

'What's for lunch, then?' asked Peter, looking pointedly at Conrad Gorinsky.

Conrad lolled back and made no reply. He gave the impression of thinking it an academic question and, moreover, one that didn't concern him.

'Well, then,' said Peter, 'what *is* for lunch?'

The – I was going to say 'the air' – became charged: it would be truer to say 'the vacuum' on the verandah became charged, and nobody volunteered an observation, while each expeditionary self-consciously looked at anything but one another.

'Well, *I'm* hungry,' said Peter.

At last Conrad muttered that a meal was being prepared.

'Where?' persisted Peter. 'Shouldn't you be organising it? Aren't you the expedition cook?'

It had been a long exhausting drive that day, and it was now nearing three o'clock in the afternoon. In spite of his part-Amerindian ancestry (or perhaps because of it), Conrad felt the heat and languor of the day, but roused himself testily from his lassitude to say angrily that on an expedition such as ours he expected people to give and take. If this is how they reacted in comfortable circumstances, what *were* they going to do when things really got tough?

This hardly seemed an adequate defence when one had only to open a ration-box (unfortunately they were still a quarter of a mile away down on the hovercraft) and dole out biscuits, cheese, jam, tinned fish and dried fruit. However, Jesco came to the rescue. He reminded the BBC party of the 'iron rations' he had suggested each man carry about with him. We quickly scratched to the bottom of our bags and prepared a snack of sardines and tinned cheese gouged out of the can with a spoon.

Conrad flung away muttering that a real meal was being prepared for everybody at a house down in the village.

We wiped our oily lips on the backs of our hands and struggled to our feet to sling hammocks from the rings set in the wall and supporting pillars of the verandah.

Colonel Leal was a bit embarrassed by our petulance, but he said nothing.

After slinging my hammock and mosquito net at the far end of the verandah, where a little air appeared to drift round the open corner of the building, and after disposing my pack and few personal belongings against the wall at the hammock's head, I took a walk down the garden path.

There was a dilapidated wooden gate giving out on to a rutty earth road. On either side of the gate lay the bronze barrels of two ancient ship's cannon of Armada times' thickness and ponderousness with fat chunky projections to ride in the trunnions of their massive stepped wooden carriages.

It didn't strike me then as forcibly as it did later that those two gun pieces had no business to be there. If they weighed anything they weighed at least half a ton each. Who could possibly have brought them and how? They had been cast in Europe, probably during the days of King Philip of Spain and most likely had reached the New World serving their time on Spanish galleons. But how had they penetrated to this God-forsaken spot far from the coast and what pressing reason had forced somebody to sweat them here? There have never been any roads to San Carlos; it's unlikely that there *will* be any in the

foreseeable future. Those guns could only have come by river. From the
Amazon mouth to Manaus is a thousand miles; from Manaus up the
Rio Negro to San Carlos is another thousand miles. Sailing and rowing
that distance in small boats must have been a labour of Hercules. Given
that someone was hare-brained enough to attempt such a task, how
could they have possibly got those gun barrels up the *Cachoeras do
Morte*, the Rapids of Death at Waupés? Well, then, could they have
come from the north coast via the Orinoco? When I first set eyes on
those guns, I wasn't certain – none of us was certain – whether the
hovercraft would be able to go from the Negro into the Orinoco by
way of the Casiquiare Canal. In any case, from the Orinoco mouth to
San Carlos by river on the map was a thousand miles. But what seemed a
much more formidable obstacle than distance in this case was the
Orinoco rapids between Samariapo and Puerto Ayacucho. Even Sir
Walter Raleigh knew of these rapids by repute, they were *the* Rapids –
Raudales with a capital R – and nobody had been known to shoot their
forty-five-mile stretch of fall, whirlpool, eddy, race and rocks – and
live.

I went back to the verandah and found Colonel Leal idly whittling a
piece of wood with his service dagger-cum-saw.

'Colonel,' I said, 'have you any idea where those two cannon at the
bottom of the garden came from?'

'I will ask,' he said, and flung a stream of Spanish towards the open
door of the quartermaster's store. A bush-hatted sergeant clicked out
and stood to attention. The two men stared sternly at each other, and a
loud-voiced Spanish inquisition followed: you'd have thought the
Colonel was the presiding judge, and the sergeant pleading for mercy
and not to be burnt at the stake. Actually, this was normal. During these
shouting matches Venezuelans aren't quarrelling, they're just having a
conversation.

The man saluted and turned on his heel into the store (later he flogged
me a services' knife for ten American dollars – a vast overcharging.
Quartermaster sergeants are the same from China to Peru.)

'Yes,' said Colonel Leal, pursing the red lips in his blue jowl and
nodding satisfaction, 'he knows where the cannons came.'

'He knows where they came from?'

'He knows.'

'Well – where, then?'

'From the fort across the river on the Colombian side.'

I really was astounded at this bit of news: a fort with bronze cannon
here, of all places, towards the very centre of God knows how many

hundreds of thousands of square miles of forest which is literally impenetrable a few yards from the river bank.

Bob Saunders came from the showers with a damp towel over his
arm. He was powdered and puffed. His dark (now silvering) hair was
neatly brushed back. Not a whisker of his pencil-line moustache out of
place. 'Bob!' I said, 'We've definitely got to go across the river tomorrow. Not only to use your pendulum – there's a fort there. Never
know what-all we might find.'

Henry, Peter and Jesco were sitting in their hammocks. They all
pricked up their ears. Jesco put his tin mug of rum and fresh lime juice
on the floor: 'We could give some of the Indian boys a few bolivars to
hire a couple of canoes – they'd take us across,' he said. We agreed to do
it. But it wouldn't be until latish in the following afternoon, for the
party of journalists who were flying in from Caracas couldn't get to us
before noon, and we had to be on parade during their stay for questioning. They would return about three p.m. in order to get back to the
swing of the night life in that great Babylon – at least in our deprived
condition that is the sort of mental picture we had of them. Lucky
devils! Still, who knows? We might find a fortune.

It was nearly five o'clock, and hungry Peter had discovered that a
meal had been prepared for that hour in a kind of *cantina* in the village.
The *cantina* was larger than the other houses, having a garden shaded by
a tall and bushy breadfruit tree. Two bustling, wide-bottomed, comfortable Spanish–Indian ladies served at a long table which, with chairs
near enough together to nip your haunches if you weren't careful,
accommodated all the expeditionaries. Graham was already there – on
time as ever; Stuart Syrad was there; David Smithers too – shirted,
shaved and shampooed, no doubt, his black straight hair well oiled, his
face beaming with satisfaction – as well it might, for the first half of the
journey had gone without a hitch and we were on time for our rendezvous with the journalists tomorrow. Arthur Helliwell was there, his
silver sideburns giving his bronzed face a look of perfect health – a look
which later was to be belied. The two hovercraft crew men, Jim
Sweeney and John Hoyland, had walked in before us, Robin Tenison
was in the kitchen airing his Spanish with the cook, and Conrad
Gorinsky (in his role of expedition cook and universal provider) was
counting the places.

The meal proved tasty and plentiful, starting with great poes of soup
and going on to a main course of hillocks of fried rice, chickens, fish
and tortillas at least three-quarters of an inch thick, fried outside a
golden yellow and, when your teeth sank into them, solid enough to

sink a battleship. The normal sweet – piercingly sweet – black, black coffee followed and, of course, gallons of water. You poured drinking water into you like emptying buckets down a drain. Then you sweated waterfalls.

That night the heavens opened and rain fell vertically like spears. The temperature dropped and I spent a comfortable night naked but for my blanket, with rain hissing down a yard from my side, every drop drilling into the clayey soil and leaving puddles of yellow mud by the time morning light came.

It was to be a lazy morning with nothing special to do except wait for the journalists to fly in. After breakfast at the *cantina* (which I have a hazy recollection consisted of black coffee and large bowls of custard), Jesco wanted me to go to the river-landing where he had made a 'discovery'.

He limped along ahead of me down the eroded village street, his rolling gait and burly frame putting me in mind of a sailor threading his way through some seedy dock area in 'the Islands' of a Joseph Conrad novel. He was wearing his *cangaceiro* hat – the sombrero-shaped hat favoured by the semi-bandit horsemen of the north-east of Brazil, the front and back brims of which are pressed upwards. Jesco's *cangaceiro* hat – it was a plaited yellow straw one instead of leather – was a little bit incongruous, because he had inked the letters BBC on the upturned front brim with a cameraman's magic marker. I could well imagine some executive gentleman from an office ankle-deep in carpet on the third floor of Broadcasting House gazing with awe and disfavour on such a 'House Image'. There would have been no need to worry: the landing was empty except for the tied-up hovercraft and Jim Sweeney, without shirt, pottering about on the far catwalk.

He raised a hand and called, "Mornin' Jesco! 'Mornin' Brian!'

We greeted him and asked him how he had slept. 'Bitten to buggery,' he said. We laughed. It's true there seemed to be more and meaner mosquitoes in San Carlos than before, though we were still on the 'black' Negro. The white water of the Casiquiare didn't begin for another fifteen or twenty miles.

Beyond the hovercraft, the blue-black river rolled steadily on, brimming after the night's rain and sparkling in the sun shafting between high clouds. Everything was new-washed and sharp. The coconut palms along the far bank were etched in dry point against the blue sky, and we could see at a break in their ranks the shape of a thatched-roofed mud-walled house well up from the water's edge. This was to be our destination later in the day – we hoped.

I was called back from my reverie on that prospect of the Colombian shore by Jesco's saying, 'You want to see this, Brian?'

'What, Jesco?'

'The thing I told you about – you know – it's very funny. *You* may think it is funny. I know you are interested in these things.'

'Where is it?'

'Up on that rock,' and he pointed to a gigantic granite boulder as big as a house which, near the landing, dropped almost vertically into the water while its top sloped for ten or fifteen yards up to the surface of the bank. The local boys use this rock as a diving board; the side beyond us slanted rather more gently into a little cove and there their mothers sometimes wash the clothes, rolling them into coils and beating hell out of them on big pebbles before spreading them to dry on the main rock.

'Come on,' said Jesco, and we plashed along the muddy shore and scrambled like bears to the top of the rock.

'Look!' he said, and pointed to his feet.

At what I saw, I experienced the 'wild surmise' of Keats' sonnet and the first thought that flashed across my mind was 'Lope de Aguirre'. On the flat top of the granite rock was a deeply incised cross with arms of equal length – about four inches each side of the centre, and to the right a date. The date was the really exciting thing. Two figures, a one and a six, were clear cut in the fashion of the sixteenth and seventeenth centuries. What was to the right of the 16 was difficult to decipher. I hurried back to the military guard post to collect Henry with his camera and a small plastic talcum powder puffer. With Johnson's Baby Powder puffed into the crevices of the inscription and the surplus wafted away with Jesco's *cangaceiro* hat, we read what appeared to be the letter M. So we had a cross and 16 M.

The obvious conclusion was that some Christian traveller had been this way three hundred odd years ago and had done a 'Kilroy was here' on the one outstanding landmark in the area. As I say, I believed at first that some God-fearing expeditionary with that madman Lope de Aguirre might have cut the inscription, in which case we would have had irrefutable proof that at least one desperate band of men had rowed and sailed up the Negro before us, had found the Casiquiare Canal and proceeded down the Orinoco to the open sea. But the date of Aguirre's expedition is well known, namely 1560–61 – a century before our inscription. For the remainder of that morning I couldn't put out of my mind those sixteenth-century desperadoes whose 5,000-mile journey had been sparked off by the urge to find El Dorado and which Clements

Markham described as 'this cruise of Aguirre (in which) all that is wildest, most romantic, most desperate, most appalling in the annals of Spanish enterprise seems to culminate in one wild orgie of madness and blood'.*

* Sir Clements R. Markham – Introduction to *The Expedition of Pedro de Ursua and Lope de Aguirre in Search of El Dorado and Omagua in 1560-1*, translated by William Bollaert – London, Hakluyt Society, 1861.

CHAPTER NINE

San Carlos : Journalists and a Fort

EARLY on the morning of Tuesday, 16th April 1968, while, from a climatic point of view, life was still livable (the tyrant sun not yet having got on his high horse) I stood alone on top of the rounded hump of the great grey granite boulder at San Carlos watching the river swish by. At my feet mouldered that enigmatic inscription, a cross and 16 M; on the other bank of the river, three-quarters of a mile away, stood some kind of fort. What its purpose had been, or who had built it, nobody could tell me. I had no intention of leaving San Carlos without having first inspected it.

The dark River Negro had an unbroken surface of blued steel as it glided past the smooth rock side ten feet below me. I couldn't help thinking of that other expedition which, 408 years ago, had grunted at oars and paddles, had tacked its pot-bellied brigantines back and forth zig-zag to use the breeze as it clawed past this very rock. Since cleared spaces on the river bank are few and far between, perhaps those Machiavellian men and spirited women had even put in here and tied up: maybe that ugly, small-faced, fierce-eyed, indomitable Lope de Aguirre had stood just where I was standing now.

My thoughts returned to the present.

Last night the leaders of our expedition had gone to bed disgruntled, at the least; at most, with a wish to do mayhem. And the Venezuelan boatman Castillo (according to Jesco) had sobbed himself to sleep: of course, he had to get drunk first, and Jesco had been sympathetic enough to assist him.

There had been a certain amount of smouldering discontent among members of the expedition ever since we arrived at San Carlos. A good deal of it centred on the river pilot Julio Castillo, who had turned up so fortuitously at Manaus. It was here at San Carlos that Castillo's real work ought to begin, for it was here he had brought his forty-foot launch to carry some of the scientists during the next stage of the trip as far as the Maipures and Atures rapids. Having become impatient at the hovercraft's non-arrival after he had waited three months, Castillo had drifted to Manaus – as I have told. Unfortunately, during his absence from San Carlos some thief had made off with the two forty-gallon barrels of petrol he had brought from the Orinoco to work his huge outboard motor.

There was no more petrol to be bought in San Carlos.

Naturally enough, the expedition manager David Smithers and the scientists were more than a little annoyed. Smithers, who spoke some Spanish, had made his exasperation quite plain to Castillo. Castillo, having seen the hovercraft working on kerosene, stated trustingly that his outboard engine would do so too. For some reason, members of our party believed him. He was given a couple of drums of kerosene to replace his stolen gas and as the setting sun reddened the dark waves of the Negro he had headed his launch away from San Carlos carrying four of the scientists, two from England, John Thornes and David Harris, and the two Venezuelans, Ernesto Medina and Captain Yepez.

Within an hour the kerosene-clogged engine had choked to a stop and the launch had had to drift back with the current to San Carlos.

This time Julio Castillo was really in the dog-house. He had consoled himself with *cachaças*, got weeping drunk and, as Jesco told me, had gone to bed like a blubbering baby.

The situation was rather serious. The hovercraft tanks had been re-filled at San Carlos, but there was no more fuel for her between here and the Orinoco. The distance we had to cover before we reached the next drums at Tama Tama was close on 300 miles. This particular leg of the journey was likely to be the most dangerous so far, for we had to turn out of the black water of the Negro and enter the pestilential white water of the Casiquiare Canal. If Castillo's launch was indeed unwork-able, then with four more bodies than had been calculated and all their gear aboard, the hovercraft ran that much more danger of not being able successfully to complete this, the most hazardous, leg. No wonder Graham Clarke and David Smithers were put out.

Still, a ray of hope did appear on the morning of the press conference. It was rumoured that across the river from San Carlos a Bolivian would very likely have two barrels of petroleum for sale. Very likely. I wonder where they came from? It was agreed that Castillo should cross the river and try to do a deal, but not until the journalists who were to visit us had taken off for their return flight to Caracas.

Wonders never cease in these parts, and shortly after landing the previous day we had been surprised by the presence of a young apple-faced English woman, said to be called Hilary Branch, and her newly married husband. According to the gossip (and I didn't inquire too closely into it), this young couple had flown a thousand miles from Caracas by bush plane to have a look at the hovercraft and half hoped to hitch a lift for the rest of the way. Failing that, they hoped to return in the aircraft due to bring in the journalists. Neither of their hopes materialised, so how and when they got back to Caracas I don't know.

Hilary and her husband came down to the rock. Hilary changed into a bathing suit round the other side of the rock where the local women do their washing and swam in the river. She was accompanied by a tame otter. Her husband stood on the bank. Like some of us expedition men, where total immersion in the river was concerned, he preferred discretion to valour: his appearance I found romantic – a wide-brimmed hat, a careless wisp of beard, open shirt, jeans thickly rolled up round his calves, feet and legs otherwise bare. He reminded me of Huckleberry Finn, needing only a corn-cob pipe. The otter, a smoky-grey, sleek, web-footed, flat-tailed, snub-jawed creature of beauty, was three months old and three feet long. Before persuading it to swim, Hilary Branch's young husband had held the otter like a gigantic kitten by the scruff close to his waist so that the body, legs and tail drooped melting into one shiny sinuous tube. He wanted to show me how long it was. The otter reached from his belt to his toe. He told me that such otters (which are found in the rivers hereabout) at full growth reach a length of six feet. When put down on the ground it lolloped and buckled after its master and mistress in a most fetching way, giving babyish squeaks and squawks, bristling its snub jaws and showing its pointed milk teeth.

We hung about during the morning waiting for the journalists to fly in from the Venezuelan capital. I myself wandered up to the air-strip lying yellow and dusty about a quarter of a mile beyond the military barracks where we had spent the night. The landing ground was, in fact, extensive and had obviously been prepared with the help of a bulldozer or some such earth-moving machine. How the Army had got so heavy and bulky a piece of equipment to this last outpost I did not know.

At twelve noon we heard a buzz over the jungle and saw a four-engined Heron fly low along the river looking for the landing strip. The aircraft belonged to the Shell Petroleum Company in Caracas and had been laid on as a 'public relations' job to allow journalists, photographers and TV news men to exchange for a few hours the concrete jungle for the real jungle while still being cocooned in the comfort and safety of a quite luxurious little plane.

After they had landed, a press conference was held in a sort of palm-roofed bandstand, with concrete floor and wooden benches round the circumference. It stood high on the bank overlooking the hovercraft and about fifty yards from the huge landing rock. That conference went on interminably, our English having to be interpreted into Spanish. Naturally enough, the journalists were eager for a demonstration of the hovercraft. Our manager, David Smithers, said sorry, the hovercraft captain was unable to oblige because of necessary maintenance which had to be carried out. He did not mention our trouble with fuel and Julio Castillo. You could see the look of disappointment and incredulity on those journalists' faces. We in the BBC party were incredulous too. Here was a bunch of fifteen people who had got up at five o'clock that morning, who had flown five hours over almost continuous jungle and who in a couple of hours time would fly another five hours back to Caracas, and they weren't even to see how the hovercraft performed. These men looked like a boy at Christmas-time whose father has bought him a train-set and then refuses to let him play with it.

The press conference was rapidly turning into the non-event of the year. There was even a television news camera team with a bulky 35-mm Arriflex camera. They were obviously beginning to think themselves fools.

In the middle of this near-vacuum a messenger brought news that the expedition's lunch – the expedition's mind you, not the journalists' – was ready back at the guest house. Unbelieving, I watched as David Smithers informed the men from Caracas that we would have to go off and eat.

As we of the BBC party walked up the rutted road past the empty plaza and the rollo to what we now called 'the sad café' we fumed like little railway engines with steam up waiting for somebody to throw open the regulator. Henry Farrar said at last in his gritty Yorkshire voice, 'Brian, you've got to do somethin' about it. What sort of a press do you reckon we'd get in England after a do like this? It doesn't matter to us really – but what I'm thinkin' about is the hovercraft. The South American newspapers'll pan it. *That's* no good. Country needs all the support it can get.'

So, egged on by the others, I decided to make a strong plea for a demonstration by the hovercraft. In these cases one's motives tended to be suspect, for we would obviously film the show ourselves, since we so rarely got a chance of covering the craft in movement from the bank. Graham Clarke had to watch every pint of fuel and David Smithers every penny expended, so neither of them was easy to persuade.

Most people were seated at table in the guest house when we arrived and already toothing it out with the tortillas. Rather self-consciously I cleared my throat and addressed them. I said we were asking for trouble by not letting the journalists see the hovercraft working and by not giving them a flip. It seemed to me that we were Britain's ambassadors, and the sort of press she would get in Venezuelan and other South American newspapers without a demonstration would be lukewarm at best, and at worst distinctly hostile.

Graham Clarke and David Smithers looked down into their piled-up plates and made non-committal noises. However, I felt I had publicly put them on the spot, and this proved to be the case. At two thirty p.m. the journalists were given a demonstration of the hovercraft.

Shortly after three o'clock the four-engined Heron flew off as quickly as it had come, and Julio Castillo was issued with a ration of petrol from the hovercraft (which carried a few gallons to run its fuel pump). He slunk across the river in his forty-foot launch to chaffer for the two drums of gas in the possession of the mysterious Colombian.

This was the time for the BBC crew to follow in Castillo's wake across the Negro and explore the fort we had been told about. I called together Henry with his camera, Peter with his microphone and Nagra recorder, Bob and Jesco. We gathered at the river bank by the hover-craft.

A little below the landing place one or two narrow dugout canoes were tied up in front of a couple of palm-thatched huts. There were coconut palms all round the huts, and some teenaged boys were walking up them in that typical monkey-up-a-stick method. Green coconuts dropped like bombshells round our heads. Two fat and comfortable Spanish–Indian ladies, overflowing their chairs, sat outside the huts and giggled at our nervousness. The boys descended and with dangerous machetes deftly sliced the ends off the shiny green nuts, offering them to us to drink.

Jesco inquired what the prospects were of using the canoes, and three of the boys agreed to paddle us over the river for a consideration.

The river was brimming and running swiftly. It was about three-quarters of a mile across, and at surface level looked quite frightening. The canoes seemed especially shallow and wobbly. Still, we got in. Jesco, who knew more about these things than we did, expressed some apprehension. Nevertheless, he carefully disposed his bulky weight in the centre of one canoe, with Peter in front of him and a paddling boy in the stern.

The second canoe was some ten feet long, and Bob Saunders sat pinched in the middle of it, with Henry and his £2,000 camera behind him. Behind Henry, our paddler thrust hard into the water to keep the canoe from drifting downstream. They all faced forward. I myself sat in the prow facing backwards, because my thwart was so near the nose it gave no room up front for my long legs.

We followed the other canoe.

Once away from the bank, we realised that our position was somewhat parlous: there was only one inch of freeboard amidships between the surface of the water and the edge of the canoe. Any slight ripple sloshed water into the craft.

Bob Saunders was foundered. There was nothing he could do about it. It was a physical thing. He reminded me of a horse I was once riding in India which plunged with me on its back into a quicksand in the River Godavari. I was looking straight into Bob's face under his floppy green forage cap and I saw that he really was alarmed. As he gripped the edges of the canoe with rigid arms and hands, his fingers were under water. Bob can't swim, and he had every right to be uneasy. He kept repeating, 'This is crazy! This is madness! We shouldn't be doing this, Brian! We're out of our tiny minds!'

No doubt he was right when you consider that one keel over of the canoe and we would have swamped, losing our irreplaceable camera as well as running a real risk of drowning – I'm only a poor swimmer myself. Still, nothing would have kept Bob behind, for he intended using his dowsing pendulum in the fort to search for Spanish gold.

In the other canoe Peter, who was stripped to the waist and gazing forward owlishly through his horn-rimmed spectacles, never saw danger anyway. He and Jesco looked as though they were actually sitting *in* the water.

Half-way over, and we could see the hut on the other bank clearly. It was a substantial building with thick buff-coloured adobe walls, the highest thing there apart from the palms, which over-topped it. And as we got closer you saw why: that dwelling was actually built on top of a wall of the fort.

I was anxious to reach the shore, not because of the danger but to explore. Indeed, I felt elated, invigorated – and even in that pounding sun which, on the unsheltered surface of the river, had us at his mercy. I trailed my fingers in the current on both sides of the boat through the soft lime-free water, silky to the touch. 'It's like silk, Bob!' I cried.

'Bloody crazy,' he muttered.

The canoe, long and narrow, fairly shot across the last quarter of a mile of river and beached below what we now saw was a couple of clay-walled palm-thatched huts set on the firmest foundation from here to Aberdeen. The granite bouldered wall on which the two houses sat was part of the fort, as I have said. We scrambled out to explore.

That fort, in that humid jungle, where something ripens or rots every second, where fierce sun heat bakes and cracks, where deluging rains erode the earth's foundations, where winds whistle exposed hills into fairy castles, that fort still stood four-square, extensive, well preserved. The walls were built of granite chunks, rough-hewn to the size of rugby footballs, with a harsh granular surface blackened by weathering. Above our heads the walls were eight feet high and about twenty feet thick. The tops of the walls were flat and grass grown, and when we got up we could see that the fort was built in the form of a squeezed-out square – one wall following the river bank and the others accommodating to slight irregularities on the ground. Each side of this rectangle was about seventy yards in length, and the area enclosed just over an acre.

Whoever lived in the huts had turned the interior of the fort into a banana plantation. From the wall top we looked down inside on to the pale green flabby fronds of the banana trees hung with heavy clusters of ripening yellow fruit.

And the owner: surprise, surprise! Who did *he* turn out to be but the buccaneer we had encountered the day before when we crossed the Venezuelan border at Cucui. Obviously he had carried our three Venezuelan companions downriver in an outboard-motor-driven canoe and had fairly recently got back. Julio Castillo, baby-faced, round-eyed, dark, crinkly haired and drunk, laughingly introduced us to the pirate.

Like true-born Englishmen, we were a little reserved, especially in the presence of inebriation at four o'clock on a sunny afternoon.

But a bottle of *cachaças*, corkless, was thrust under our noses, and we swigged in turn, carefully and as unostentatiously as possible wiping the neck of the bottle before we drank. There was no need. That fiery spirit would have melted varnish from a heat-resistant table top. It was as antiseptic as carbolic.

Before very long we were giggling and poking Castillo in the ribs – pulling his leg over the lost petrol and winking exaggeratedly, saying he had obviously come to the right place to get it back again.

The buccaneer, wearing slops and soiled open shirt, beamed welcome from his rubbery face. He talked to Jesco, but about what we had very little idea.

Looking down on the banana plantation, we saw half a dozen little pits and a trench. This was where the buccaneer had found his Spanish gold and, judging by the recently turned earth, he was obviously still searching for more. Bob's eyes sparkled as he thought of his pendulum. The buccaneer went into one of the two huts and came out with a solid dome of pitted iron about three inches across. It was half a cannon ball. He fumbled in the bottomless pocket of his trouser slops and produced a stone which sparkled blue in the sunlight. He told Jesco it was a sapphire. The gem was very evenly cut in droplet form – a pendant or an ear-ring – and about the size of a haricot bean. I told Jesco to offer him five American dollars for it, but the buccaneer was no fool, and no doubt expected to make his fortune. Whether the stone was a real sapphire or not I was unable to tell. I put my offer up a hundred per cent before leaving, but he held out.

Henry, Peter and I filmed a short sequence on the fort wall, while Bob scrambled about the plantation below us swinging his pendulum for sign of gold.

Julio Castillo had already got hold of the two petrol drums and had rolled them across two planks into his capacious launch. This vessel had a beam at its widest of nine or ten feet, with a rough shelter stretching almost from the stern to within ten feet of the prow. This shelter had a slightly arched corrugated aluminium roof. The sides were normally open for ventilation, though at night and during the worst kinds of tropical rain you could let down tarpaulin shelters like roller blinds.

So Castillo was ready to return. We ourselves wanted to go with him. We reckoned we had tempted fate far enough this time in the canoes. We asked him to wait a little longer.

Bob Saunders continued to swing his pendulum methodically. He stood in one corner of the fort banana plantation swinging the wooden ball on the end of its cord with his right hand, slowly moving his left arm in an arc parallel to the earth.

He had set the cord length for gold – twenty-nine inches.

The theory is that when your left arm points to gold the pendulum will change its swing backwards and forwards to a circular gyration.

Bob's pendulum began to gyrate.

He moved off to another corner of the plantation and repeated the procedure.

He got a gyration on his pendulum.

He paced across until his line intersected the previous one. Pointing to his feet he said, 'Dig here!'

Unfortunately, in that sweaty heat nobody wanted to dig. He looked around expectantly, then accepting the situation, dropped his floppy green forage cap to mark the spot while he went off to borrow an extraordinary long-handled shovel from the buccaneer.

He had been digging with Peter's help but without result for half an hour when the combined calls of Henry, Jesco and me from the wall top finally penetrated his concentration.

'Come on, Bob!' we shouted, 'we're going! If you want a lift on Castillo's boat, come now. Otherwise you'll have to come back by canoe.'

That threat was more than the lure of gold could withstand. He threw down the shovel. I won't repeat the four-letter word he used on that occasion.

When we were chugging back to San Carlos we discussed who could have built that fort and why. From its position, I felt it had been intended as a block-house for intruders coming *up* the river. In that case it had most probably been built by Spaniards moving southwards to prevent a further Brazilian spread northwards. Seventeenth century? Who knows? And how had those Spaniards come? By way of the Casiquiare Canal?

'I'll tell you one thing that's bloody certain,' said Bob Saunders.

'What's that?' asked Henry, always trusting and eager for useful knowledge.

'That bloody buccaneer'll be digging like mad back in my hole! Yeah – you bet he will.'

CHAPTER TEN

Casiquiare Canal

MY diary for 17th April 1968 began: '10.30 a.m. left San Carlos in a tropical downpour. A thunder and lightning storm played all round our hammocks last night and the cachou-nut trees threshed in the wind beyond the verandah of the guard post; but there was no downpour until two or three a.m. Then the bottom fell out of the sky, and nobody up there has managed to get it back in yet. Colonel Leal, sitting rather long-faced and looking miserable up front of the hovercraft, says the river has risen ten metres since the start of the rains and will rise another five metres still. Rain waterfalling down. Sky and river one grey. Everything warm and clammy to the touch inside the cabin. Nobody speaking much – just wondering what's up ahead. All three windscreen wipers sweeping hard – water washing down windows in layers and splashes. Alongside, I can see occasionally through the breath on the window to my right that the river surface is pitted with raindrop rings. Unusual view, attractive pattern. I wonder how the four scientists are doing in Castillo's more or less open boat?'

We had said goodbye to the long-suffering David Harris, John Thornes, Captain Yepez and Ernesto Medina as, for a second time, they left San Carlos, about two hours before sunset the previous evening. Castillo's second-in-command was at the tiller of his huge Johnson outboard motor with one of his crewmen at the prow to signal him left or right to avoid rocks in the rapids. Somewhere before dusk they would have had to tie up by the bank, and because of the torrential rain were now more than likely drenched to the skin. Wet mosquito nets, sodden hammocks, slimy ropes – oh, discomfort!

In the hovercraft we reckoned we had only fifteen miles to go before we should strike the Casiquiare Canal. With conditions as they were, with a rain-fogmasking the banks, the finding of the entrance would be a matter of chance. The craft was simply bulging with kerosene, somewhat sluggish in answering to the controls because of being over-weight and handling tetchily. Twice we were startled from our only half-awake condition by a harsh shout and a rubbery grimace from Stuart Syrad sitting on his box alongside the pilot: 'Weight right!', at which everybody had scrummed rapidly across the narrow gangway, vacating all the seats on the left and leaning heavily on those (Henry and me for two) sitting on the starboard side.

Altogether, what with the weather conditions, the mist, the soggy controls and the uncertainty as to the canal entrance, it was a rather nail-biting time. The trouble was that if we overshot the Casiquiare Canal and continued our way blindly up the Negro, even for only one hour, then our chances of completing the expedition were practically nil. Supposing we made a mistake and discovered it after an hour, there would be another hour backtracking – two hours' fuel gone – in distance the equivalent of, say, eighty to 100 miles. On this leg there just wasn't that much leeway, so we should be stranded. No wonder the pilot and his map readers in the forward seats were chewing their lips and peering sharply from their mapboards to the windows.

With me, I'm afraid, curiosity got the better of anxiety. In any case I was content to let those in charge do the worrying – wasn't that why the BBC had paid £1,000 a seat for us? You hardly expect your driver to get you lost on such expensive tickets – even in the Amazon.

But this canal was a mystery, the *unknown*, and because of that the rumours about it had invested the name with a certain menace. In England, as I have said, some people argued that the water in the channel flowed from north to south (that is to say from the Orinoco into the Negro); others argued that the current went south to north, from Negro to Orinoco; yet a third body of opinion believed that at some time of the year the Casiquiare ran both ways at once! Presumably the waters dried up in the middle, parting like the Red Sea and running both north *and* south.

Now, Robin Hanbury-Tenison, our maestro-del-campo, had in fact been through the Casiquiare Canal but in a rubber boat, from the other direction and at a different time of the year. I had talked to him about it, but the only solid information I seemed to have gained was that it did exist, it *was* there.

In San Carlos Hilary Branch had added to the folk-lore of the Canal. She said there were reputed to be many *piedras pintadas* or painted rocks alongside or actually in the canal. You can find such rocks marked on maps in a number of places throughout the upper reaches of the Amazon. When you discover them they are not actually painted, they are rather *pictured* – carved with designs. Hilary Branch told of one *piedra pintada* in the Casiquiare Canal which was said to have depicted on it a serpent twelve feet long. She mentioned a professor in Caracas whose theory it was that the engravings on the *piedras pintadas* date from Stone Age cultures without tools hard enough to dent the granite rocks. But the tribal artists may have painted figures and designs using acid pigments which, with centuries of continued application have eaten into the rock and produced engravings. Jesco knows that the forest Indians have the secrets of chemicals undreamed of by the West. He is convinced of this, and Jesco not only has ten years of intimate contact with Indians behind him but he was also trained as a chemical engineer. One example of such a chemical whose composition is still in doubt is the killer curare, another is that which the Aztecs used sometimes to skin their victims, injecting it subcutaneously; an operation which lifted the skin by some process of oxidation: thus, if their statuary can be believed, an Aztec priest could wear another human being's skin so that it fitted like a glove or a fine rubber suit, covering him in front from head to foot and tied down the back with little apron bows.

Half-tranced by the constant hum of the hovercraft's motor, I muse on the barbaric ingenuity of humankind.

I am brought back from this reverie by a stir up front. Our leader, Mike Eden, in the middle of the bus, is showing signs of breaking out of his Easter Island immobility and being interested in what the pilot and business manager are about to do, namely to turn the hovercraft right. What appears to be a wide creek can be dimly discerned as a dent in the tree-lined bank. Through the wash of rain and the banners of spray it isn't easy to tell whether you are meeting a bend in the jungle bank or an actual channel. By this time we are all craning our necks, even the hardened journalists Arthur Helliwell and Douglas Botting, while Henry has staggered up the gangway with his Arriflex camera to film our entrance – if indeed we are going to enter, and this really is *it* – the Casiquiare Canal.

Whether we are right or wrong, the fateful decision is taken and the hovercraft throttles back and skids obliquely into the creek. I make a mental note that the current is still against us, so if this *is* the Casiquiare Canal, one question at least is answered – the water does flow from north to south, from Orinoco into Amazon. I made one further significant observation: the river beneath us was no longer 'black'; it was a lightish mud colour.

After five minutes' steady travelling I felt confident enough to write in my diary, 'Entered the Canal about 10.45 a.m. Width some 450 yards. Little change from Negro apart from narrowing.' A bit later I added, '11.00 a.m. passing Solano (a miserable couple of deserted huts). The water is definitely "white". Well and truly in Canal. 11.20 a.m. overtook Julio Castillo's launch.' It was still raining hard as we slid past the long, narrow boat with its corrugated aluminium awning. The occupants waved somewhat dismally, it seemed to me; they were dank and probably dispirited, for the weather was beating in. Under their raincoats they were no doubt steamy and parboiled. I could see David Harris, naturally dark complexioned, with a blue shadow round his jowl – nobody likes shaving in these conditions. In any case, I had asked him not to shave for some days for the benefit of the film. Captain Yepez contrived still to look military, probably because he was wearing his jungle green kepi, while Castillo's man and Ernesto Medina with their round-brimmed straw sombreros added a touch of the steel bands. Dr John Thornes, peering without his glasses, might well have been the band conductor, for he was gesticulating with one arm. We fluttered our hands against the steamed-up windows and rapidly left the launch astern. Their being there at least confirmed that we were up the right creek – this was indeed the Casiquiare Canal.

The more I have thought about it, the more I have become convinced that the Casiquiare Canal has been for the Indians a well-travelled waterway. It is like a pass in high mountain country – the traffic is bound to funnel through it. It is that unique phenomenon, a connecting navigable channel between rivers which actually crosses the watershed. The first Europeans to traverse it were undoubtedly those of Lope de Aguirre's expedition in 1561. The next (so I believed – mistakenly at that time), nearly three hundred years later, were the German scientists in Baron von Humboldt's party. The last, I really believe, another century and a half later, ourselves. In contrast, Indians have continually migrated and counter-migrated this way for centuries, probably for millennia, coming and going between the Amazon and Orinoco basins. One tribe even today occupies jungle hunting grounds off both ends of the Canal. In Brazil they are called Guaicas and in Venezuela, Waikas. It's a name used by other tribes and means 'butchers', though they call themselves Yanamani or Yanamamo, 'the people'. If we got through the Canal safely, we of the BBC were determined to seek out the Waikas in the depths of the forest.

But at the moment, as we ploughed gingerly through the narrowing Canal, I did not know how the plan to visit the Waikas was to be carried out.

At eleven fifty-two by my watch we slackened speed and pulled in to the left bank at two or three huts indicated to the captain by our map readers Robin Hanbury-Tenison and Stuart Syrad. The name of this ghost settlement is Porvenir. Robin Tenison leapt ashore on to a steep bank covered with brush. We five BBC men followed with our camera gear.

The huts were decrepit, dirty and deserted.

An overgrown path, but still a path, alongside the river bank led away from the hovels. Robin shouted to Graham Clarke that we ought to try the neighbouring settlement a quarter of a mile away. It might be cleaner. He began striding up the jungle track, and we followed, lugging our gear and making as much noise as possible to frighten away snakes, spiders and anything larger.

One thing was brought home to us immediately. No sooner had we scrambled ashore than we were assailed by the blood suckers – clouds of them. They settled on any area of exposed skin – hands, neck, face, and began drilling. This was what those who had experienced it simply called 'the plague'. Oh torment! Oh bloody hell! And there was nothing effective you could do about it. On whose blood did these millions of flies sup when we weren't there? How *did* they subsist? Hellions! We should never know. Before we even reached the next miserable huddle of three empty palm-thatched huts and an open shelter stocked with fat bundles of palm fibre the backs of our hands and our necks and faces were rising in lumps. Soon we should be sprinkled with pin heads of dried blood itching and irritating like crazy. 'Don't scratch,' they said, 'whatever you do, don't scratch!' *Don't scratch?* Don't scratch, my flaming arse!

Humboldt, in his account of his travels through the Casiquiare and up the Orinoco, rattles on primly for page after page about 'the plague': 'Persons who have not navigated the great rivers of equinoctial America can scarcely conceive how, at every instant, without intermission, you may be tormented by the insects of the air; and how the multitude of these little animals may render vast regions almost uninhabitable. Whatever fortitude may be exercised to endure pain without complaint, whatever interest may be felt in the objects of scientific research, it is impossible not to be constantly disturbed by the mosquitoes, zancudos, jejens, and tempraneros, that cover the face and hands, pierce the clothes with their long needle-formed suckers, and getting into the mouth and nostrils, occasion coughing and sneezing whenever any attempt is made to speak in the open air. In the missions of the Orinoco, in the villages on the banks of the river, surrounded by immense forests, the *plaga de las moscas*, or the plague of the mosquitoes, affords an inexhaustible subject of conversation. When two persons meet in the morning the first questions they address to each other are: "How did you find the zancudos during the night? How are we today for the mosquitoes? . . ." In going down the Rio Negro we breathed freely. But this improvement of our situation (Humboldt goes on) was of short continuance; our sufferings recommenced as soon as we entered the Casiquiare. At Esmeralda, at the eastern extremity of the Upper Orinoco, where ends the known world of the Spaniards, the clouds of mosquitoes are almost as thick as at the Great Cataracts . . . If in an obscure spot, for instance in the grottos of the cataracts formed by superincumbent blocks of granite, you direct your eyes toward the opening enlightened by the sun, you see clouds of mosquitoes . . . I doubt whether there be a country upon earth where man is exposed to more cruel torments in the rainy season . . . At Esmeralda, to make use of an hyperbolical expression of the monks, "there are more mosquitoes than air".'

But we still had three or four days' journey before we got to Esmeralda.

As we struggled along the bank we could hear the hovercraft buzzing behind us, so, having reached the next huts, Henry and I set up the camera on its tripod to film the approach while Robin Tenison waited for a line to be flung by John Hoyland. We stood with our backs to the large open shelter where the bank dropped steeply away to water-level. As ever (although the rain had stopped) the slopes were slippery and you had to move carefully and slowly or else find yourself tobogganing towards the water. Robin secured the line to a massive tree whose trunk disappeared into the river's edge. People began to scramble ashore. A fireman's chain was formed, one man a step above another, and then the personal packs and bedrolls were heaved out.

I think it was here, for the first time, that it occured to me that Arthur Helliwell really looked all in. He would insist on taking his place in the chain, and perhaps because he was the oldest member (admitting to fifty-nine) he felt he had to do more – just that little more – to show that age made no difference. In these climes it does: and you can't get away from it. Arthur was heaving and panting and saying nothing. The rest of us joked, a bit lamely, but still joked about things like Jesco's 'sausage' – that huge canvas kitbag which seemed to be filled with lead. I calculated once again that before we were unloaded each man had handled just about a ton in the space of ten minutes. It was tough stevedoring for normally chairborne troops: in that heat and humidity it was killing. No wonder Arthur panted and turned an unhealthy puce.

Our campmaster had allotted one of the three huts to the BBC party. It was downstream a hundred yards from where the hovercraft lay moored, along a creeper-crossed, vine-hung jungle trail. Another trail ran immediately in front of our door to the canal. I noticed exotic jungle flowers, splodges of crimson and purple; hibiscus and bougain-villaea. Here and there, in the divides of branches, stars of orchids, beautiful and sickly sweet as sin. On the ground there were heaps and layers of seeds of every size and shape from walnut to pea – nature was killing itself in its blind urge to live, orgasmically seeding itself to death. And it smelt like it – a bouquet of manurial lushness and decay.

The inside of our nut was dark and dusty. Furtive and unexplained rustlings sifted down from the palm thatch. The earth floor was uneven and lumpy, but worn smooth presumably by naked feet. We rapidly slung our hammocks and covered them with the protective mosquito nets. The nets fell quite to the ground and, as usual, I stored all my gear underneath. Then we fled to the shelter by the hovercraft for lunch.

Everybody was flailing the air and slapping face and neck to counter the *jejenes*. Some of us had anti-mosquito creams and aerosol-spray repellants. They were useless. You just had to put up with it.

After dry Ryvita biscuits coated with tuna fish almost as dry and woody, varied with soapy tinned cheese and a revolting drink made from so-called lemonade crystals, Peter Smith, our sound recordist, young and eager as ever for adventure, asked if he could go fishing. Arthur Helliwell (now a bit recovered) wanted to join him, having the notion that, to live up to the *People* standards, he ought to catch at least one cannibal fish. Jesco, as the jungle expert, said he would make one to show them how to do it. I said I would come for something to do. Douglas Botting came for photographs.

We collected line and fish hooks from Robin Tenison in charge of the expedition stores. Young Peter led the way, hacking with a machete like a madman.

The whole enterprise was a failure. If we had really been dependent on living off the land we should have starved. In the first place, the jungle was so thick it took us about half an hour to hack a way to a spot not more than twenty paces from the larger shelter. Jesco said we had to do this to get to the best fish 'beat'. As soon as we reached the water's edge he fell in.

Then, in fumbling to attach the nylon line to a hook, Peter Smith got the barb firmly lodged in the palp of one of his thumbs.

Finally, Arthur Helliwell, too, got into trouble with his line. The fine, weightless thread wouldn't stay where he put it. It seemed to float into the surrounding twigs and thorn barbs: it festooned itself on trees like spiders' webs; it cocooned itself around him.

'This is the photograph you want,' I whispered to Douglas.

'It's not what the bloody *People* wants,' said Douglas. 'They want to see him wrestling with a piranha.'

'Arthur,' I called, 'you'd do better to use that line as a net – you've almost got it knitted.'

'Piss off,' he said, not unkindly. I decided this was good advice, and I carefully picked my way back through the splintered tunnel of bush, avoiding prickles and spines, and watching the ground for snakes and the lower branches for tree ants.

In our shadowy hut Henry Farrar was already hidden within his mosquito net, conserving or building up his energy. Henry is downright sensible. Of all the BBC crew, his work entailed the hardest sustained physical effort, for during most of his working time he was man-handling the heavy Arriflex camera with its massive ten-to-one zoom lens and built-in sound-blimp. In addition to holding it steady at shoulder level during shooting, Henry was quite unable to put up even the smallest defence against biters. Consequently, before long his face and neck were swollen and lumpy. I shall always associate the smell of medicinal alcohol with Henry Farrar. Whenever he was able to retire to his mosquito net, that distinctive odour would cloud the air and I would hear the rasp of his hands as he rubbed the spirit into his body in the hope of getting relief from his unnumbered bites.

I clambered into my own hammock and lay in a muck sweat divested of all clothing. Little runnels and trickles of perspiration tickled their way across my belly and sides and soaked into the fabric of the ham-mock. I tried to read *Sir Gawayne and the Greene Knyghte*, but the book kept falling on to my face, and before long I was asleep.

I dreamed of my dear wife. We were in some nightmarish futuristic hotel, all glass and chromium, and we were lost in the lifts. She was going up in one lift, I was going down in another. Getting out at one floor, I was just in time to see her tear-stained face as the doors of her lift closed. No matter how I pressed and hammered the button, her lift

Jesco and young Suyá girls in the Xingú village where he lived for a year.

Orlando Villas Boas with Aura Indian girls kidnapped eight years previously by fierce Txicão tribesmen.

The hovercraft finds the wrong fuel dump at Moura, first stop on the Negro River.

Bones of Padre Calleri's expedition massacred by Atroari Indians; collected by
paratroopers and laid on the air-strip at Moura.

The canoe we chased to ask directions to Barcelos.

San Carlos, Venezuela.

The hovercraft tied up by the rock on the Casiquiare.

The two canoes alongside each other on the Orinoco at the start of the journey to the Waika.
Left foreground Arthur Helliwell, right Peter Smith, centre Douglas Botting, standing Danny
Shaylor, New Tribes missionary and guide.

BBC expedition to the Waika – our first sight of the Indians.

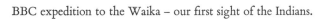

Delora Neese, American New Tribes missionary, and Makiritari Indian girl at Shanamaña, Rio Padamo.

Waika Indian girls filling grated manioc into a sieve to extract the poisonous juices.

Makiritari women removing manioc from sieve after having extracted the poison.

Makiritari Indian girl and pet monkey, Rio Padamo, Venezuela.

Makiritari Indians roasting a monkey for food.

Waika Indian village on the Rio Padamo. The roughly circular lean-to, or *shapuno*, houses a number of families.

Preparation of curare: granulated liana in a leaf cone filter. Water is trickled through into a calabash producing the deadly coffee-coloured poison.

Waika Indians painting curare on to the tips of blowpipe darts which are hardening over the fire.

Blowpipe darts held in baulks of banana tree to harden over a fire while curare is dabbed on with a cotton-tipped twig.

Makiritaris delousing and dressing up, Rio Padamo.

Waika Indian receiving the drug *ebena* or *yopo* through a hollow cane, Upper Orinoco.

Paul Dye holding a piece of bark stripped from the *yopo* tree by the Indian guide 'Hefty'.

Waika women spinning wild cotton, Upper Orinoco.

The BBC expedition to the Waika: at the top of the portage when the canoe was swamped and nearly lost over the waterfall. Arthur Helliwell (back to camera), Jesco (star in hat), Brian Branston (behind Jesco), Paul Dye (arm in sling) and Danny Shaylor.

Waika Indians of the Upper Orinoco war-dancing: the last sight seen by many intruders into the area over the past four hundred years.

American New Tribes Mission schoolboy with carvings on rocks at Tama Tama on the Orinoco.

Aura women chanting the Yamaricumá song, Rio Xingú.

Puerto Ayacucho: Jim Sweeney looking for possible damage to the hovercraft bottom after she had shot the Great Rapids.

Waika Indians already under missionary influence and wearing western cast-offs.

continued inexorably on its way. I woke depressed and miserable. 'If ever I come safely out of this jape,' I said to myself, 'I'll never leave you again for long, Dodo!' This beloved woman had for three weeks before I left England fed me on practically raw steaks and green salads, honey and apple-cider vinegar; she had engineered it that my car (in dock for a repair) should not be released until two days before we had to fly to South America – consequently I had had to do a daily hike up and down Henley Hill to and from the station. How wise she was. When I stepped into that plane at London Airport I was as fit as any boxer on the eve of the big fight. In the tough time ahead of me her care paid off.

During the afternoon the launch had caught up with us; and after Henry and I had staggered leadenly out of our hammocks down to the landing we picked up something of the expedition plans. The launch would leap-frog with us along the Casiquiare to our next day's stop. The day after that it was hoped to achieve our break-through into the Orinoco, turn right upstream for thirty miles and proceed to Las Esmeraldas. The launch would, however, motor only very slowly through the remainder of the Canal, for it was here that three of the scientists were to do one of their justifying geographical, geological, botanical and particularly hydrographical studies. We were happy to leave them to it. The hovercraft and the main party would wait for ten days at Esmeralda. During this time the BBC party would go after Indians.

Graham Clarke told me he intended to make two runs next day to Capybara, our next stop on the Canal. The distance was thirty miles, the time taken to cover it short – about thirty-five minutes each way. But there was believed to be no shelter at Capybara, the weather was stormy, living conditions bad, and the leaders and campmaster felt that an advance party should go there to set up our huge tarpaulin shelter. I elected to wait with the film unit until the second run. Such a delay had several advantages: it would allow us to film the hovercraft leaving and approaching the bank (when she returned), and it gave us time to film a lip-sync sequence to camera on the subject of the extraordinary Casiquiare Canal.

Jesco and the fishermen had caught nothing after three hours. I forgot to mention that they had used as bait a plump pigeon shot with our 16-bore double-barrelled gun bought in Manaus – the only wild creature, I am happy to report, which anyone managed to hit with that weapon during our entire trip. Later, I was to hear it constantly banging off, but the marksmen were such bad shots that none of our fellow forest creatures suffered more than a fright. However, this pigeon had fallen to the gun. It was a beautiful chocolate brown, a thing of limp beauty, which Jesco had plucked in three minutes and cut into bloody chunks, for the bird was well nourished, with a crop full of seeds. Arthur Helliwell had expected with such bloody bait to catch a piranha at the drop of a hook.

I forget their excuses for returning empty handed. Jesco merely winked and mixed pungent pingas for anybody who was prepared to have the first layer taken off the walls of his stomach. That included me. So we retired, with the dusk, to our hut. Small bats took avoiding action between the tree tops. The cicadas sawed out their grinding symphony. Little lizards darted away from our feet. Henry stopped along the trail and called me. He flashed his torch into the leafage and put a spotlight on a cicada. It was four inches long and looked like a mighty grasshopper. The frogs were croaking in the undergrowth, *co-ax, co-ax, co-co-co-ax*, just like the chorus in Aristophanes' play of that name. The gloom inside the hut when we reached it was forbidding, faintly hostile. Our mosquito-netted hammocks waited like the ghosts of coffins. We climbed into them. It was about seven o'clock and there was a long hot night of Trappist isolation ahead of us: within the solitary confinement of your muslin cell you were as lonely as a mummied Pharaoh walled up in the stifling dark depths of his pyramid.

Early next morning, as soon as it was light, I found myself awake listening to the birdsong. Contrary to what the books say, it was not a bit raucous – you know, the old story of tropical birds being brilliantly beautiful to look at – flying rainbows – but like klaxon horns to hear. In fact, the sound beyond the palm thatch, when day was breaking, fell upon my ears as melodious as any English dawn chorus, strong and voluminous. I lifted the folds of the dusty net, harsh over my naked back and slid out of my hammock. Jesco's tomb was already empty. The other three were buzzing gently. I got dressed, collected my soap and towel and walked down the narrow trail leading from our open door to the river's edge. Down the bare clay bank to the water I saw several fresh claw marks. I was examining these with interest when I heard a rustle behind me.

A bit startled, I glanced to the top of the bank to see Julio Castillo's round red face, round straw sombrero and round brown eyes looking down at me. I pointed to the pug marks, and Castillo simply nodded his head and uttered one word, 'Tigre'.

Tiger – jaguar: sometime in the small hours a prick-eared forest cat had sidled sinuously down the path to drink, threading his silent way within feet of our hammocks.

Later, when I told the others, Arthur Helliwell insisted on my show-ing him the marks and had Douglas Botting photograph us on the spot. The *People* carried his report (which only served to amuse our BBC colleagues and terrify our wives) as follows:

MAN–EATER PROWLS IN JUNGLE CAMP

A big spotted jaguar, one of the two man-eaters reported to be in this area, prowled through our camp here last night. No one saw or heard him as he came down after dark to the river to drink. But when the BBC television team, who were camped nearest to the water, woke up this morning, fresh pug-marks of the big cat were clearly visible in the damp ground.

When our predecessor, the Baron von Humboldt, passed through the canal 168 years ago almost to the very month he reported a similar experience: 'At our last resting place on the Casiquiare, whilst we were sleeping on the edge of the forest, we were warned by the Indians in the middle of the night, that they had heard very near us the cries of a jaguar. As our fires burnt brightly, we paid little attention to the cries of the jaguars. They had been attracted by the smell and noise of our dog. This animal (which was of the mastiff breed) began at first to bark; and when the tiger drew nearer, to howl, hiding himself below our ham-mocks. How great was our grief, when in the morning, at the moment of re-embarking, the Indians informed us that the dog had disappeared! There could be no doubt that it had been carried off by the jaguars. Perhaps, when their cries had ceased, it had wandered from the fires on the side of the beach; and possibly we had not heard its moans, as we were in a profound sleep. We waited part of the morning in the hope that our dog had only strayed. Three days after we came back to the same place; we heard again the cries of the jaguars, for these animals have a predilection for particular spots; but all our search was in vain. The dog, which had accompanied us from Caracas, and had so often in swimming escaped the pursuit of crocodiles, had been devoured in the forest.'

The name of our deserted settlement, visited so silently in the night by a jaguar, was Baiola, according to Castillo, and the explanation of the fat bundles of coir fibre on which we sat at breakfast in the mess-shelter by the hovercraft was that people from down the Negro came sporadically to collect this new material for making besoms. Two such Caboclos, young men of twenty-five, arrived that morning in a dugout canoe, having driven with a tiny *put-put* outboard from Waupés. They told Jesco that up the next tributary on the right, a two-day journey away in their boat, were wild Indians. Probably Shamatari – the tribe who held Helena Valero captive. People had seen a rude creeper or pole bridge across the stream and cooking hearths. But that was the sum total of their knowledge – nor did they want to find out any more. I was left with the feeling that the two parties would have shot at each other on sight.

After breakfast I stood alone on the river's brink and gazed across the swollen Canal. It was maybe 300 yards wide at this point, flowing from left to right at four miles an hour, the brown surface midstream spotted with a procession of floating foam patches. I thought at first that these patches were leaves, but they were in fact little rafts of bubbly froth churned up at eddies when the water swirled by rapidly submerging rocks. The level was rising every day, and the trees on the far bank appeared to have their boles under water.

I sheltered from the broiling sun in the shade of a large silvery tree. Immediately after breakfast the hovercraft had left with the first party to make camp as arranged at our next stop, so all was quiet. A kingfisher who had his beat from the tree was hunting like a blue flash six inches above the surface of the river. I watched a flock of butterflies jigging about some splashed pebbles. They had their proboscis down delicately sipping up the damp. When they took it into their heads to flutter here and there they looked like flying flowers – blues, crimsons, shining irridescent blacks – their petal wings reflecting brazen sunlight and transmuting it into the new-born colours of an Italian pre-Raphaelite painter. My heart lifted at the sight. I watched one orange-yellow beauty with a thin brown border and a curious rolling flight – the sort of wave motion you get when you shake a piece of skipping rope. Another butterfly drinking at the pebbles had wings which, when they opened flat, were shaped like a Greek lyre.

The hovercraft returned to pick us up, and Graham Clarke, when asked what the next camp site was like, said shortly, 'Pretty grim.'

We left Baiola with rain clouds ahead in the shape of a monster of a bird with outstretched wings – menacing. Occasionally lightning forked into the river and there was distant thunder. The air was humid as a Turkish bath. As I stepped into the craft I noticed that little Jim Sweeney's face (the left side, he must have slept on his right side the previous night) had a thousand lumps from insect bites.

Almost as soon as the engine roared, the rain came. We passed clusters of bald-headed grey rocks and bumped over some small rapids. At three fifteen it was raining solid, and I noted we were passing the entrance of a tributary on our right. Up that stream, two days journey in a dugout canoe with outboard motor, were those wild Indians – little men and women, as naked as the day when the Spanish and Portuguese conquistadors first pushed into the jungle four hundred years ago.

Tree-tops stuck up from the water right in the middle of the channel. Visibility dropped to thirty or forty yards, and the craft slowed down to a crawl. The windows on my side were rippled with driving rain, and I could see the footwalk outside, level with my shoulder, rushing with water.

I made the following notes in my diary: '3.20 just passed two kidney-shaped rocks with small trees growing out of cracks. Slight rapid. 3.25 more protruding rocks – water coming in through my window which has jammed and can't be shut – pilot Castillo has difficulty in indicating the route. 3.30 sky brighter ahead – a band of yellow across the jungle and river in front of us. Ride very bumpy – I can hardly write. Craft noise changes frequently and suddenly to a rasping roar as the pilot throttles back on approaching rocks and broken water. 4.00 a let-up in the rain. John Thornes (who with Castillo has left the launch on this leg) asks Graham to stop midstream so that he can take water samples. He strips to his underpants and scrambles outside with his sinker which he can let down into the river and open to receive water at whatever depth he wishes. He pours his samples into white screw-top plastic jars, and labels them. John Hoyland helps him and Henry films the operation from the catwalk on the port side. 5.15 Those who have already made the trip say we are three miles from Capybara, tonight's stop. The rain is driving hard again, almost horizontally past my window. The river surface is a dark muddy brown, livid with a sheen of red in this half light. The omnipresent jungle has become a band of purple shadow from which groups of trees materialise and melt back as we pass. A sinister jungle this – unpeopled, for the most part, unexplored – waiting to pounce – almost as if the two sides would close like an enveloping maw if they could. 5.20 arrived at Capybara – a vast rock sliding down into the river – mottled, flaking and black with rain. At the top of the rock, where the lush-leaved forest yeasts above the edge like some green dough rising over the lip of a giant's bread pan there appeared the ruins of two palm thatched huts.'

As usual, our first concern on landing was to find a snug spot to hang our hammocks. Robin Tenison indicated a cramped corner under one of the ramshackle shelters which was all the living-space left. The roof was tattered and broken and the floor was already patched with puddles.

The first arrivals had slung the huge tarpaulin so that it hung like a murky cave ceiling from the pillars of our shelter to those of the other shelter on our left, while at the back, in Stygian darkness, its guy-ropes were hitched to forest trees. What had once been the settlement's path leading from the jungle to the rock and the river ran diagonally under the tarpaulin. A smoky fire was burning in the centre. A billycan was doing its best not to boil. Piles of gubbins strewed the wet coarse grass of the floor, and the hammocks and mosquito nets of those who had come first were slung higgledy-piggledy like boats on a lee shore after a storm.

We five from the BBC began the distasteful task of preparing our own nests. Piums and mosquitoes, as usual, pastured on our flesh.

Humboldt had a similar experience; he wrote, 'During the five following nights our passage [through the Casiquiare] was the more troublesome in proportion as we approached the bifurcation of the Orinoco. The luxuriance of the vegetation increases in a manner of which it is impossible for those unacquainted with the aspect of the forests between the tropics, to form an idea. There is no longer a river bank: a palisade of tufted trees forms the margin of the river. You see a canal two hundred toises broad, bordered by two enormous walls, clothed with lianas and foliage. We often tried to land, but without success. Towards sunset we sailed along for an hour seeking to discover, not an opening (since none exists), but a spot less wooded, where our Indians by means of the hatchet and manual labour, could clear space enough for a resting-place for twelve or thirteen persons. It was impossible to pass the night in the canoe; the mosquitoes which tormented us during the day, accumulated toward evening beneath the toldo covered with palm-leaves, which served to shelter us from the rain. Our hands and faces had never been so much swelled. Father Zea, who had till then boasted of having in his missions of the cataracts the largest and fiercest (las mas feroces) mosquitoes, at length gradually acknowledged that the sting of the insects of the Casiquiare was the most painful he had ever felt. We experienced great difficulty, amid a thick forest, in finding wood to make a fire, the branches of the trees in those equatorial regions where it always rains, being so full of sap, that they will scarcely burn.'

Well, we did have a fire, or more correctly a *smoke*, whose pungent tickle in my nose brought back memories of more congenial camping with my wife and children. Not that I am a camper by nature: frankly, I rather dislike it. Over the years circumstances have forced me into it. For four years during the war in India and Burma I had to live under the sky; then for ten or twelve years afterwards we had such a large family of children our only hope to keep them on holiday during the long school vacation was to go camping. Some are born campers, some have camping thrust upon them. I am of the latter class.

Jesco instinctively recognised my distaste and insisted on helping me to sling my hammock. Because the area was so cramped. three of us had our mosquito nets touching. I was in the middle, Peter Smith on my right and Bob Saunders on my left. It was obvious we should have to use our transparent plastic sheets as roofs to keep off the imminent rainstorm. Jesco very cleverly produced a long branch cut from the forest and made a ridge over my net to support the plastic sheet like an A-roof. Bob and Peter were too tormented by insects and exhausted by the clammy humidity to do anything but spread their plastic covers flat along the tops of their nets.

After supper (the best part of which was hot watery cocoa and rum) I took my torch and slid along the slippery path to the rock by the river for a last look round and a pee. It had been raining a slight drizzle when we disembarked, but now it was fine. There was, however, distant thunder, like noises off, and looking back the way we had come, I saw the lightning reflected on the under belly of far-distant flocky clouds, a beautiful sight, a bit of natural stage-lighting.

After we went to bed at eight thirty the rain set in hard, sluicing through the holes in the tattered palm roof and deluging on to our plastic covers. As usual, I lay naked in my hammock with a towel over my loins, and the water shot straight off my ridge roof. Unfortunately, on one side it poured into Peter's flat cover and on the other into Bob's. Before long, their bulging roofs were like plastic aquaria. I heard them at intervals during that wretched night pushing a naked arm up to their reservoirs (well supplied by the catchment area of my cover) to dislodge the pools. The water would clatter down, a good deal of it, I am afraid, finding its way on to the cursing camper below.

I felt guilty about it, especially as I myself kept pretty dry, apart from sweat; but there was nothing I could do.

On the morning of 19th April a wet clammy bunch of expeditionaries breakfasted on porridge, ship's biscuits and coffee. I saw that David Smithers, normally shining-faced, shaved and sleek at that hour, was lying fully clothed in his hammock. His hair was ruffled and ungreased, his cheeks blue with beard. In his hand he grasped a camp spade. He was in a raging fever.

Suddenly he scrambled out of bed and rushed down the path to the river. I followed him as he cut across the rock to the left, but as he crashed into the undergrowth he turned back a round-eyed agonised face and shouted, 'Don't follow me, Brian! It's too messy!'

He was in the throes of an acute attack of diarrhoea and vomiting. What specifically had caused it, it is difficult to say. Water perhaps, or something he had eaten. Jesco told me he had given David the day before a chunk of tapir meat which he himself had acquired from the two Caboclo brush makers encountered at our last stop. At this rainy time of the year there is a lot of food in the forest and the tapirs become very fat. Eaten, this fat can cause belly pains, vomiting and diarrhoea. One also wonders what germs the meat had picked up in the handling.

As I stood on the rock listening to David threshing about in the bushes and wondering if he needed help, I noticed in mid-stream sticking up out of the water like the dome of a billy-cock hat or a Churchill bowler another huge rock. Only nature had split this one down the middle as if with a huge cleaver, the two halves having fallen apart into a V cleft.

I scrambled back up the slippy rock of Capybara and walked under the tarpaulin and out into the jungle beyond, only stopping to pick up a toilet roll and what was left of my bottle of Bacardi rum. Why I had the Bacardi in my hand at that time I forget. I only know that in scrabbling about among the rocky boskage to find a suitable crouching place, my rubber-soled baseball boots skidded and I fell forward on to one elbow and jounced the base of the bottle on the rock I was trying to climb. For one awful moment, I thought I'd broken my precious bottle. Fortunately not. It was a little thing, but in these strange circumstances values are altered, and that half-bottle of Bacardi rum must have meant a lot to me. Far more than my bruised and aching elbow.

Jesco rolled up behind me, his capacious belly lipping over his belt, his gaucho sombrero a bit limp after last night's rain, but still with the front brim sticking up.

'Brian,' he said, 'you want to see this. Come, I show you!'

I followed him along the narrow trail, brushing wet off the fleshy leaves and sinking deep into the sodden mould. At one point, where we paused, I was startled by a loud explosion in the tops of the trees. It was merely a natural process of ripening and rotting: some jungle giant had come to the end of his upright days and begun his latest stage, leading to decomposition and integration, with the continual cycle of growth and decay.

As I looked up, I saw a termites' nest, four or five feet long, flattened on to a tree trunk like a huge sand-coloured Cornish pasty.

Jesco beckoned me on.

He stepped to one side of the path and pointed up into the gloom. It was a magnificent sight, a beautiful sight – a wild cocoa tree with glowing yellow fruit like oval lamps drooping from the branches. There were two main stems, fifteen or twenty feet high with fruit suspended at intervals of a foot or so. I was reminded of Marvell's poem:

> Where the remote Bermudas ride . . .
> He hangs in shades the orange bright
> Like golden lamps in a green night . . .

And as I gazed up into the cathedral roof of the jungle I came also near to understanding fully those other lines of his '. . . annihilating all that's made, To a green thought in a green shade'.

When the golden cocoa pod was first brought back to Europe along with Inca gold in the holds of Spanish galleons, if the English bucca-neers – Hawkins or Drake – seized a treasure ship, they threw the cocoa pods overboard as useless. Nevertheless, they did take from the un-suspecting Indians their maize, potatoes and tobacco. This is the plun-dered country of which Raleigh reported, 'A nation of people, whose heads appear not above their shoulders. Which though it may be thought a mere fable, yet for mine own part, I am resolved it is true. They are called Ewaipanoma: they are reported to have their eyes in their shoul-ders, and a long train of hair groweth backward between their shoulders.'

If we had continued to walk along that forest trail for a couple of days we should, no doubt, have struck wild Indians – or they would have struck us. I couldn't help wondering what the origin of Raleigh's story of the Ewaipanoma was and whether some kind of pygmy or dwarf Indians, or a deformed hump-backed family, might not have given rise to that traveller's tale. One thing is certain, Raleigh has been proved to be an accurate observer and an honest reporter; he never said he had seen the men with heads beneath their shoulders, but he did say eye-witnesses had told him of their existence. Another thing is certain, that after Raleigh's account was published in 1595 many of his contem-poraries poked fun at the story, though some, including Shakespeare, found fascination in 'the anthropophagi and men whose heads do grow beneath their shoulders'. Others of Raleigh's stories which, at the time, seemed equally tall, we ourselves witnessed to be true: I am thinking of his report that some Indians grind the bones of their grandfathers and eat them in soup – they do indeed.

We left Capybara with no regrets at ten forty a.m. My diary says: 'The craft is skidding and swinging round the bends like a curling stone. The canal is much narrower now – about 100 yards wide and much more twisty than it has been – I'll bet it looks like a snake from the air, curling and coiling back on itself. [I later found this to be true.] Remarkable variety of trees – big leaves, small leaves, thin leaves, fat leaves, spade-shaped, star-shaped, floppy, stiff, palm-like, grass-like, but all green, green – *inferno verde*, the green hell.

'11.15. Henry filming outside as we travel, with Jim Sweeney holding him. Both have safety harness but the wind is so strong it just blew Jim off his feet to land spread-eagled on the curved plenum chamber. His harness held and he scrambled back to the catwalk.

'My thoughts go back to Capybara. It is impossible to keep either dry or clean in the Amazon rain forest. This morning I slipped on a great granite rock greasy with forest ooze and nearly broke my bottle of rum – what a tragedy that would have been. It was only half full and I have another half full one in my pack – but we still have a long way to go. Fortunately, Jesco still has plastic jerrycans with cachaças – I don't know how much. He started off with five litre containers full, but we have drunk pingas morning, noon and night – so I can't tell what's left.

'When I fell down the gliddery rock I splotched my clothes with jungle dirt, leaf-mould, soil, God knows what; it leaves a dark indelible stain.

'12.30. High mountains which we first sighted ahead about an hour ago are now getting nearer. Thin blue tops are surfacing from a white woolly cloud base.

'Jesco is tending to David Smithers who is lying in a fever on the back seat.

'I wonder what the Aguirre expedition thought when they saw the mountains? Any change from the monotonous jungle draws men's eyes and thoughts – and *they* (unlike us) had had the green hell for months.

'It hasn't rained since we left Capybara; lots of high cumulus cloud and sunshine. As the craft crabs round the many corners, a cool refreshing spray shoots in on me through my muslin curtained window. In places the Canal narrows to fifty yards.

'Many macaws – I've just counted one flying flock of fifteen. Macaws in the air are distinctive, not because of their brilliant colours (they are usually too far away to appear anything but dark grey) but because of their shape – they look like flying crucifixes – and the fact that they pair off and proceed through the air almost as close as Siamese twins. This part of the Casiquiare (we can't be far away from the Orinoco) is embarrassingly rich in bird life and palms. Jesco says he's never seen a jungle so chock-a-block with palms: if ever anyone could legitimately use the old word "foison", this is the spot. I have counted at least five different kinds of palm trees, some, I notice, with great Prince of Wales feathery fronds sprouting almost from ground level.'

Jesco gets up to look at David Smithers and I go with him. David's bush jacket and pants are black with sweat patches. His eyes are half-open, but he is plainly not with us.

'How is he?' I whisper to Jesco.

'Bad,' says Jesco with a characteristic screwing up of his eyes. I know when Jesco draws down his blond eyebrows and nearly closes his eyes that he is emphasising what he says.

'Is there anything we can do?'

'I already gave him anti-diarrhoea pill.'

'What about his temperature?'

'You want to boil a pan of water? Put it on his forehead.'

Of course this is no joke, but Jesco is clearly well acquainted with fever – I've seen it myself, but years ago – yet in this situation without a doctor to refer to, one feels helpless. The BBC party has an excellent medical box got together by Bob Saunders on expert advice; Jesco augmented it in Manaus, especially with disposable hypodermic syringes and 'wide spectrum' antibiotics – those with a blunderbuss effect. Myself, I'm suspicious of pills and potions, but Jesco would stick a needle into anybody at the drop of a hat.

We go back to our seat.

It's a pity that David of all people, the one who really organised the bulk of this trip, should be laid out now, for we are just about to burst into the Orinoco.

CHAPTER ELEVEN

Tama Tama and Curare

WE ran out of the Casiquiare Canal and into the fabulous Rio Orinoco at ten minutes past noon on 19th April 1968.

The event was marked by the stage entrance of Duida, a crouching mountain seven or eight thousand feet high like some gigantic blue cat watching the hole of the canal for a mouse or an explorer to pop out.

At this point, at that rainy season of the year, the Orinoco was about a quarter of a mile wide. From here to its source was perhaps the distance from London to York, two or three hundred miles; but so incredibly difficult for travellers, what with jungle, rapids, rocks, floods, fallen trees, disease and hostile Indians, that the first discoverers of the source had reached it only seventeen years before. At first we found its banks were no different from what we had encountered so far – solid walls of greenery – and its waters were 'white' waters, a sort of light mud grey which, near the banks, reflected the ubiquitous green. From the air, the parting of the waters appears like a T-junction. At the time, I believed we were the first white men ever to proceed all the way by water from Amazon to Orinoco since Aguirre made the journey in 1561. We had travelled in less than ten days well over a thousand miles. No one, I am convinced, will do it quicker for many years to come.

But still, Europeans have rowed from Negro to Orinoco via the

Casiquiare: after Aguirre, Humboldt did it, and he himself tells an interesting tale which not only serves to show the extraordinary character of such a penetration but also indicates to what lengths men can push themselves in search of gain.

Humboldt writes: 'The incursions undertaken from the middle of the 17th century, to procure slaves, had gradually led the Portuguese from the Rio Negro, by the Casiquiare, to the bed of a great river, which they did not know to be the Upper Orinoco.' These intrepid slavers did not actually capture the slaves themselves, instead they adopted a particularly hypocritical procedure which allowed them a pretence of humanity and dragged God on to their side as well. Because of the way they went about their cruel business, the slavers called themselves *tropas de rescate* or 'troops of ransomers'. They incited Indian tribes to make war on one another and then, instead of allowing the captured prisoners to be killed, the slavers 'ransomed' them and to make the business appear respectable in the eyes of God and men, they took monks with them solemnly to examine 'whether those who sold the slaves had a right to do so, by having made them prisoners in open war'. According to Humboldt, from the year 1737 the visits of the Portuguese to the Upper Orinoco became very frequent. They brought with them hatchets, fish-hooks and coloured glass beads to induce the Indians to make war on one another. One tribe, the Guipunaves, led by their chief of the time, a brave and cruel man called Macapu, went down and farther down the Orinoco inflicting incredible injuries on other peaceful tribes, 'devouring some,' says the missionary Gili, 'and selling others as slaves to the Portuguese'. The Spanish Jesuits of the Lower Orinoco became uneasy at this state of affairs, and the Superior of the Spanish Missions, one Father Román, decided very courageously to attempt to force a way up the Great Rapids (the Atures and Maipures) without a military escort and to contact and pacify the savage Guipunaves Indians. He was successful in passing the cataracts and having arrived at the spot where the rivers Guaviare and Atabapo join the Orinoco 'he saw from afar a canoe as large as his own, and filled with men in European dresses'.

This, for Father Román, was as dramatic a meeting as Stanley's famous encounter with Livingstone: it was even more unexpected. Here was the Superior already pushing beyond that tremendous obstacle to progress the Great Rapids into an unknown, unexplored wilderness, and there, coming to meet him, were white men.

'He caused a crucifix to be placed at the bow of his boat in sign of peace (probably to keep off devils too, if the truth be known) according to the custom of missionaries when they navigate in a country unknown to them. The whites, who were Portuguese slave-traders of the Rio Negro, recognised with joy the habit of the order of St. Ignatius. They heard with astonishment that the river on which this meeting took place was the Orinoco; and they brought Father Román by the Casiquiare to the Brazilian settlements on the Rio Negro.'

Five minutes after we debouched from the Casiquiare into the Orinoco, we ourselves were to receive a similar surprise to that of Father Román.

We were heading for Tama Tama, the next fuelling stop.

The settlement came into sight about twelve fifteen, a dozen huts wedged one above the other in three or four tiers round a steep knob-shaped hill. Some of the houses had palm-thatch roofs, others corrugated iron, painted but rust-stained. The walls were the familiar sand-coloured baked clay. Below the huts, the beach was cluttered with massive tumbled rocks; in fact, Tama Tama hill, beneath its buildings and thickly crowding palm trees, reminded me of a collapsed Aztec pyramid overgrown by jungle. Later, when we walked about the paths, we heard hollow rumbling echoes under our feet, and beyond the hill saw there lay a wide valley chock-a-block with a debris of scattered stones from the size of bricks to the size of houses.

But it wasn't the appearance of Tama Tama which astonished us.

As we turned in a wide circle, wallowing over our own wash towards the specks of red on the shore which were our fuel drums, we saw the spaces in between the houses filled with people. But *people*. Just as the various local Indian tribes call themselves 'people' and other tribes 'Butchers' or 'Monkeys' or more kindly 'Watermen', so I have to confess that I, at least, had this feeling when I first saw the inhabitants of Tama Tama that they were *people*; men, women and children – many children (they flourish like weeds in the tropics), all white, many blond, *all like us*. I apologise for this racial chauvinism: I am simply trying to express the burst of sympathetic integregation I felt with people who looked like me and talked the same language – except, of course, that they were chattering excitedly in Southern and Mid-Western American accents.

For these were the New Tribes Missionaries – whole families of them – and Tama Tama was their forward strike headquarters.

As we floated nearer to the rocks I could see through the hovercraft window that the women and girls were wearing new-pressed cotton frocks, crisp and gay (they couldn't have long changed into them). Of course, there was no suggestion of the mini-skirts we had left back in

London and even in Manaus: these ladies wore calf-length respect-
ability. The men, on the other hand, looked sporty: there were half a
dozen of them with cowboy hats, brightly patterned shirts and jeans.
We grown-ups could never appreciate what our arrival meant to the
wondering imagination of the children who jumped about excitedly
and yelled, 'Gee! Look at that, Paul!' 'Johnny – I din' never think it 'ud
be like this at all!' The mission school for the children of all families
spreading the gospel in the Upper Orinoco was here at Tama Tama, and
today was a red-letter day in years and they had all been let out of
school to see this marvellous machine like something from their space
comics and the strange-speaking men who manned her.

Graham Clarke ordained a stop for ninety minutes to refuel and take
lunch. We bundled ashore.

A young married woman wearing a pale yellow frock and with a
little blue-eyed boy of three astraddle her hip said, 'Howdy?'

'How do you do?' I said a little self-consciously.

'Where you from, sir?' she asked.

'I'm a Yorkshireman,' I said, even more awkwardly.

'No, sir. I mean where 'd'y' come from in that machine?'

At that time I didn't know it, but this was Pat Dye, the wife of a
young missionary called Paul Dye with whom we were to become well
acquainted. Another, more mature lady was introduced to us as a Mrs
Peg Shaylor. She said, 'Ifn any yo' menfolk wan' a cookie an' a cool
drink – yo' better come on up to th' house.'

The BBC crew (less Jesco, who had wandered off elsewhere to
photograph little boys) accepted Mrs Shaylor's invitation. When I look
back on it, it was one of those coincidences which in real life are always
happening but which in fiction are condemned. Mrs Shaylor was the
wife of Robert Shaylor the senior missionary in charge of the post. As
we walked up the narrow winding paths ('Don' tread on the grass,' she
said, 'it only stirs up more flies') Peg Shaylor asked us what our plans
were. We said we wanted to get in touch with the Missionary Aviation
Pilot based at Puerto Ayacucho.

'That's Paul Johnstone. O.K. – I'll call him up.'

'Pardon?' we said.

'I'll call him up on the radio.' Well, would you believe it?

'We also want to meet wild Indians.'

'Waikas. Sure – plenty o' them – still feudin' and wife-stealing. They
don' wear no clothes,' she said. 'When Robert gets back from Puerto
Ayacucho tomorrow I'll tell him to fix it for you.'

By this chance meeting, within five minutes the events had been set in train which were to get us our air support and our expedition to the Waika Indians. If we had not accepted Peg Shaylor's invitation we would have proceeded upstream to Esmeralda and probably never linked up with our airman and certainly not brought our Indian expedition to fruition.

Mrs Shaylor's home was a long spacious bungalow, open plan in style. Its foundations were a raft of shiny surfaced concrete, its walls stopped a yard short of the eaves all the way round to give an air space guarded by mosquito netting. Inside the mosquito-netted double door there was a room divider to waist height, with a modern sink and chrome taps and a cooker fitted into it. There was also a fridge – worked probably like the cooker from bottled gas. As we entered the bungalow and walked through a gate in the room divider to a large, easy-chaired sitting space we heard the crackle of static from a turned-on radio receiver.

Peg Shaylor brought a large glass jug of sweet-scented iced raspberry drink from the fridge and clinked it into long glasses. She put a plateful of new-baked iced buns on the table round which we sat and said, 'Help yourselves.' We set to like schoolboys.

Within five minutes she had called up Paul Johnstone the pilot on her radio, and Bob Saunders got up with a mouthful of bun to make his acquaintance, tell him our plans.

'Brian!' called Bob from the other side of the room-divider, 'Paul says he's flying up to Esmeralda tomorrow and will see us then at half past ten. Is it all right if he brings his wife and young daughter?'

Who am I to be asked such permission, I thought. 'Certainly. We'll be delighted to meet them all,' I said.

We spent an hour chatting with Peg Shaylor, enjoying the quiet and cool of her home, and then walked back past the other houses down to the rock-strewn beach. We left Tama Tama at two fifty that afternoon, our stern swinging round sharp, too sharp, presenting the full blast of the propeller at those waving us off. We didn't know it then, but Pat Dye and her little boy had been blown clean over in a whirlwind of river spray and sand. Fortunately, they were more startled than hurt.

We motored up the Orinoco to Esmeralda or Las Esmeraldas (people call it both – neither the singular nor the plural fitting, for there has never been an emerald at Esmeralda, only outcrops of sparkling quartzite to set off wild rumours of vast fortunes, rumours known for these past 200 years to be as baseless as the fables of El Dorado. But still the name Esmeralda remains.) The sun shone brightly and the river flashed pleasantly. It was cool inside the hovercraft, with the door at the front wedged open a couple of inches to send a refreshing draught over our sun-prickled heads and scorched arms. We stopped for ten minutes to talk to a young American apparently adrift in an outboard canoe. What we didn't realise, of course, was that our appearance had been to him as shocking as if a flying saucer had suddenly descended on to the Orinoco and he had made for the bank and shut his engine. We found out afterwards that he was Mike, one of Peg Shaylor's teen-age sons from Tama Tama.

The distance from Tama Tama to Esmeralda is about thirty miles. It took us, in actual travelling time, half an hour. In an outboard canoe it takes between two and three hours. Esmeralda is important to the missionaries at Tama Tama because of its fine air-strip, but as a settlement it no longer exists. Once there was a largish Catholic mission here, now not even the walls remain, only overgrown foundations and a lumpy chessboard of tufty grass which you suddenly realise is the graveyard. For the missionaries, Esmeralda was always the end of the line and long regarded as a punishment station. Humboldt visited Esmeralda in the year 1800. He writes: 'Opposite to the point where the Orinoco forms its bifurcation (with the Casiquiare) the granitic group of Duida rises in an amphitheatre on the right bank of the river. This mountain, which the missionaries call a volcano, is nearly eight thousand feet high. It is perpendicular on the south and west, and has an aspect of solemn grandeur. Its summit is bare and stony, but, wherever its less steep declivities are covered with mould vast forests appear suspended on its flanks. At the foot of Duida is the mission of Esmeralda, a little hamlet with eighty inhabitants, surrounded by a lovely plain, intersected by rills of black but limpid water. This plain is adorned with clumps of the Mauritia palm, the sago-tree of America . . . There is no missionary at Esmeralda; the monk appointed to celebrate mass in that hamlet is settled at Santa Barbara, more than fifty leagues distant; and he visits this spot but five or six times in a year . . . We were surprised to find at Esmeralda many zambos, mulattos and copper-coloured people, who called themselves Spaniards and who fancy they are white, because they are not so red as the Indians. These people live in the most absolute misery; they have for the most part been sent hither in banishment.' In fact, once the mineralogical error which gave celebrity to Esmeralda had been discovered, the place appears to have taken on the role of the Siberia of the Orinoco. Nobody came here unless he had been sent: once here he did his utmost to escape and get away. This is the spot which, as I have already mentioned, claims to have more mosquitos than air. 'Esmeralda,' says Humboldt, 'on account of the immense number of insects that obscure the air at all seasons of the year, was regarded by the monks as a place of banishment. The Superior of the missions, when he would make the lay-brothers mindful of their duty, threatens sometimes to send them to Esmeralda, "that is", say the monks, "*to be condemned to the mosquitoes*".'

Esmeralda has not changed in this one respect. When we landed, we found ourselves also condemned to the mosquitoes. There is absolutely no defence, no antidote, no relief that I know of for the continual pricking, piercing, burning, boring of your exposed skin, your eyelids, ears, neck, eyebrows, hair, by those tiny blood-sucking hellions the *jejene* flies. You dance and slap in a frenzy, you yell and groan in mixed anger and despair. In the end you put your head in a bag and wear gloves: at least, that's what I used to do.

The only people left at Esmeralda today are a couple of Makiritare Indian families soiled by civilisation and living a kind of squatting existence in some shacks next to a sort of barrack building which the authorities had put up in 1951. This was on the occasion of the successful Franco-Venezuelan attempt to discover the source of the Orinoco. We ourselves took over this building, a single-storey army hut with three or four rooms to sleep in and a dining room and filthy kitchen at one end. Behind were 'ablutions' and squatting-type water closets, which still sometimes worked.

An earth-floored verandah stretched the full length of the front of the barrack, and between it and the river ran the long air-strip laid down by the Orinoco source hunters. Joseph Grelier, the young Frenchman who planned the search, recalls his first sight of Esmeralda on an air reconnaissance flight, 'Though we were not looking for emeralds, we might also have called this bright green plain which cuts into the sombre green of the forest by the same name. Its lushness gave us some misgivings about its suitability as an airfield, for surely it must be subject to flooding! Then, flying closer, we noticed a series of termite hills which we thought must be incompatible with regular flooding. The task of levelling them, we decided, would be preferable in the long run to periods of inundation.' When I myself first saw Esmeralda from the bank I recorded in my diary, 'Esmeralda seems to be a most attractive and refreshing spot. Open savannahs run back to rocky outcrops which form the foothills defending Duida mountain. That mountain is always blue, always trailing scarves of white cloud – but the blue changes from powder blue in the early pearly morning to blue-black when the sun falls behind its ridge. The flat savannahs are covered with fresh green grass a foot high, broken only by the earth-coloured cones of termite hills. None of them is very tall – perhaps two feet above ground.'

Someone (who, I don't know – perhaps the local Makiritare Indians for payment, perhaps the occasional National Guard visiting party) has kept the termite hills levelled along the air-strip ever since the day, seventeen years ago, when it was first completed. This air-strip is one of the three tenuous links which the New Tribes Missionaries at Tama Tama have with the outside, the other two being radio and the river. Civilisation downstream is represented by Puerto Ayacucho, itself a frontier town. It is the capital (pretentious name) of Venezuelan Amazonas, blocked off effectively from its jungle dependencies by the Great Rapids: in fact, there is no direct water link from Esmeralda to Puerto Ayacucho, all surface traffic having to leave the river at Ayacucho coming up, and at Samariapo going down, to circumvent the forty-five-mile stretch of the Atures and Maipures cataracts. By river and the Samariapo road from Esmeralda to Ayacucho takes a fortnight barring accidents; by air it takes three hours.

Arthur Helliwell and I were once again on kitchen duty for our first night at Esmeralda. We took over the squalid room at the end of the barrack building and prepared great cauldrons of packet soup and cocoa and opened tins of Spam, herring and cheese. There were two defunct oil stoves and a long bench all coated with a distasteful film of grease which I found so revolting I preferred to work on the floor, setting up one of our Primus stoves in a dark corner. Its circular ring of roaring blue flame gave me a feeling of at least one clean thing in that dirty kitchen.

Conrad Gorinsky was also there in his role of camp cook. The three of us discussed the forthcoming BBC expedition into Waika Indian territory. Because our leader, Mike Eden, wanted to study savannah conditions, and because we had to wait for the launch working along the Casiquiare behind us, we should have ten days to spare at Esmeralda. Provided we could hire guides and boats from the missionaries at Tama Tama, I proposed to explore upstream for a distance of four or five days' travel. Arthur Helliwell and Douglas Botting were eager to come with us, and Conrad (under his ethno-botanist's and not his cook's hat – thank goodness) wanted us to bring back information on curare and a drug known to be used by the Waikas to produce LSD or mescalin-type trance states and said to be called *yopo*.

Everybody has heard of curare, that deadly poison against which there is no known antidote and which the forest Indians smear on the ends of their blow-pipe darts. Raleigh came across it in 1594 and claimed there *was* an antidote, though he never discovered it. He writes, 'There was nothing whereof I was more curious, than to find out the remedies of these poisoned arrows, for besides the mortality of the wound they make, the party shot endureth the most insufferable torment in the world, and abideth a most ugly and lamentable death, sometimes dying stark mad, sometimes their bowels breaking out of their bellies, and are presently discoloured, as black as pitch, and so unsavoury, as no man can endure to cure, or to attend them.'

About the supposed antidote Raleigh said, 'In all this time there was never Spaniard, either by gift or torment that could attain to the true knowledge of the cure, although they have martyred and put to invented torture I know not how many of them. But every one of these Indians know it not, no not one among thousands, but their soothsayers and priests, who do conceal it, and only teach it but from the father to the son.' Raleigh may have been right: I myself have never heard of a cure once a person has been wounded with a freshly made poisoned dart. I have heard horrific stories of collectors who, years after they acquired their darts, when showing them off have scratched their fingers and have had to have an arm amputated to save their lives. If the curare had not been weakened by age presumably they would have died quickly. The Victorian traveller in Amazonas, Sir Robert Schomburgk, in the interests of science, no doubt, experimented with a weak solution of curare on a fowl: the poor bird died within five minutes. As to an antidote, I am very doubtful whether the Indians have ever discovered one. That to outsiders they appear to be able to effect cures or at least to recover from poison-dart wounds is because from childhood they have built up immunity. They do it by eating the blackened meat from around curare wounds in animals they have hunted. They urge their children to eat it although it tastes bitter. 'Go on,' they say, 'and if anyone ever shoots you with a *mamocori* [i.e. curare-tipped] arrow, you'll likely not die.'

Conrad Gorinsky had heard that the local Indians make curare from jungle vines growing on the slopes of Mount Duida behind Esmeralda. There were certainly Piaroa Indians on the banks of the Orinoco opposite Tama Tama who were the acknowledged experts in curare manufacture in that area. Nowadays, these Piaroas have been influenced by the missionaries and probably don't use curare for hunting (either animals or men) but barter it. They were supposed to exchange the distinctive dark-blue calabashes of the poison as a form of currency in trade with the Waikas farther up the river. Trustworthy information on the subject tends to be scanty, but I have since found out that Waikas

living in the untouched area between the Rio Padamo and the Rio Ventuari do in fact make curare themselves using a very sophisticated process. These Waikas collect the raw material from four different forest
lianas and pound the dried and toasted stems into granules rather
larger than coarse breadcrumbs. On a fine day, squatting in the open
air in front of his lean-to home, a man will set up two twigs about a foot
high. Between the tops of the twigs he holds tightly suspended by a
cord a thin ring of springy vine about six or eight inches in diameter. He
then twists himself a cone (rather like the paper cone some pastry cooks
make for piping iced cakes) using a broad-leaved forest plant. He pinches
a hole in the point of the cone, which is then hung through the ring
with a half-calabash cup under the hole in the cone. The Indian already
has his crumbs of vine stems in a leaf parcel, and he fills them into the
cone. Water from the river is then sprinkled on top of the liana crumbs
almost with the care and precision of a chemist titrating a fuming acid.
As the coneful of material becomes thoroughly soaked, strong coffee-
coloured liquid drips into the calabash. This is curare.

While this has been going on, one of the women will have been preparing chunks of a termite hill (like those on the air-strip at Esmeralda)
jamming huge pieces across the top of an eathenware pot and striking
the honeycombed substance with a stiff leaf. The object of this is to
frighten the termites out of their home into the pot, where they lie
white, fat and wriggling like maggots. The termites themselves have no
part to play in the making of curare – it's their hill which is needed to
produce a hot smokey fire – without flames – the termites themselves
will of course (being a valuable food) be eaten and not wasted.

Over the fire of pieces of termite-hill, the Waika man then lays a
cheveux-de-frise of darts which he has stuck in tens or dozens into the
pulpy stem cut from a banana tree. These outsize combs are laid
horizontal so that the heat from the fire hardens the ends of the ten or
dozen darts simultaneously. At the same time, the Waika paints the
liquid curare on to the first three inches of the foot-long dart, using
either a twig crushed and teased at the end into the form of a brush or
a twig with a bit of jungle cotton balled on the end.

As far as I know, this is the first record of this particular process for
making curare, and I got it from my friend the German anthropological
film-maker Hermann Schlenker, whom I directed into this area after
having failed myself from lack of time to uncover the secrets of curare
making. Another friend of mine, an American girl, Jean Liedloff, who
had lived with Waikas, but on the Caroní side, said she had never seen
them making curare, and for this reason believed Schlenker's Indians

were making a poison for hunting monkeys. But I am nevertheless convinced that the process I have described is one to produce true curare: my reasons for saying this are two. First, before he began the preparation the Indian put on war paint, streaking his arms with inch-broad black bars from forearm to biceps and painting a fearsome black band across his mouth and cheeks; secondly, a village war was imminent, for his people had invited those from a neighbouring village to a feast and during the night had kidnapped and hidden five of their women. This little neighbourly war which would result in the killing of men had brewed up in May 1969.

The incident emphasises the state of our half-knowledge of these primitive and yet at the same time sophisticated peoples. Their wildness and the utter remoteness of their habitations make it almost impossible for us to establish a long enough lasting relationship from which benefit can come for both sides. Those from the West who do penetrate into Indian country all have an axe to grind – and this applies to us film-makers as much as to political administrators, prospectors and missionaries.

As I say, we film-makers had little success with the actual preparation of curare (I managed to procure a calabash of the stuff later), but with *yopo* it was another matter. We were not only to track it down but to bring back specimens of the materials from which it is made, as well as some curious not to say horrific information as to its uses and effects.

Note: After the above was in print I went back to Humboldt to discover something I had before unaccountably missed. In 1800 Humboldt actually saw curare being made at Esmeralda itself, just as Schlenker has filmed it. 'The bark . . . is thrown into a funnel nine inches high, with an opening four inches wide . . . it was a leaf of a plantain-tree rolled up in the form of a cone, and placed within another stronger cone made of the leaves of a palm tree. The whole of this apparatus was supported by a slight frame-work made of the petioles and ribs of palm-leaves . . . A yellowish water filters through the leafy funnel. This filtered water is the poisonous liquor.' This process has always been regarded by the Indians as a magical one and has remained a closely guarded secret. The only other European known to have seen curare being made is Richard Schomburgk, who, in an almost forgotten booklet published in Adelaide, Australia, in 1879 describes the granulated bark in the palm-leaf filter with water dripping through it.

'The mystery of all the curares is by no means solved' – Prof. A. R. McIntyre in *Curare*, publ. Chicago, 1947.

CHAPTER TWELVE

A Bit of a Bust Up

AFTER breakfast next morning, Saturday, 20th April, I was sitting on my hammock in the dark room I shared with the other BBC men at Esmeralda. Outside, the sun was challenging anybody who cared to come on to the unequal duel; pastel blue Duida mountain was sailing through the jungle sea waving her long cloud pennants; and the *jejenes* were hunting the air in packs. Altogether, you were better off inside, although the stuffy, stifling room brought trickles of sweat running down from your neck and armpits. We were waiting for the buzz of the Cessna aircraft to warn us of Paul Johnstone's approach.

I was surprised to hear an unrecognised American drawl on the verandah outside and one of the other expedition members calling my name. The American, a grey-haired, strong-featured, middle-aged man under the usual cowboy hat, tall and Gary Cooper-like, turned out to be Robert Shaylor. He had driven an outboard canoe up from Tama Tama, bringing for company his ten-year-old daughter. They planned to take our missionary pilot and *his* wife and daughter back to stay at Tama Tama. But Robert Shaylor had also come prepared to furnish us BBC men with two large dugout canoes, engines, gasoline, Indian boatmen and two young American missionaries to act as guides. One of the missionaries would be Robert's son, Danny Shaylor, the other would be Paul Dye, husband of the young woman I first spoke to on landing at Tama Tama.

Sitting on the verandah (*jejenes* forgotten in the excitement), I studied a large map brought by Robert Shaylor and drawn by the celebrated New Tribes missionary Jim Barker, who has spent twenty-four years in the Upper Orinoco. The map showed the main branch of the Orinoco running from its source in the east almost horizontally to the west past Tama Tama. To the right of Esmeralda there joined the Orinoco from the north a straggling tributary shaped like a letter Y. This was the Rio Padamo. At the point where the Y splits there was a village called Sixto. Here Paul Dye and his wife Pat had built a house and preached to the Waikas, but, for reasons I did not inquire into, they were no longer living there. Nobody was there – no white people, I mean. Just beyond Sixto village (said Bob Shaylor), in the right arm of the Padamo's own tributary called the Rio Cuntinamo, was a fierce waterfall, a broad, roaring race of white water sixty feet from top to bottom, up or down which canoes could not go. A portage had, however, been hacked out of the jungle and, provided there were enough men available, you could just drag a boat up the steep slope and continue on your way. I gathered that the idea was for us to be taken beyond the fall to a village still 'unpacified', still little affected by white men.

The prospect was, to put it mildly, exhilarating, even frightening.

By this time, Bob Saunders, Henry, Peter and Jesco were all crowding round watching me draw a sketch map on the back of Raleigh's *Discovery of Guiana* so that I could calculate how long we would be away. According to Robert Shaylor, it would take us four days to get to the village he had in mind. Once we turned north into the Padamo River progress would be slow because of a dozen or so rapids we would have to struggle over before reaching the waterfall. Then there were two or three rapids after the fall.

Arthur Helliwell (his horsehair fly-switch going like the conductor's baton during the gunfire part of the *1812 Overture*) had joined us, and so had Douglas Botting. We were all chattering as excitedly as choir-boys on a Sunday-school outing.

David Smithers hovered in the background with a rather Puritanical look on his face. He had almost recovered from his diarrhoea and fever. I don't think he approved of the New Tribes Missionaries, and he certainly didn't like the idea of Arthur Helliwell and Douglas Botting deserting, as it were, the journalistic side of our joint enterprise.

Suddenly, we all pricked up our ears. There was no mistake. Above the buzzing of the flies we could hear a man-made buzz. It was Paul Johnstone approaching the strip.

Before we all got diverted by this new arrival I clinched the details of our Indian journey with Robert Shaylor. He was a little anxious (as was only right) that expenses would be met, and I reassured him on that score; he was probably going to find it difficult (and of course hellish expensive) to rustle up enough gas in that remote area; then he had to worry about the possible loss of one or both outboard engines. I told him that the BBC would pay – and in American dollars, of which I had brought a fair supply for just such eventualities.

By this time the distinctive blatter of a diving single-engined plane was rattling in our ears as Paul Johnstone put his Cessna down, with what appeared to be no run at all, right in front of our hutment. The three wheels of the red-and-cream Cessna Skywagon touched ground almost like the feet of a fly landing on the back of your hand. I noticed that the plane had the underbelly luggage attachment which presumably gives this Cessna its name as well as the appearance of a pregnant bat. Paul's new machine (it replaced the wreck of his predecessor Don Robertson recently lost with all hands in the sea of jungle) had an extra refinement. The wing-tips curved up right at the ends and reminded me of the finger feathers of landing crows, their function being to allow a touch down in extremely limited areas.

Within minutes we had all been introduced to Paul, his wife and ten-year-old daughter, and Paul (a man of about thirty with the strong nose of an earnest believer) was asking what we, the BBC, wanted him to do.

'What,' we said, 'now? Right now?'

'Sure,' he said.

'Well,' I said, 'can you fly with one door off?'

'Anything you like.'

'In that case I would like to fly a filming mission with Henry downstream to Tama Tama then to the junction of the Casiquiare and along the Canal until we come across the launch.'

'Fine,' said Paul Johnstone.

'How many of us can you take?'

'Three passengers.'

'Then, Douglas,' I said, turning to Douglas Botting, whose peaked cap was pushing over my shoulder, 'would you like to come to take stills?'

'Yes, please,' Douglas answered and dived immediately into his room in the long hut to get his cameras.

Within ten minutes Paul had removed the right-hand door by knocking up the hinge-pins, Henry Farrar was strapped in the front seat next to him, I sat behind the pilot and Douglas sat next to the open door behind Henry.

For some seconds nothing happened, then Paul said, 'We will say a prayer for God's blessing on this flight.' I myself am old enough to be ready for most things, but I must admit I had not really expected this. 'Cor!' I thought to myself.

'Dear God,' prayed Paul, 'we ask Thee for a profitable and safe flight in Jesus' name, amen.'

'Amen. Amen,' we three infidels muttered into our shirt necks. Afterwards Douglas remarked to me, 'You noticed that prayer was typically American? The profit motive came before safety?' I don't know what Paul carried with him in the shape of survival equipment. We other three went gaily off with nothing but a bottle of drinking water and an aluminium mug. It was my mug. I had bought it in Manaus the day before we left. It seemed just the right sort of receptacle for expeditionaries. Actually, it was worse than useless, for when you filled it with hot tea or cocoa the heat was conducted almost immediately to the aluminium handle and it was too hot to hold. Having protected your fingers with a handkerchief, you still couldn't drink from it, because the rim burned your lips. Somewhere over the Orinoco the wind snatched that mug out of the open door of the plane, and I wasn't sorry to see it go.

It was a glorious morning up in the air. No *jejenes*. Fresh and cool. The sky high, wide and handsome with some billowing, whiter than white clouds slanting up the horizon like God's washing. Below us, bubbly green forest covered as far as the eye could see in any direction. Duida, now navy blue with woolly sheep clouds grazing along her flanks, rose out of the jungle. Here and there lay patches of pea-green savannah, little paradises with palm trees spotting their smoothness like stars. This jungle did in fact look different from any other I have seen from the air, for a number of reasons. First, it was disturbed by occasional outcropping mountains like Duida; then it was broken by brighter green tablecloths of savannah; thirdly, it was veined with parasolled processions of Mauritia palms which stood out light, lush green as they followed hidden streams or broadened into crowds over marshy ground; lastly, round about the junction of the Casiquiare Canal, the land obviously had some difficulty in exerting its independence of the river, and as we flew over, for square mile after square mile, one could see sunlight glinting up between the jungle trees from the inundation round their trunks.

It was all breathtakingly beautiful, and I enjoyed it the more for the suggestion of sinister hostility. It was a Garden of Eden, but you always got the feeling that the Serpent was merely out of sight, lurking in the underbrush.

We caught a glimpse of the scientists' launch drawn in to the Canal side – you couldn't call it bank, there is no bank, the trees come right down to the water's edge. We circled a couple of times and some-body waved a straw sombrero in a wide slow sweep. Ernesto Medina, probably. Then we flew back to Esmeralda.

The Cessna door was replaced, and the plane parked in front of our dwelling. Paul locked up and left, together with his wife and daughter, in Robert Shaylor's dugout. Paul promised to be back together with a forty-gallon drum of Avgas for his plane, plus the missionaries and boats for our trip, by eight o'clock next morning.

All our arrangements seemed to be going like clockwork. I took my sketch map to our leader, Mike Eden, and showed him where we ex-pected to go and indicated the particular villages where we intended to spend each night. I did the same to Graham Clarke, who was mainly interested in our being back at Esmeralda by dawn of 27th April, when the hovercraft would resume its journey down the Orinoco.

Arthur Helliwell and Douglas Botting had both decided definitely to come with us. They, together with Jesco, Bob, Henry, Peter and me, began packing. Apart from our hammocks, mosquito nets, plastic rain sheets and camera gear, I suggested we should cut down drastically what we took with us. We knew it was going to be a hard trip physically – lugging everything we had up and down a dozen or more rapids. I myself packed most of what I reckoned I needed into one plump haver-sack to sling over my shoulder. It held mainly changes of clothing – each item slipped separately into a cellophane bag to keep dry. In the side pockets I had my water filter, spare rolls of film, footrot cream, toilet-roll, a couple of tins of eau-de-Cologne pads, toothbrush and tube of toothpaste, 'Stings', metal barber's comb, battery shaver and *Sir Gawayne and the Greene Knyghte*. I also had two tins of sardines. On that occasion we others got an insight into what Jesco had in his 'sausage'. The bulk of it was food and drink, iron rations such as chubby tins of sardines, limes and rum; there were gifts for the Indians – dozens of tiny plastic mouth organs, kilos of fish-hooks and boiled sweets; there was also a small bundle of soiled underwear and socks.

'You won't take this, Jesco?' I said.

'Oh, yes, I take it,' he replied.

This I found puzzling. It was unlike Jesco. Every day he did his washing – vest, pants, socks – and yet this bundle appeared to have been there since we left Manaus, maybe longer.

He watched me staring at it and he picked it up and drew me aside. He burrowed into the bundle with his strong freckled fingers and un-covered two cardboard boxes about three inches long and an inch broad and thick. He pushed the boxes aside and showed me what was there: a snub-nosed Browning revolver. Loaded. In the cartons were extra shells.

'I don't never show this to no one, Brian,' he said. 'The Indians must not know; and the officers at the frontiers would only be upset. Any-way, they don' like to look into shitty underpants any more than you do. So – I 'ope I don't never 'ave to use it.' He winked broadly and bundled everything away into his 'sausage'. He pulled the cords tight and laced them up.

He proposed that he should arrange with Conrad Gorinsky to draw eight days' rations per man from the expedition stores as well as the cooking pots we would need. In the meantime I found Graham Clarke again and suggested that it would be simpler for us to go all the way back to Tama Tama with the missionaries on our return and that we would load our large packs for safe storage on the hovercraft while we were away. This was agreed to.

I had got the impression that some of our expedition members who had been to South America before were 'agin' the New Tribes Mis-sionaries, regarding them as particularly bigoted and inflexible in religious outlook, fanatical subscribers to dogma which went out with the Puritans, uneducated, intolerant and relentlessly pursuing two main aims – the collecting of Indian souls like scalps and putting the men in trousers and the women in skirts.

The total nudity of most South American Indian tribes was, from the very first contact, a subject of wonder and curiosity to Europeans. To sailormen confined for weeks in cramped quarters aboard ship and de-prived of female contacts, the first sight of the shapely Indian women, walking like Eves about a Garden of Eden must surely have shaken the men rigid (as they say), at least partly. It was all the more startling be-cause the two great objects of interest to men of all the female anatomy were so innocently and openly flaunted: their breasts swing firm and free, while no bush of pubic hair is allowed to hide those other inviting lips. The first letter ever written from Brazil (dated 15th May 1500) to Europe is Pedro Vaz' famous *Carta a el Rei Dom Manuel* – Letter to King Manuel of Portugal, and the nudity of the women is continually at the tip of the writer's pen. He writes of the Tupi Indians encountered on the coast of Brazil, 'Among them there were three or four girls, very young and pretty with jet black hair hanging down over their shoulders; with their cunnies so plump and so tight and so clear of hair that we felt not the least embarrassment in having a jolly good look.' A little farther on, 'One of the girls was all stained from top to toe with decorative paint and certainly she was so well formed and so curvaceous and her cunny (which she had *not* painted) so pretty that many ladies of our own country, seeing such attractions, would be ashamed that their cunnies were not like hers.' And yet again, 'There you might have seen braves painted with black and crimson, with quarterings both on their bodies and their legs which was indeed most pleasing. Also among them were four or five young women, new ones, just as naked, not at all bad looking. Among these was one with her thigh from knee to hip and buttock all coloured with the same black paint but all the rest of her body in its natural hue. Another had both knees, calves and her ankles as well painted in the same way. Her cunny likewise naked but so innocently exposed as to cause no awkwardness at all.'

Flesh and the Devil – although I have no recollection of Christ Himself teaching the indentification of these two, his followers certainly have done it for nearly 2000 years. For Christian men since Paul, women have always represented temptation, it is logical therefore that Christian missionaries should minimise temptation (of themselves surely, for the Indians have always been used to nakedness) by breeching the men, but especially by frocking the women. As a result, apart from the encouragement of disease, discomfort and the discovery of shame, frequently in the Upper Orinoco the image of the noble savage is replaced by that of a dependant, a beggar in ill-fitting, old-fashioned, filthy cast-offs.

Nevertheless, this physical assault is, in the eyes of those who regard all missionaries with suspicion, not nearly so bad as the psychological affronts. Back in the 1870s the father of anthropology, William Tylor, was pointing out that Primitive Religion is not a jumble of superstitions but a coherent body of beliefs worthy of respect. These beliefs have developed from Primitive Man's environment and his attitude to his environment. If you take away his beliefs and try to replace them with *your interpretation* of another set of tribal beliefs from the Middle East, from an entirely different environment, you are asking for trouble. The Indian in his jungle (no matter how barbaric and how pagan he may seem to missionaries) is integrated with the nature which is his habitat. In that habitat he is a first-class citizen and a noble one; take away the beliefs and rituals which give meaning to his everyday life and supplant them with others which have no environmental tie, and you make him miserable, morose, self-doubting, but above all a dirty dependant, a second-class citizen of an alien civilisation whose thinking members have long suspected that their own well-springs may be tainted.

The New Tribes missionaries are fundamentalists to a man: they believe implicitly in the Bible, with all its thousand inconsistencies and contradictions; their faith doesn't move mountains, it is itself an immovable mountain. The Mission was founded in 1942 by Paul Fleming, an American missionary invalided out of Malaya. His doctrine demands belief in 'word by word inspiration and Divine authority of the Holy Scriptures', in the irrational acceptance of One God who is also Three, Father, Son and Holy Ghost: in the virgin birth of Jesus, His resurrection and His second coming, in Man's fall from God's grace and his absolute need for salvation which can only be brought about by Christ's sacrifice on the cross, and the belief that only faith in this sacrifice will achieve an individual's personal salvation; in the resurrection at the Last Trump of both the sinners and the saved – the saved to live in 'eternal bliss with Christ', but hell and damnation for the rest – 'eternal torment for the unsaved'.

For many of the Stone Age peoples of the forests of South America their advent into the twentieth century is by way of the path laid down for them by New Tribes Missionaries. Whether these Children of Nature should be hauled willy-nilly into 'civilisation' is a vexed question: that it should be done by proselytism seems to me indefensible. But, in a shrinking world, what is to happen to people like the Waikas? One is forced to accept that by 'civilised' standards their lives are nasty, brutish and short; like monkeys or forest pigs, they spend at least two-thirds of their waking time in the quest for food; they live in fear. They live in fear of neighbouring tribes, who will inevitably attack to steal their women, as they themselves steal from those same neighbouring tribes; they live in fear of the wild animals of the jungle and rivers – jaguar, alligator, poisonous snakes and spiders; they live in fear of the spirits – the Hekurá; they live in deadly fear of some white intruders – the rubber tappers and mineral prospectors, who may shoot them on sight. What, then, one might reasonably ask, do the Waikas get out of life? It seems to me that the *quality* of life as lived by these primitive forest tribes is quite different from the quality of life as lived by us. In the first place, we have forgotten largely how to live for the present. We live mainly for the future or the past; the Waika lives for *now*. He does not know the tyranny of time. Then we 'civiliseds' are most of us corralled in towns cut off from nature, sunrise and sunset, rain and wind, planting and harvest: the Waika is part of nature. We, most of us, have given up our faith in Man as centre of the Universe – the universe does not know we exist; so at the present time we are spiritually disorientated, 'lost': the Waika is complete to himself, he is not lost in his forest, he is still part of the natural cycle. We have cast God out from our garden: to the Waika God *is* the garden.

The tragedy of the Waikas, the tragedy of any Primitive Men today, indeed THE TRAGEDY OF MAN, is that Man fouls his own nest. He pollutes the ground on which he walks, the air he breathes, the water he drinks. Most tragically of all, technological Man can pollute quicker and more extensively than ever before. And primitive peoples cannot withstand or be protected against the technological onslaught: you cannot keep them in reserves or human wild-life parks, for inevitably governments will snatch their lands; you can only hope to integrate a few. The rest, it seems to me, will be destroyed. To governments, the Indians' traditional home is a potential source of wealth waiting to be exploited. It is a Naboth's vineyard. Unfortunately for Naboth there is only one way of evicting him, and that is by destroying him. At least that's how it seemed as I walked with Colonel Leal, Castillo and Doug Botting back over the traces of what had once been Esmeralda, past the overgrown graveyard back to our hut.

I decided to skip supper (slush and tinned herring holding no attraction) to have a shower in the 'ablutions' and go to my hammock. It was almost dark when I plopped wetly out of the shower into our room wearing rubber sandals and a damp towel round my waist. These rooms at Esmeralda are the full width of the hut, with a door at front and back. As I came in the back door, Bob Saunders came in the front. He said, 'Oh, Brian, could you come to the dining room for a conference?'

'What, *now*? *A conference?* I'm just going to bed.'

'I think it's about tomorrow.'

'Oh, well, then,' and I followed him out and along the earth verandah without stopping to put on any clothes.

The other expeditionaries were seated round the long trestle table in a pool of light from the pressure lamp. A litter of flies lay on the bare board round the chrome lamp base and a few, bent on suicide, buzzed round its glass shade. There was a flotsam of cellophane covers from Ryvita biscuits, crumbs, tins of cheese, tin plates, dirty knives and forks, mugs of cocoa. Burly blond Jesco sat at one end, near him little grey Arthur Helliwell, Graham Clarke, no bigger, then Mike Eden with a profile like a jag of lightning, Stuart Syrad with his round and rubbery face, handsome Robin Tenison, dark Henry Farrar, young balding Peter Smith and round-eyed sleek David Smithers. In its chiaroscuro it was Rembrandtesque; like a sketch for the 'Night Watch'.

I put one sandalled foot in the space on the bench next to Smithers and looked across at our leader.

'Would you mind, Brian,' Mike Eden said, 'going over the BBC arrangements for David's benefit?'

'*What?*' I said, 'David knows all about it.'

'No, I don't, Brian,' said Smithers.

'Now look, David, I've just come from the shower and the flies are biting me. I have already told our leader exactly when we leave, where we are going and when we plan to return. I have given the same information to Graham Clarke and agreed where and when we shall rendezvous again with the hovercraft. What more do you want?'

There was an awkward silence.

Smithers said, '*I* don't know who's going. I don't know when you go or anything about it, I don't think you realise what danger you may be going into. Who's going to know if somebody breaks a leg or the Indians attack you? I don't want to have to call out the Venezuelan Parachute rescue service for the BBC.'

'Oh, for God's sake,' I said, 'everybody knows by now where we're going. You yourself knew months ago in London that I intended a trip from Esmeralda.'

'Very well,' he said, extremely angry. 'I'll have nothing more to do with it,' and he pushed past my bare knees away from the table and strode out of the room.

I sat down at the table and scratched my ankles vigorously. 'These mosquitoes are biting me to hell,' I said.

Mike Eden looked glum. 'We'll have to do something,' he muttered.

'Brian,' he said, 'if I got David back here, would you tell him your plans?'

'Sure,' I said, 'I don't mind telling anybody.'

So Mike Eden stepped out into the dark and returned in a while, followed by a David still standing on his dignity. I'm an easy-going chap when it suits me, and I didn't want anything to jeopardise our expedition to the Waika, so I showed David on the map what our intentions were. 'Tomorrow morning at eight o'clock a couple of missionaries will come here from Tama Tama with two outboard canoes. The BBC party plus Arthur Helliwell and Douglas Botting will wait for them by the hovercraft. The pilot Paul Johnstone will also return with the missionaries and will fly Bob Saunders and Jesco to Coshalowateri here,' and I stabbed my finger at the first missionary settlement on the Rio Padamo. 'There's a short and (we have to admit) dangerous landing-strip here. It runs across a peninsula formed by the river looping. If you fly in too low you hit the cliff, and what's left of you falls back into the river. If you touch down too late to stop, then you run out of landing-strip and dive into the water again. Bob and Jesco will fly from Esmeralda tomorrow after the two boats have left in order to allow Jesco to film our departure. They will fly as far as Coshalowateri, filming us in the boats on the way, as well as filming our arrival there. We shall stay the night at Coshalowateri. The plane will return here and then fly back to its base. After two more days we ourselves get to Sixto, the village below the waterfall. It'll be Wednesday before we reach the village we're finally making for – it's here, Nacoïshimateri. All being well, we hope to rendezvous with the hovercraft back at Tama Tama at the crack of dawn on Sunday 28th April. At least, that's what I've arranged with Graham.'

'And what if anything happens to any of you?' asked David.

'Don't worry. Nothing'll happen,' I said.

CHAPTER THIRTEEN

Journey to the Waika: New Tribes Missionaries

THERE were two things we did on the Expedition which we realised at the time were fraught with some danger: one was our journey to the Waika Indians, the other was shooting the Maipures and Atures rapids in the hovercraft. But it wasn't until afterwards that we came to understand how near to death we had been on both occasions.

As far as the Indian trip was concerned, we expeditionaries were, in a way, idle spectators – curious to peer through the bars of jungle trees at some very strange men. But we did have two laudable aims: to bring back film which we hoped would give an audience of millions some little knowledge of the Waikas and arouse sympathetic understanding of their way of life; and to gain for the hovercraft scientists information about 'yopo'. Other Indian drugs, such as cocaine, quinine and curare, have been invaluable in modern medicine and surgery; there was reason to believe that what we knew vaguely as 'yopo' would prove beneficial in the investigation of mental illness. One thing is certain. If such information is not collected before the next ten years are out, then it will be too late, and part of Man's little store of accumulated knowledge will have been lost for ever.

At eight o'clock on Sunday morning 21st April our party of seven who were to visit the Waika Indians foregathered on the river bank near the moored hovercraft and waited for our guides. The seven were the BBC party of five (Henry Farrar, Bob Saunders, Peter Smith, Jesco and myself) and Arthur Helliwell, journalist, and Douglas Botting, writer–photographer.

We stood about for a while and nobody came.

We sat down on the nearest fallen logs now baked and weathered like driftwood. Nobody came.

I looked occasionally at my watch. Eight o' clock was the hour arranged, and we were still waiting at nine.

The *jejenes* were biting all the time, and the boiling sun added to our torture. I began to have some personal doubts which shifted my anxiety, as the leader and the one responsible for the success of our mission, to anxiety about the trip falling through and our having to return ignominiously to the hut by the air-strip.

Henry Farrar's face and neck were like purple leather embossed with bumps. I went down to the river and examined my own reflection. The left side of my face was a mass of tiny blood spots. Everybody was suffering agonies, and there was little one could do about it.

At ten thirty we built a fire, partly in the vain hope that the smoke would drive away the voracious *jejenes*, partly to brew coffee. Afterwards I put on a pair of motoring gloves my wife had bought me in Reading shortly before we left England, and drew a macintosh bag over my hat down to my shoulders. It seemed better to suffocate and broil rather than be driven off my head by the incessant pricking punctures of the flies. At least, it was a change of tortures.

At eleven thirty we heated a pot of soup, spooning it and the damned flies as well into our mouths.

Shortly afterwards we heard the distinct burr of an outboard motor from downriver, and we all arranged our packs and hurried to a high point on the bank to gaze.

Two large outboard canoes were surging abreast in midstream throwing off bow waves solid as shining ploughshares. One canoe had a curved awning of bright corrugated aluminium. It was our two missionaries, and Paul Johnstone the pilot.

When the canoes curved into the bank we saw that they were easily thirty feet long, each chipped and burnt into boat shape from a single tree. The one without the awning was narrower and had the larger engine of the two – a 40-h.p. Johnson. We found it well able to do ten or eleven knots against the river current.

Paul Johnstone introduced us to the two young men in charge of the boats – Paul Dye, about twenty-seven, quiet spoken with a mid-western American drawl, blue-eyed with a handsome lean brown face and one arm in a sling – he was suffering from a jungle boil on the back of his hand; the other, slightly younger, perhaps twenty-five, with a rounder, freckled face, was Danny Shaylor.

We all helped to off-load the forty-gallon drum of Avgas, needed for Paul's flight, and trundle it past the termite hills to the waiting plane, then those who were to go by water on the first leg got into the boats. Henry, Peter and Douglas scrambled with their gear into the covered canoe together with Danny Shaylor, while Arthur Helliwell and I joined Paul Dye in the fast canoe.

Jesco and Bob Saunders filmed our departure from the bank and, as soon as we were out of sight, packed their camera and kitbags into the Cessna to follow us.

It was one thirty by the time we left Esmeralda, and I remember with gratification the four hours it took us to reach our night stop. I sat up in front of the dugout canoe on the foremost thwart with my knees tucked under my chin. In midstream it was not only delightfully cool and refreshing but *there were no jejenes:* oh joy! From water level one saw and smelt a different jungle. It was a ravishing experience to the senses: my body was cool and braced for the first time in weeks, a scent of – was it verbena? – stimulated my nostrils, and my eyes were excited by the unrolling tapestry of jungle trees; many palms like huge Prince of Wales Feathers towered over us and were gone; there were great shafted trees with smooth silver bark like marble pillars; there were fallen forest giants, now impotent with arms and fingers rising appealingly out of the water.

The aeroplane swooped startlingly over the trees from behind us, buzzed us and flew past both canoes not more than six feet above the river. We refrained from waving, remembering we were being filmed. The Cessna rose abruptly and hedge-hopped over the jungle on our right. Bob Saunders told me afterwards that she was so close to the tree tops that the white insulator of her dangling aerial (which had somehow come adrift) was torn off as it caught in the leaves.

A violent rainstorm fell on us, but not without warning. The sky in front grew dark and thunder drops splashed about us. I pulled on a pair of nylon overpants, a bright yellow oilskin cyclist cape and a sou'-wester to match. I rode that storm out with enjoyment, bone dry except for my face. I sipped the rain off my lips. I actually felt *cold*.

Douglas Botting later described his feelings before we drew away from the slower canoe: 'There was something rather curious about one's first impression of whizzing upstream in a canoe, in that one felt rather embarrassed, rather self-conscious, rather histrionic, as if in fact one were playing a part or entering a scene. It was a scene we'd viewed in the movies; a scene we'd often conjured up in our own minds when reading certain kinds of books – the Martin Rattler variety, W. H. G. Kingston variety. Suddenly, there one was actually living this picture we had seen quite clearly since childhood without ever having been near the place. I remember particularly the totally motionless – as if turned to stone – bodies of Brian and Arthur, slumped on their seats looking neither right nor left and just skidding along against a forest background which looked almost as if it was on rollers and that somebody, somewhere miles down the river, was winding in the backdrop, the painted trees and occasional mud bank and hill and the blue mountain behind Esmeralda.'

For half an hour the storm continued, then the sky brightened again. I watched one heron after another, set up by the noise of our outboard, fly on ahead of us. You could always recognise them at once, partly by the distinctive U-bends in their necks (like a toilet-basin waste pipe), and partly by their unhurried, regular two-wing-flaps-per-second. After a time they would rise into the tall tree tops, brake with their wings, stretch their trailing legs forward stiffly and sink into the dark forest cover like a wraith. There were many other kinds of Amazon birds, seen now for the first time, which previously the noise of the hover-craft must have driven away before ever we came within sighting distance. I saw flocks of small white-bellied fliers, the size of swallows, skim in unison a foot or two above the sparkling river. I saw a dense blue-black bird rather larger than a magpie and with the same sort of wedge-shaped tail. I saw the bird which swims with its body underwater and its neck and head protruding like a periscope – one, as we passed a partly submerged tree, fell into the water from very startlement.

Occasionally, I looked back over my shoulder to see how Arthur was enjoying it. He would give me a sad little smile, wrinkling his grey moustache.

Behind him, Paul Dye sat expressionless at the tiller of the outboard, his blue eyes, under the frayed brim of a weathered forage hat, keenly watching the surface of the river ahead of us. Most of Paul's life had been spent in the forests of South America. All of it had been passed within the ambience of missionaries and mission stations. I once asked him if he had any doubts. I don't think he even understood my question, so remote was any doubt from his mind: 'No, sir,' he said shortly.

Paul Dye's life was like something out of the Old West. His father had been murdered by the Indians. When I got to know him better he told me about it. Five young, trusting American missionary men were in that first fatal contact with the Ayoré tribe made in dense jungle 300 miles east of Santa Cruz, Bolivia. Paul's father, Cecil Dye, and his uncle Robert were two; the others were George Hosbach, Dave Bacon and Eldon Hunter. At first they had painfully hacked a way through the matted spiny growth at less than a mile a day; they were scratched and torn to pieces, their hands, arms and legs festering, their fingers spotted with blood blisters and water blisters. They suffered from malaria and pneumonia, but always they sang and praised the Lord. Cecil Dye wrote home, 'With all my heart – and I have told Him – I would gladly suffer many times more intensely for the same manifestations of Himself. [He believed he had seen God during the crisis of his pneumonia and had established personal contact.] I love Him. His Name is all-glorious. There is power in His wonderful Name . . . I hear Eldon and Dave coming down the trail with water, singing, "Praise ye the lord, Hallelujah".'

The five men disappeared (like Fawcett), and after November 1943 it was seven years before the details of what had happened to them were made known to Cecil and Bob Dye's wives.

Early one morning in November 1943 a man of the Ayoré tribe called Ejene was hoeing in his plantation when he was startled by five white men coming through the jungle. They were holding up machetes and articles of clothing. Expecting to be shot as soon as seen, Ejene flopped on his belly and began wriggling through his corn stalks towards the village. Once out of the men's sight, he scrambled up and legged it to the huts as fast as he could go, yelling the warning, 'Cojñone! Cojñone! Whitemen!' It was a word which struck terror into most of the Ayoré who heard it: women and children and some of the more timid of the men immediately fled behind a nearby hill. Other men, who had been working in other plantations, on hearing Ejene's warning shrieks ran to the village to snatch up their wives' bags full of their meagre belongings to hide them in the woods. Then they themselves hid behind their huts with spears, bows and arrows and clubs at the ready. They watched the five white men walk into the clearing between the huts.

After looking round, these strangers set up two sticks and strung lines between them. Over the lines they spread shirts, trousers, three machetes, some smaller knives and a pair of scissors. While they were doing this an Ayoré arrow whizzed out of the trees and hit one of the white men in the shoulder. He cried out with the pain and surprise. One of his companions ran to him and plucked the arrow out. All five then rapidly walked back down the trail leading through the plantation away from the village.

To a Stone Age Indian, the thought of possessing a steel machete arouses emotions of longing and desire calculated to overcome fear, given a little time. Some of the men came out of hiding and snatched up the knives. One man, Upoide, was too late to get a machete. He became very angry and shouted to the others 'I'm going after those white men to make them give *me* a machete!' He followed the missionaries down the trail. He found them sitting side by side on a felled tree, part of the débris of Ejene's plantation. They were calling him on with their hands, holding out more knives, speaking and pointing to the heavens.

Upoide's anger and frustrated envy were still boiling inside him. The smallest white man, with gold in his lower teeth (Dave Bacon), walked towards Upoide holding out a machete and tried to hug him. Upoide freed himself from the embrace, stepped back and planted his spear firmly in the little man's body.

The other Ayorés arrived in time to see the blow without knowing if there had been any good reason for it. As Dave Bacon tried to pull the spear out of his side another Ayoré, Aburasede, clubbed him over the head and crunched in his skull. Instinctively, the Ayoré warriors thrust and battered at the remaining four. One white man managed to break free and run for the edge of the plantation. He had almost reached the cover of the jungle when an Indian called Datide overtook him and brought him down with his long heavy bludgeon. He died under the blows.

Altogether, eight Ayoré men took part in the killing of the five young missionaries. And here, one hardly knows where one's sympathy lies – with the killers or the killed. If the missionaries were seeking martyrdom, and one must believe almost that they were, then it could hardly have come quicker or cleaner. As for the Ayoré, in order (as they believed) to save their own lives they had had to offend not only the spirits of the men they had killed but also the Something in whose transcendental power all men and all things are held to account. Guilt for the killing had to be transferred from the men to the weapons. They danced and shouted through a ritual in which they wiped the missionaries' blood from their hands on to the weapons. Then they threw away the spears and clubs which had done the deed. Next, they had to 'pay' for the killing, so they all went to the forest to collect wild honey, which they then gave away to fellow tribesmen. Lastly, to lay the dead men's ghosts, they drew a representation of the man they had killed using a stick to trace a body and a head on the ground. Then they stamped and scuffed the outlines until they had been erased and so, with sympathetic magic, rubbed out the haunting ghosts.

As I have indicated, when I first heard Paul Dye's story I hardly knew whether to sympathise with the missionaries or the Indians. Paul's mother, Dorothy Dye, knew intuitively where her sympathy must lie. Instead of retreating to the States, she stayed in Bolivia with her three small children and eventually had the satisfaction of treating a sick Ayoré Indian who was one of the eight who had slaughtered her husband and his friends. This, at least, is practical Christianity to the letter.

As we chugged along, every now and then Paul would gingerly take his arm out of the sling and pick up an old dried milk tin lying in the wet at his feet. Painfully, he would bale the river spray and rain water from the curved bottom of the canoe. Less frequently, he throttled back and swung the racing propeller out of the river to free the cooling system of clogging leaves and forest rubbish.

For three hours we had been driving along at a steady ten or eleven knots and had long since left the other canoe behind. We were all alone in that wild, sequestered region, far from the haunts of so-called civilised man.

I looked at my wrist watch. It was five o'clock and we were turning left out of the broad stream of the Orinoco into a tributary called Padamo. Apart from being slightly narrower (perhaps 250 yards), the Padamo was little different from its parent river. In half an hour the Padamo's banks grew a little steeper and higher, and shortly after five thirty we were nosing between three or four dugout canoes moored at the landing of Coshalowateri.

I jumped on to the bank and looped the chain stapled into the nose of our canoe over a stake driven into the mud at the water's edge. There was a steep yellow clay slope leading to the houses twenty feet above us. The first few steps from the boat at such landings are the slippiest. Because the river continually rises and falls by a couple of yards until the highest flood level has been reached during the rainy season, the immediate margin is ever being wet into a skiddy-surfaced slime. Once you negotiate this trap there are thin logs embedded in the slope to form stair treads. At some time or another every embarking or disembarking passenger (not the bare and sure-footed Indians) slips and shoots down, backwards or forwards. If backwards, you jolt your spine and plaster your pants with a sticky yellow goo and frequently bark your shins on the sharp edge of the hard wood boats – if forwards, you fill the spaces between your scrabbling fingers with the ochreous clay.

At Coshalowateri I was extra careful, for the bank is almost perpendicular. I shouldered my haversack, slung my camera round my neck and went up on all fours.

Looking down on us were clothed Waika Indians – small, square, blocky, untidy, scruffy, but inquisitive, bright-faced and smiling. They watched us excitedly, together with friendly dogs, two tame coatimundis, green and blue parrots and parakeets, a big-billed toucan and two white women and one man. The whites were, of course, missionaries of the New Tribes Mission. The man turned out to be Derek Hadley, twenty-nine, an Englishman from Bournemouth who spoke with an American accent, had a dark crew cut, was dark-skinned with a stubble of black beard, had intense dark eyes and sharp nose and reminded me of a character from Shaw's *St Joan* – the burning, earnest priest who tried to argue Joan out of her heresy. Derek Hadley's face and arms were covered with black pin-head spots of old pium bites. The ladies were Derek's wife, Jilleen (from Wisconsin), and Mrs Loretta Haslam (pretty and bobbed, with two children), whose husband, Billy Joe, was a radio mechanic away at this time doing maintenance work down at Tama Tama.

Jesco was busy filming our disembarkation, and Bob Saunders waited behind him to show us to a palm-thatched wattle-and-daub hut assigned as quarters for the night. They had, of course, flown in over three hours before with Paul Johnstone.

A couple of Waika men in shapeless slops and stained army drill castoff jackets carried our hammocks up from the boat. Paul Dye went off with the Hadleys, while Arthur Helliwell and I followed Jesco and Bob into our gauze-windowed, mud-walled home for the night. We immediately began to sling our hammocks and mosquito nets from the cross beams of the hut alongside those of Bob and Jesco. We were hindered with the help of a crowd of Indians, mainly young girls with babies astraddle their hips, and children. As Arthur Helliwell said, it was like trying to sling a hammock on Paddington Station during rush hour. Suddenly, to our relief, they left us, swarming like bees to another point of interest. It was Jesco. He had dived into his kitbag (the sausage) and was distributing largesse. I shall always be reminded of Jesco and Indians whenever I hear the notes of a mouth organ. He had hundreds of tiny plastic mouth organs, red, yellow, blue and green, which he distributed to the little boys and girls. The air was filled with their sucked and blown wheezy notes. He also gave out fish-hooks, nylon line and boiled sweets. He attracted Indians as jam attracts flies.

When there was no prospect of more presents the Indians returned to gaze at Arthur and me. The young mothers would stand there with their babies glued on to one swollen breast and sometimes put out a finger to touch us, no doubt to see if we were real. Their dirty shifts hung on them like sacks. The whole pathetic group looked as if they had recently raided a rag-and-bone cart. Most of these Indians (the girls with pudding-basin-cut hair, the men cropped like GIs) had been given Spanish names by the missionaries – Rosita, Elena, Ricardo, Rafael – but if you asked their names they were still extremely shy, not to say suspiciously reluctant to tell you. To give you their names put them in your power. My common sense ought to have reminded me of that. But, without thinking, I had asked Derek Hadley what the Waika phrase was for 'What is your name?' and to gain their confidence I preceded it with 'My name is Brian' – '*Brian jã: wã: hã: kua*'. So when I asked '*Wadi wã: wã: hã: kua?*' if they deigned to reply, without exception they would put their lips to my ear and whisper 'Ricardo' or 'Elena', feeling no doubt that since these weren't their real names it probably didn't matter, anyway. I later came to know of one Indian woman who was ignorant of her husband's real name until she had been married to him a long time and had a child by him. Even then, she only found his name out by accident.

Once these Waika Indians were confident of your friendship they openly embraced you, standing with their arms round your waist – they were so short and I was so tall that they usually hugged my belly.

Before long we were joined by the occupants of Danny Shaylor's boat, and Peter Smith, Henry Farrar and Douglas Botting put up their hammocks in what space we had left them.

As darkness was falling, Derek Hadley came into our hut with a pressure lamp. It hissed gently and attracted all kinds of night-flying moths and insects. Derek passed on an invitation to supper with Mrs Haslam.

Douglas asked me if I had located the 'little house at the bottom of the garden' yet? I hadn't, but Bob Saunders had, and pointed it out across the cleared space between the houses. Later, when I visited this little house I found it to follow the general design of lavatories in other missionary villages. The 'throne' was a holed wooden seat set on top of a substantial hollow wooden column. The column appeared to be made from two eight- or ten-foot lengths of dugout canoe sunk edge to edge into the ground with the last three feet left above the level of the surface. It seemed a very effective arrangement, though I preferred not to visit it after dark.

The missionaries' living accommodation reminded me forcibly of what I had seen in a long succession of cowboy films – the cruder, more authentic ones, not the television *High Chaparrals* and *Virginians*. When we walked to Mrs Haslam's across what, in England, would be the village green we were conscious of a buzz of mysterious life coming from the darkness of the eight or ten Indian houses circled round it. It was a nervous noise compounded of breathing, babies' cries, pet bird squawks, sharp Waika phrases, dogs barking and unseen people moving about. We paddled through the pools of moving light thrown by our torches. I remember distinctly Arthur Helliwell's suede-leather calf-length boots stained with mud and sweat. Loretta Haslam's mud house was what, in more sophisticated circles, is called 'open-plan'; in other words, it really only had one room with a flat-topped bar separating the entrance from the rest. The bar served to keep the Indians from the living area, for they flocked in and out of the door at will. Inside the living area there was a butane gas cooker, a sink and various cupboards, rough chairs and a table. With its mud walls and raftered roof, the house had a distinct flavour of the opening up of the West, pioneers, sod-busters, the covered wagon. In fact, these missionaries' covered wagon is the dugout canoe, and the same air of piety is ever present as it appears to have been with the men and women of the wagon train. God is always in the room or on the river with these American New Tribes missionaries, and they speak to Him simply and practically in prayer. I forget which one it was at Mrs Haslam's who called down God's blessing on the cooked bananas and cassava bread with egg and rat sandwiches – either Paul Dye or Paul Johnstone. It didn't matter – we expeditionaries would have been a little embarrassed whichever it had been.

The tasty rat meat we enjoyed in the sandwiches also cropped up again in a hot stew. Later we saw the carcass of the little beast who had supplied so much of the feast. He was a bit crozzled on the outside through being roasted (I take it) over an open fire, and a pair of sharp rat-like claws were still visible: but inside, the meat was white like pork or chicken.

On our way back to our sleeping quarters (it was probably half past eight and pitch black) we passed a hut in which the evening prayer-meeting was being conducted by the Waika who was the spiritual leader of the village. He was wearing spectacles, which looked odd, and still had his army bush jacket with dangling epaulettes. Earlier in the evening we had watched with disfavour a little game he enjoyed with the small boys, in which he used a piece of stick like a billiard cue against their close-cropped heads. The surprised howl of pain from his victims stretched his mouth in a grin from ear to ear, which made him look like a particularly revolting toad. He continued cueing heads with his stick end until one diminutive mother (she was all of thirteen) stood up to him in noisy protestation and he stopped. Whereupon all the other men bystanders laughed. But now he was distributing the gospel in Waika while dark-eyed Derek Hadley intently watched.

We slunk quietly by to our hammock beds.

The third missionary family at Coshalowateri were the Roundys – Will, his wife Mary and seventeen-year-old daughter Elizabeth. I record verbatim a conversation I had with them:

Myself: Mr Roundy, how long have you been here?

Mr R: For ten months, sir. We came down from the Washington, D.C., area on 2nd June last year and we really love it here.

Myself: Have you been in the mission field many years?

Mr R: No, we started training in September 1964 and we finished our training in March '67, and then we came down here in June.

Myself: Well, you've got a fine grown-up daughter, so you can't be as young as all that. How did you happen to come so late into missionary work – what were you doing before?

Mr R: I was an engineer when the Lord spoke to my heart that he wanted me to be a missionary, and as soon as we'd located the New Tribes Mission – I'd never heard of it before – well, we applied and they accepted us, and then we started our training in their Boot Camp and language schools.

Myself: And was Venezuela your first station?

Mr R: Yes, that's right. And the Lord laid the Cadimani Indians here in Venezuela, which are north-east of here, on our hearts, and Lord willing, we are looking forward to moving into that territory some time.

Myself: And Elizabeth, how old are you?

Elizabeth Roundy: I'm seventeen.

Myself: And what are you going to do?

E.R.: I don't know for sure what the Lord has in store for me, but I'd like to be a missionary too.

I found the blind faith and unselfdoubting assurance of Will Roundy disturbing. Before we left Coshalowateri he demonstrated to a wondering audience of Waikas how to preserve a miraculous jungle creature, a giant insect one of them had brought to him. It was about five inches long with narrow gauzy wings, angled legs, questing head and delicate antennae supported on a strong horny body ribbed like the Michelin-tyre man. Will Roundy went into his house and returned to the 'village green' with a hefty hypodermic syringe full of formaldehyde. He deftly thrust the inch-long needle into the living creature's body and slowly pumped the killing preservative into it – all the while peering through his spectacles with a fixed smile.

I thought of St Francis of Assisi. I thought of a passage in a book by Paul Dye's aunt, widow of Bob Dye and herself a New Tribes Missionary. She is describing how while in Bolivia she had decided to have her pet dog put down and persuaded the local garrison commander to assign a soldier to do the job. She writes, 'As I led the dog out of town, the soldier, hating his task, asked me, "Señora, isn't it a sin to kill a dog?" "No," I reassured him "because a dog doesn't have a soul. Now if it were a *bárbaro* [i.e. a jungle Indian], that would certainly be wrong."'*

The larger of the two canoes (the one with the awning) left Coshalowateri at eight forty-five next morning. At seven thirty a.m. I had followed Arthur Helliwell down the steep bank to wash and shave in the river. Not to be encumbered with clothes, I had gone down naked except for my underpants. It was a mistake. The *jejenes* were on me in a flash. I finished up completely submerged except for my head, supporting myself with my left hand over a canoe gunnel while I soaped and shaved with my right. It was the only way to escape the bloodsuckers, and for once I was willing to risk the dangers of the river rather than be bitten to death.

I decided to stay behind with the faster canoe to wait while Jesco flew upriver to film all the rapids we should have to overcome, the waterfall which would finally force us to a portage, and the village we hoped to reach. So Danny Shaylor went ahead with his boat carrying Bob Saunders, Arthur Helliwell and Douglas Botting. At eleven fifty the aircraft had returned and would now fly back to Tama Tama. Jesco, Henry Farrar, Peter Smith and I set off once more upriver with Paul Dye.

When I asked him what the rapids were like, Jesco screwed up his eyes and said, 'I think they are not so good, what?'

He looked more like a burly *cangaceiro* than ever, and because the canoe was narrow he appeared to overflow the sides. Below his pressed-up hat brim with its star and 'BBC' marked on it, his round face shone like a blond moon. He was wearing a striped open-neck shirt with a shot-gun slung across his back on a bandolier. Four cartridges were tied with a bit of coarse string to the butt of the gun. A machete in a shiny red leather sheath with his name 'Jesco' in magic marker hung from his belt. Always at hand he had a half-pint tin mug (again labelled 'Jesco') with a leather thong which he regularly filled with native rum from a red

* *God Planted Five Seeds*, by Jean Dye Johnson, Harper and Row, New York, 1966.

polythene jerry can on which he had printed BBC WATER. Now and then he passed the mug down the canoe for the refreshment of any who pleased, following it with dainties such as sardines on water biscuit or cheese on Ryvita. He usually had to taste the rum both before it started its round (to see that it was mixed correctly with the right amount of lime juice and sugar) and on its way back (to see whether what was left needed to be thrown away). By lunch-time he was expansive, happy and in great good humour; by evening he was exploding with energy, ready to fetch, carry, make camp, make fire, cook and feast like a lord: then suddenly he would deflate and with a muttered 'I go to bed', he would retire quietly, limping to his hammock.

CHAPTER FOURTEEN

Journey to the Waika: The Rapids

AT ten minutes to two on that Monday 22nd April we rounded some ruffled water and a natural jetty of smooth flat rocks to pull into Shanamaña, a village on the left bank of the Padamo.

Beyond Shanamaña the rapids begin, and it was here that we had to exchange Danny Shaylor's large boat for a narrower, lighter one which we would be able to manhandle over the rocks and broken water; we also had to pick up four Makiritare Indian river men, without whose strength and expertise we should never be able to get beyond the first cataract.

Danny's covered boat was tied up alongside three or four dugout canoes, empty; all the gear and extra gasoline tins having been transferred to a canoe similar in size to our own. The men were up in the village.

Paul Dye led us past the land side of the half-submerged rocks, where we could now see brilliant coloured butterflies thirstily sipping at the splashes. Under the hot sun, in the middle of the day, hardly a dog was stirring. Reaching the top of the bank, we saw a rather higgledy-piggledy collection of rectangular mud huts. Paul led us into one of them, the home of the two resident missionaries Cecil and Delora Neese and their two little girls.

Douglas Botting and the others were already wiping their lips, having been served by Mrs Neese with a surprisingly sumptuous feed. The table in the second room had been relaid and the hospitable Delora Neese, a comfortable lady of forty or so, hailing from Southern Alabama, invited 'you-all tu wash yo' han's an' pull up to table'. We smartly did as we were told and were served with long glasses of cold iced tea straight from the gas refrigerator. The main dish was fried fish fresh from the river with peas and carrots as a sort of salad set in jelly. There were sheets of white cassava bread (it comes in round floppy pancakes which look like thin foam rubber but taste good after biscuit and dry Ryvita) and afterwards, American cookies.

The situation of these New Tribes Missionaries is, to an outsider, to one who cannot share their burning zeal, pathetic. The trappings of city life, such as the refrigerator, only serve to emphasise the hill-billy existence they are really forced to endure. Their walls are mud, their floors are mud, their furniture is crude, their living conditions and sanitary arrangements are like those of peasants in the Middle Ages. Delora Neese had lived at Shanamaña for two years and been out in the field since 1954. When Douglas asked her if she ever felt homesick, she replied, 'Well, I guess it gets harder every time to leave the States.'

We left Shanamaña in the two narrow boats shortly after three o'clock with the sky darkening and not much chance of forcing the first three bad rapids we had hoped to do before our night stop. There were no more missionary posts ahead. The Neeses were at the end of the line.

Bob Saunders was wearing an orange-coloured Mae West. I saw him slumped amidships of the other canoe, his green jungle hat pulled over his ears, looking the picture of misery. When the Neeses heard he couldn't swim they were concerned that he should at least borrow a life-jacket. My own belief is that drowning is probably the last thing to fear in rapids: if anything goes wrong you are much more likely to have your chest or skull stove in.

On rounding one of the many bends we saw the first rapid perhaps a quarter of a mile away. The water was broken for the whole width of the river.

Since we left the Neeses there had always been one Indian seated at the prow of each of the canoes. He was there to give signals to Dan and Paul as to what lay ahead. We inexperienced city dwellers simply sat amidships and waited to be told what to do. The Indian communicated his orders (they were nothing less – and mandatory ones too, if the canoe wasn't to be wrecked) by minimal flutters of his right or left hand. He would see a wrinkle on the river surface ahead, would dart his hands towards the bank, the tiller would be pulled smoothly just enough to turn the nose to the right, and a second later we would see the shadow of a submerged rock flash by on our left like some baulked shark. The four Indians from Shanamaña village were men of the Makiritare tribe whose name means 'water men'. Their skill and experience was matched only by their strength. One of them in particular was a man of tremendous physique. He would embrace the prow of a canoe being dragged through rocks and lift it bodily to right or left to free its passage. All of them wore western pants and shirts, but rather more presentable than the Waikas at Coshalowateri. They all had short cropped black hair – a sort of bristle cut. One of them wore an American cowboy hat, had an oriental buttery round face which easily broke into a smile and was called (I believe) Raphael by the missionaries.

As we approached the first rapid I saw the canoe in front curve into the bank on our right just below the broken water. I could see Danny Shaylor standing in the stern, resting his right foot on the gunnel and peering intently ahead as he aimed for a tiny beach. Wet branches and dripping leaves overhung the land, kept ever moist and clammy by the spray drifting down from the rapids. They brushed over the backs of the men seated in the boat.

Our canoe ran alongside Danny's, the motor having been cut, and stubbed to a halt.

The noise of the rushing water was deafening.

Nobody said anything, but it was obvious that Danny and Paul wanted everything and everybody out. We stood up stiffly in the curved wet canoe bottoms and grabbed our belongings and anything else that came to hand. We staggered along the wobbly platform, striding over the thwarts and on to the stony, sandy beach.

At close quarters that first rapid was frightening. It looked as though some forest giant, some *Cupirá* with his feet fixed on backwards, had flung a mountain of rocks across the roaring river in a vain attempt to dam it. White waves dashed and broke furiously against the largest boulders, spending some of their force in drifting spray. About twenty yards from our band there was a solid chute of water pouring between rocks with the smooth speed and energy of a runaway tube train. Along the bank itself the river curled and spluttered wetly over a moraine of large slippery pebbles and stones.

We city dwellers stood about uncertain what to do and raised our eyebrows at each other. Drops of moisture beaded Arthur Helliwell's crinkling grey side whiskers.

Danny and Paul and the four Indians began to pull and push Danny's empty canoe through the rocks and shallow water near the river's edge.

'Hefty' – the one with the big physique – had wrapped the mooring chain round his left arm from elbow to wrist and was hauling like a Japanese wrestler, occasionally using his right hand to gain purchase on a rock or an overhanging branch.

Seeing that progress was satisfactory, Paul and the Indian called Raphael (the one with the buttery smile and cowboy hat) waded back to our beach and we gathered that Paul was intending to *drive* his canoe up the water chute.

Jesco (our oracle on all jungle matters) listened wide-eyed with disbelief. Young Peter Smith, who had stripped off to a pair of swimming briefs, stared owlishly through his horn-rimmed glasses and asked Paul if he could shoot the rapids upwards too?

Before we fully understood what was happening, Paul and the Indian Raphael, assisted by Peter, had pushed the canoe off into the river and Paul had started the 40-h.p. motor. The Indian squatted at the prow, and Peter sat on a thwart in the middle grasping the sides with stiff-braced arms.

Jesco was almost beside himself with anxiety, but I presumed that Paul Dye knew what he was doing. The canoe swung into a wide arc and was brought back into a straight run aimed dead at the centre of the water chute. Because the dugout was empty and the motor was so powerful, the curved stem rode high out of the water like the prow of a Viking ship, with Raphael, a figurehead, perched five feet above the boiling river. The bow wave was easily a quarter of the way back from the front, spouting to left and right like a pair of wings almost under Peter Smith's feet.

Ashore, Henry had set his camera up on the tripod with one leg in the water and was filming the adventure from the bank.

I watched fascinated and rather envious as the bow of Paul's canoe contacted the base of the water chute and bounced even higher in the air. For a split second its speed was checked, then it rose like a horse at a fence and literally soared up the smooth strong race of water. In ten seconds it was all over and Raphael was guiding Paul between eddies into the bank beyond the rapid.

Of course, the engine *might* have died; the propeller *might* have clogged, cut the shear pin and stopped; the canoe *might* have hit a submerged rock and turned over: in any of these cases the occupants would have been lucky to escape alive. Still, none of these things had happened, and we others were faced with a grunting, heaving, hauling of heavy camera cases, tripod, cans of film as well as our personal gear and bedding through the jungle to a point above the rapids. I came to hate that tripod: it weighed a ton, it was long and unbalanced, it was hard and angular and had digging and scratching metal excrescences so that it caught in your clothes; in the prickles; in the ground. More than once I was tempted to fling the bloody thing in the river. I resolved next time to ride up the rapids myself.

We reloaded the dugouts and began to take our places. I was still travelling with Paul, and Henry and Peter Smith were also in the same canoe. Bob, Douglas and Arthur were with Danny. As Arthur stepped in I saw him begin to lean back towards the bank while his weight pushed the dugout away. It was like something in slow motion. A look of mild surprise gradually opened his eyes wider and his body assumed an angle of forty-five degrees on its way to the river. But before he could complete his arc a convenient outstretched bough parried his fall, and one of the Indians grabbed him and set him securely on a thwart. His sixy years sat on him lightly and he grinned like a schoolboy.

We set off up the twisting river under grey skies. The atmosphere was dull and heavy. We had no idea where we were going to lay our heads that night.

We came to the second rapid.

The water was a little less wild and turbulent than the first. I elected to join Paul in his attempt to drive up, and asked Henry if he would like to come too and film. He agreed. Danny was also going to drive his empty boat up, and Arthur Helliwell asked to go with him. Jesco, Douglas, Peter and Bob Saunders had to stagger through the jungle edge loaded like henpecked husbands.

It was an exhilarating ride. I knelt behind Henry, encircling his waist with my arms to give him some support as he filmed, and to stop him falling into the water. The bottom of the dugout bumped and baffed over the charging waves, the water occasionally splattered us and the wind whistled past our ears. Above the rapids, Paul throttled back to wait for the other canoe, giving the engine just enough gas to hold us against the flow of the current.

The head-on sight of Danny's canoe coming like a galloping horse with leaps and bounds was an unusual one. 'Hefty' was squatting at the front, and Arthur Helliwell sat amidships with straight arms locked to the sides. When they came alongside Arthur was grinning happily in spite of being drenched to the skin. Even his bush hat was wet – its pink band with blue spots now faded and stained with water and sweat.

I noticed that when the tension was off and Arthur could let go the canoe sides he raised a hand to his mouth and coughed every now and then.

Once more we reloaded and set off again, Danny leading. We wound in and out along that river as if we were travelling up a snake's back. After half an hour our engine coughed and stopped. The forward canoe was just disappearing round a bend ahead of us, and in two minutes we were alone. Raphael was sitting up front on a paddle placed across the boat. He pulled it out from under him and dipped it in the water to keep our nose upstream.

We began to drift backwards with the current towards the jungle on our left.

Nobody said anything, and Paul simply swung the propeller out of the water and began to poke into the cooling system. It had clogged up with leaves and twigs, and the overheated engine had cut out.

For a time there was no noise but the water lapping against the sides of the canoe. Then, a sort of maniacal laughter rattled up from the depths of the gloomy trees – some sort of bird, I presumed. I heard one of us singing softly to himself to keep his spirits up. The tune was from 'The Bohemian Girl' by Balfe, 'I dreamt that I dwe-elt in mar-arble halls . . .' only the words had been changed to 'I dreamt I was tickling my grand-father's balls, with a little sweet oil and a fe-eather'.

After twenty minutes the last of the light began to drain out of the sky and the river took on an inky shade.

Paul pulled on the starter cord of the outboard engine, which sud-denly shattered the silence by roaring into life. In a second we were under way again and a bow wave a yard either side was sprouting from the breasting boat.

We rounded two more bends and came upon a small jungly island perhaps four or five acres in extent. Paul took the left-hand channel and drove the canoe to the upstream end. It was now nearly dark. A huge tree, some three feet in diameter, had been laid end long from the top of the bank down into the water and roughly notched with steps. It was so huge it could only have been felled into that position. As our canoe came alongside I stood up with my haversack over my shoulder, my camera round my neck, my plastic brief-case under my arm and my right arm free. I stepped from the dugout on to the first notch. I put my weight on the notch to take a second stride and my wet rubber sole skidded off the tree and I shot standing upright into the black water. I went down like a knife and suddenly discovered two things: the river was running very fast and there was no bottom. I remember being con-cerned about my camera. I pushed it up above my head with my free hand and was saying 'My camera!' when the water came into my mouth. The situation was potentially a dangerous one, for it would have been difficult to keep afloat in that strong-running river entangled in my haversack and with my boots on. Nor would it have been easy in the dark for anyone to have seen where I was. Fortunately for me, as I sank between the canoe and the bank, the back of my right hand hit the side of the dugout and I let go of the camera (which fell into the boat) and hooked on to the gunnel. In a second I had my right elbow inside the canoe, and in two seconds Henry, Peter Smith and Raphael were hauling me out of the river. They set me once more on the notched log and, spouting water like a colander, I scrambled on to the bank and followed a path to where I could see the flames of a camp fire.

There were, in fact, two fires going, enriching the spear-shaped leaves and tree boles with gorgeous gold. Jesco and the people in the first boat had landed to find that the notched log led to a deserted Waika village and had, because of an unusual circumstance, been enabled to start camp fires.

A camp fire, 'man's red flower', in the Amazon jungle is extremely difficult, frequently impossible, to light. You are surrounded with trees, with timber of every kind, size and thickness, and all of it bursting with chlorophyll and soggy with sap and therefore useless for firing. But inside one of the huts they had found the smouldering logs of an Indian cooking hearth. Not stopping to ponder on the strangeness of so recently deserted a village, they had taken the logs outside and blown them into life.

Jesco had a huge aluminium pot on each fire, one bubbling with a canned meat hash and the other with a thin simmering porridge. Jesco himself was upset at our late arrival at the camp site and because we were going to have to get our hammocks slung in virtual darkness – we did have our torches, of course, and quite a lot of garish glow from the fires. He kept repeating, 'Come along, gentlemen! Come along, gentlemen!' like some elderly governess, meanwhile furiously stirring the stew and the porridge, which he called 'sweet soup' – sometimes standing between the two fires and stirring both at once.

'Calm down, Jesco,' I said. 'Look at me. Just fell in the bloody river.' And I stood on the outside of one of the fires and stripped everything off to the buff.

As it happened, only two things were ruined by my wetting: my battery shaver and my light-meter. In my haversack I had a complete set of clothing, including socks, each item wrapped separately in a cellophane bag (my wife's idea), and consequently not one of the articles was wet. I changed quickly and was soon eating a mugful of steaming hash.

Then I went into the nearest hut to sling my hammock. I didn't much like the entrance, which was tiny and rough, with a dry thatching of palm fronds which rustled along your back as you crawled in. I shoved my torch in front of me, and the floor seemed to be alive. It was hopping – jumping. The place was thick with fleas! A single dingy hurricane lamp, hung somewhere in the depths, emphasised the Stygian gloom of the cavernous maloca. I tied my hammock ropes to a couple of wooden pillars. Having been delayed by my ducking, I found that most of the others were already established and getting ready to retire. There was a commotion beyond Henry Farrar's mosquito-netted hammock. A spider on the palm-thatched wall was arousing a deep atavistic fear. Its body was as big as a snooker ball and pale grey in colour. The horror called up by the spider was released in a series of half-humorous injunctions: 'Wring its neck!' 'Get Jesco! Tell him to shoot it – but for God's sake not just to wound it!' 'You've broken its leg, you fool!' This last from Bob Saunders to Peter Smith, who was bashing out at it wildly with a pole. It was quick, that spider, darting this way and that, and took a lot of killing. Even when it was dead, you couldn't help thinking of its wife or husband or brothers and sisters lurking somewhere over your head.

I had to go outside again for a pee and found Douglas Botting standing by the embers of the fires with a bottle of Haig whisky in one hand and a mug of coffee in the other. He invited me to join him, and we gazed into the heavens powdered with brilliants, among which the Southern Cross appeared to soar like a kite on a string of stars.

That night was not one of the most restful I have ever spent. As for Paul and Danny, they told me next day that one or other of them had got up every two hours and gone down to the notched log where the boats were moored. At a mooring like that, with no beach and the river rising and falling unpredictably, it was only too easy to lose a boat or even both of them. During one of these visits they surprised a couple of Waika Indians who had paddled across the river from the right bank. The Waikas were curious to know why anyone should want to use the island village – they themselves had made a mass exodus from it a couple of days before because it had become so infested with fleas they couldn't stand it.

I don't think we could have endured the torment of those fleas for another night. We tossed and turned with a noise like splintering wood – we of the BBC team, that is. We were trying out special tin-foil blankets, a by-product of the Space Age. They pack into a cube about the size of a Swan Vestas match box. The side next to the body has a shiny mirror – like silver finish to keep the body heat in; the outside is red to absorb heat. All I remember of them is that they were scratchy and deafened you with their brattle.

Before we left next morning Jesco stuck a long branch into the soft mud by the notched tree and tied a plastic bag full of goodies to the top of it as a sort of rent for our stay.

When the two canoes were loaded and we were all seated, Danny Shaylor stood by his tiller, took off his hat and called us all to prayer. I was in Paul's boat, as usual, and a bit too far away to hear all that Danny said (some of it was in Waika for the benefit of the Indian boatmen, anyway), but I did get the gist of it, which was a plea for assistance in the dangers ahead as well as one sentence which went 'and Lord, keep the motors runnin''.

I was feeling a bit under the weather that morning. It was partly the muggy atmosphere beneath a lid of low cloud; partly that I was suffering from 'sticky eye', an infection probably started by some obnoxious fly; and partly that I had been unable to shave. Also, I was brought down by flea and other bites.

I admired our two laconic missionaries, who hardly spoke to anyone apart from the Indians and the Lord: every action they took was deft and necessary, every order they issued was requisite, succinct and obeyed at once. But about their religious campaign I couldn't help having doubts. That morose morning I was uncharitable enough to think that their life in the jungle was *only* a way of life, that they were escaping the Sodom and Gomorrah of the States, transferring their wives and families to a fenced-off existence where outside influence was minimal and slow in coming. The conversion of Indians then became either merely incidental or a meaningless rite.

The jungle jaundiced me. As we drove along between the monotonous green walls I thought of Spencer Chapman's book *The Jungle Is Neutral*, written after years in Japanese-occupied Malaya. His thesis is contained in the title, and how wrong it seemed to me. The South American jungle certainly isn't neutral. It is hostile – from its diseases, noxious animals and plants to its wild men. And if you stay long enough sooner or later it will get you.

Round a bend in the river we sailed under a spiral of large birds wheeling slowly, using one wing-tip after the other to act as a pivot as they levered themselves skywards up the warm air funnel of a thermal. Vultures, said Jesco. They looked to me like frigate birds – white with forked tails. As the clouds lifted and the sun got through, we saw a good deal more bird life than formerly: parrots and macaws, with their tail feathers waving behind like coloured paper streamers; toucans flew across the river ahead of us with their strange stooping attitude, as though their huge beaks were weighing them down in front and tilting up their behinds.

At the third rapid both boats were unloaded. The passage was too rough and rock-strewn for Danny's boat to ride up, but Paul drove through, though without passengers. The rest of us took on the panting, straining, sweating, exasperating fight against slippery rocks, skiddy clay banks and the spiny tanglewood which matted the slopes right down to the water's edge. It was aching arms and straining lungs all the way. You got to the point where you didn't care if your feet and legs went into the river or if your clothes were torn by the jungle thorns. All you wanted to do was lug that camera box or that tripod or bedroll or whatever to the spot where you could shed it into the boat and try to get your breath back.

We grunted and grinned sadly at each other.

It was like heaven to get back into the canoes and start off once more. Poor Arthur had a look of death on his pinched face.

We had risen that morning at six o'clock and begun our journey by eight a.m. Shortly after two o'clock we passed the village known as Sixto on my sketch map. It was the one where Paul and his wife had spent some time, but it now appeared deserted. We stopped for only ten minutes to empty both canoes of all the gear except camera and film.

Perhaps a quarter of an hour later we rounded a bend and saw the waterfall.

From behind, I watched Danny standing in the stern of his canoe swing it right towards the shore and glide in front of the curtain of falling water.

The occupants of the canoe were silhouetted against the white fall and seemed to be sitting in a line on the surface of the river. It was just as if the waterfall was viewed on back-projection with that artificial larger-than-life effect this cinema trick produces. But that torrent of water was real enough. It was thunderous and spectacular, split into two separate downfalls by an island cliff of rock and bushy trees. The water bounced and boiled in white and buff-coloured gouts down a raging precipitous slope of perhaps sixty or eighty feet throwing off a vast spume which drifted downstream in a fine mist for hundreds of yards. You could feel it condensing in your hair and on your face as you stood on the bank alongside the two beached canoes.

I watched Danny undo the wing nuts fastening the outboard engine to his canoe. He was wearing a floppy tattered forage hat to which time had obviously attached him; he had a faded blue open-necked shirt and off-white shorts; his legs and feet were bare. He stood in the stern of the dugout canoe and with one swing lifted the heavy engine on to his left shoulder.

If it weighed anything, that 20-h.p. engine must have turned the scale at near a hundredweight and a half.

He settled the bulk of the tank more comfortably into his neck and, holding the propeller stem with his left arm, used his right to balance. He stepped easily along the rocking length of that curved boat bottom, taking each thwart with the nonchalance of a practised hurdler. It was a feat of tremendous strength, of skill, of control. Once ashore, he placed the propeller end carefully on a flat stone, and two of the Indians relieved him of the burden and began lugging it away up the jungly hill. Nobody spoke.

Raphael wrapped the mooring chain of Danny's dugout round his arm and began to haul it clear out of the water. Paul, with his one free hand (the other was still in a sling), and Danny, with both powerful hands, gripped thwarts and heaved. The rest of us suddenly saw the point and sprang into some semblance of life, awkwardly grabbing the canoe edges or seats and pulling as best we might.

There were three or four logs already placed as rollers across the sandy beach. The dugout ground with a dull heavy echo over them. In water, that cockle, unstable contraption, capable of being pushed sideways with no effort at all, out of it now became a log, a tree, a solid almost immovable object.

The two Indians who had disappeared with the engine came back from above almost as though descending stairs – and that was the way we had to haul the boat. The slope seemed like the side of the leaning Tower of Pisa. It had living roots brought up to the surface by constant wear to act as further rollers. Hefty grabbed the prow in a fierce embrace and lifted the front end on to the beginning of the hill. There was space enough amidships between the rounded bottom and the ground to crawl under. Raphael lugged at the mooring chain. Hefty got his shoulder to the bottom. We all pulled, pushed and heaved with wild yells. The canoe slowly stood up on its end. The water that had gathered in the bottom during the morning cascaded backwards and gurgled over the stern like an undammed stream.

A foot at a time we got that helpless hulk up the hill. And it *was* helpless: if you took too many hands off it together it rolled over on to one side or the other, ready to crush a leg or foot not shifted quick enough. We were dealing with the best part of a fully grown tree whose weight, though hollowed out, I estimated to be a ton and a half. With my cheek down on the gunnel I could see Arthur Helliwell in a similar position on the other side gasping and straining.

'You shouldn't be doing this, Arthur,' I said. He just looked.

Henry Farrar was filming the struggle. Douglas Botting was taking stills and also lending a hand. A big, strong boy, Douglas – over six foot. But he was limping.

'What's up, Douglas?' I said.

'Got a couple of chegoes in my foot,' He said. This is the human bot-fly which burrows under the skin and lays a clutch of eggs. But there was no time then to give the matter further consideration.

'*Heave!*' came the almost hysterical injunction from three or four throats, and we all struggled like men possessed. By this time our clothes were grey with mud, and green with chlorophyll crushed from the juicy jungle growth. Our arms and legs were trembling with fatigue, and our throats rasped with the rough air demanded by our pumping lungs. But at last we had the canoe teetering like a see-saw at the top of the slope.

And it did actually teeter, for the ground fell away in a deep, dry trench or moat between the hilltop and the river. Someone had bridged this gully by felling two trees at intervals over which a boat could ride: except that the trees were five feet apart, just too far for a hauler to stride. The only thing you could do was to wait until combined push-ings and pullings had given the dugout momentum and then take a flying leap from one log to the other holding on the boat side. It was a dangerous trick – and there was no safety net.

At this point I got Henry to climb into the boat to film from a new angle. He sat on a thwart in the centre, and we made a combined effort to pull down the prow on to the logs over the moat.

A further six inches the dugout pushed up into the air and then, over-reaching the point of balance, dropped, a dead weight, on to the log bridge and rocked dangerously on to one side. Henry, clutching his camera, was spilled into the bottom, barking his ribs and hips against thwarts and wood supports. I saw his face looking skywards, his eyes like poached-eggs. '*Christ!*' he said in an aggrieved tone, as though we had engineered it all to upset him. He scrambled up, crawled with his camera to the front of the canoe and got over the side on to a little knob of rock beyond the gully.

I watched him and, in doing so, 'panned' my eyes to the river. What I saw shocked and frightened me. It was the sort of disturbing startle-ment you get when standing on the platform of a quiet country railway station and a screeching, rocketing express suddenly explodes through.

The constricted river was roaring by within a few feet of the gully, to leap headlong over the fall.

I just couldn't see how we were going to get the canoe into that maelstrom without it being torn from our grasp and flung upended down the race.

Danny, Paul and the four Indians leapt over the moat, and Hefty hauled on the mooring chain. We set our hands to the sides and pushed the prow down into the river. Hefty strode forward a stride at a time against the current, trying to find suitable overhanging branches to keep his contact with the bank. Danny and Paul were out in the river up to their waists in surging water. I saw Bob Saunders between the boat and the bank reach for support from a hanging liana. It broke, and he disappeared with popping eyes down the gully. There was no time to inquire after his health, for the nose of the canoe had gone underwater, and in a second she filled from end to end as the water's weight forced her stern into the river. I myself jumped in and made to join Paul. The water was up to my armpits and tearing wildly at me, so that my fingers at the sunken gunnel had all they could do to hold on. I saw Paul's blue eyes flashing like a naked electric spark.

'Mr Brian! *Mr Brian!*' he yelled (he still had my Christian name and surname mixed up at this juncture) 'Go back! *Go back!*'

He was obviously right, for six or eight feet behind me the water was swirling over the edge of the fall. I crabbed my way round the stern of the water-logged canoe and joined Arthur Helliwell and Peter Smith on the side nearest the bank. It was bad enough here with the water pushing you like a mad football crowd and a very rough rock-strewn river bed in which to try to find a foothold.

It was Hefty who saved the day. Somehow, he managed to get the mooring chain round the bole of a bankside tree and knot it there. I watched incredulously as Paul took his boil-plagued arm out of the sling and tried to bale water with the old dried-milk can. It seemed an impossibility. Peter Smith began scooping with his bare hands. Then two of the Indians scrambled from the bank with wide-bladed paddles, clambered into the sunken swamped canoe and began swilling the water out with wide sweeps. I didn't notice it at the time, but when I saw our film of this incident afterwards you could plainly see small fish being flung out with each paddle-full of baled water. After that it was really only a matter of time – perhaps ten minutes, before the canoe was almost dry and floating again. We trooped down the slope back to the other canoe, piled in and Paul drove us downstream to Sixto village. As Douglas Botting said afterwards, it was becoming clear that the journey itself, whatever its object, was a thing in its own right with its own demands, and possibly its own rewards: its demands were to keep going, to endure heat, rain, trouble and toil, insects and danger; its rewards – who knows, something the Victorians used to call 'character-building'?

CHAPTER FIFTEEN

Journey to the Waika : Beyond the Waterfall

WE had returned to spend the night at 'Paul's village' or Sixto because the journey to the still wild Waikas and back would take a whole day. As we could use only one canoe, the one we had dragged up the water-fall portage, Danny would drive and, in addition to our party and him, would take two of the Makiritare Indians to help us over the rapids. The river beyond the waterfall was called Cuntinamo, the fall being situated at the confluence of the Cuntinamo with the Padamo. The village we were heading for was Nacoïshimateri or 'the village of Black Tooth' – Black Tooth or Nacoïshima being the name of the Chief.

When we got back to Paul's village we saw two naked Waikas stand-ing quietly by one of the huts almost as if they were some sort of jungle plant growing there. They held two or three arrows apiece – arrows much taller than themselves, for the men didn't even come up to my shoulders; and they had bows. They were wearing on their faces and bodies what I now presume to be war paint: it took the form of black, red and yellow stains in lines and circles radiating from the nose and running along the arms and legs. They wore their black hair in the pudding-basin or medieval cut.

We were too fagged out to take much notice of them, though I believe Arthur perked up enough to have Douglas take a press snapshot of himself standing between them like the Edwardian pier-end photographs our grandfathers had of themselves with exotic seaside back cloths and holes through which they could poke their heads.

What we didn't know at the time was that these young men were brothers pursuing a vendetta – a vendetta which closely concerned Chief Nacoïshima and the people we were to visit tomorrow. They faded into the forest and were forgotten.

That night we expeditionaries spread out between three of the huts, for they were all empty. Bob Saunders called me over to a hut which he had intended sharing with Peter Smith. Across one corner there was what appeared to be a black band about six inches broad. When I looked closely I saw it was moving – ants! Twenty or thirty abreast. They were coming out of the jungle and under the wall and across this corner of the hut floor. Then they were making their exit under the adjacent wall and disappearing into the jungle again. How long they had been marching no one knew; how long they would go on nobody could tell: but they were still on their inexorable parade when we left the village next morning.

But before we went to bed Douglas Botting submitted to an operation on his foot and Paul Dye to one on his hand. Paul's boil had become so painful that he asked Danny to ease its throbbing by lancing it, which was done. Removing sacs of chegoe eggs was perhaps a little more delicate. Unless you get them all out any left behind hatch under your skin, and the new chegoes begin the laying cycle again. Douglas described his condition as follows: 'It was an uncomfortable feeling because I felt that I had suddenly become part of this whole cycle of growth and decay that one saw in the jungle all around one, and that I was – sort of become a part of the jungle and was sort of growing and decaying and mouldering. And it was very upsetting – it was painful to have these things growing because they began to expand against the side of one's shoe so one had to wear these open flip-flops, which meant that one got bitten by more of these chego fleas and had more of these egg sacs laid in one's foot. . . .' But Raphael put Douglas out of his misery with a large sewing needle. He got Douglas' bare foot into his lap and broddled and pricked with the needle until he had removed intact three separate sacs of eggs like tiny bunches of off-white grapes. There were three holes resembling miniature volcanoes in Douglas's right foot, but most of the pain had gone, he told me.

Arthur Helliwell's condition was much more serious, though he succeeded in keeping it to himself. One of his lungs had collapsed and that night, in the hut which he shared with Raphael and Jesco, he gasped for breath and slept very little. Occasionally he was delirious. A long time afterwards he told me about it. 'Let's face it,' he said, 'I was probably a little too old to attempt the journey anyway, but I did think that, you know, I wouldn't come back with you all and I kept thinking of Pina [his wife] and thinking how I didn't want to be buried in that God-forsaken hole. We were surrounded by these very savage people [some Waikas had come across the river and talked to Paul and Danny before we went to bed] and one chap had told Paul how he had clubbed his wife to death and laughed while he was saying it. I lay in my hammock this night feeling very, very ill, and one of our Indian guides kept whistling, a sort of low whistle which I can't attempt to imitate, but he kept it up all through the night, and I asked Jesco the next morning about this and he said, "Oh yes, he knew you were sick, he knew you were very ill. That whistle meant don't be afraid, I am here." '

Next morning at eight o'clock Paul conveyed us all in his boat to the landing by the waterfall. We scrambled up the portage and took our places in Danny's dugout. The young freckle-faced missionary stood at the prow of the still moored boat, took off his tattered hat and called us all to prayer. I remember sneaking a look at Douglas during this invocation, and he had his eyes closed and his hands held together up to his face in the angelic attitude taught us as children. Danny said, 'We will now say a prayer for the protection of God upon our trip up the river.' He then prayed in the Waika language and added in American, 'Heavenly Father, this morning we come before you and ask your protection and help upon our trip up the river. Lord there are many dangers and Lord we believe you are able to help us and we pray that you will. We ask these things in Jesus' name. Amen.' He put on his hat and strode past us seated men down the length of the boat and started the outboard motor. He shouted to Raphael at the prow to cast off, and I heard Paul Dye from the green shade of the bank calling, 'See you—all when you get back!'

It was a morning of rapids, with tremendous struggles, heavings, pushings, luggings and falls. Peter Smith had two bad falls within minutes of each other at the same spot, and I suddenly realised that in a situation such as ours a comparatively mild accident, like breaking a leg, could prove fatal. Not so much from the break as from complications such as pneumonia which might set in during the difficult business of trying to get the victim back.

The rapid where Peter fell was a tedious and difficult one. First of all we had to disembark at the jungle edge and carry all our gear to a point where a massive black rock about twenty feet square sloped back from the troubled water into the undergrowth and trees. Above the rock a channel of water had formed a natural lock alongside the roaring rapid, and the idea was to haul our canoe up the rock and refloat it in the calm channel. Unfortunately there was an obstacle across the top of the rock – a twenty-five-foot dugout canoe which had floated away (we supposed) from some Indian village upstream and had become firmly wedged to form a dam between the top of the great boulder and a rocky island. There was a mighty weight of water behind this canoe, and we hadn't a hope of lifting our own over it with the men available. Somehow we had to dislodge it before we could do anything else.

While we were surveying the situation young Peter Smith slipped on the big wet rock. He put his right hand out to break his fall and sat down heavily on his turned-back fingers. He got up and staggered away into the dripping leaves, cursing. He had hardly returned when he slipped a second time, his feet chuted away from him and he jounced the point of one elbow hard on the rock. Again he crawled into the jungle, and I went after him. He was girning with pain, but waved me away. I turned to see that Danny and the two Indians had sneaked our own dugout through the less boisterous water at the river's edge and brought it to the bottom of the big rock. We helped them to secure it in the wet-washed boulders, then we all scrambled up to the 'dam' and tried to budge the wedged canoe.

We toiled and moiled for half an hour, sodden with sweat and swamped with river. We just couldn't move that jammed dugout.

We obviously needed Hefty, but he had stayed behind with Paul.

At last we all concentrated on the end of the canoe nearest the bank and tried to push it away from the rock upstream. Danny changed his position. He stepped into the dammed-up channel to his waist and hugged the boat's end, at the same time levering himself back with his legs. We had already seen one example of Danny Shaylor's strength when he carried the engine off his canoe at the portage. Now we saw another. Slowly the derelict dugout swung through ninety degrees until it pivoted on the top of the sloping rock, which also began to act as a fulcrum. Once we had it moving, we redoubled our efforts, encouraging each other with gasps and shouts. We began rocking it like a see-saw. Then with a last heave and a push we shot the boat down into the rapid. It leapt like a breeching whale, its prow shooting high, and spouting water shot forward from its belly. Then it tumbled into the boiling maelstrom, tossing round and round, sometimes under, sometimes over until it was eventually spewed forth into flatter water and went drifting out of sight downstream. It was a sobering example of what could happen if ever we lost control of our own craft in a rapid.

It took us another ten minutes to lift and drag our dugout up between the big rock and the island outcrop. Having got it into the channel, loaded it and seated ourselves, we were off again once more.

There were three or four more rapids – none quite as daunting as the one I have just described, but all demanding every bit of physical and moral strength we could call up. After that first rapid of the day I stopped taking notes during the travelling stretches between. Like the others, I just had to sit slumped and rest, nurturing enough effort for the next bout of gut-straining toil. Douglas was right: the journey was becoming an end in itself. We began to get careless – stopped using our water-filters, for instance, just dipping our mugs into the river as it flowed by the canoe side. There's an art in this too, and without it you drench not only yourself but the man behind you. The secret of collecting half a mugful of river water when your motor is driving you on at ten or eleven knots is to swing your receptacle round in a circle so that the bottom arc just sinks below the surface of the flying water and the mug fills when (because of the backward movement you have imparted to it) relative to the flowing river it is almost stationary.

It is impossible in a narrow canoe to hold a satisfactory conversation. We just sat one behind the other in the cell of our own personality and occasionally exchanged messages through the window of the face. Only Danny at the tiller and the Indian watching the water up front maintained close contact, and they did it with no noise, simply signs.

Suddenly Raphael at the prow made a gesture quite different from his usual signs. He shot his right arm stiffly out, pointing ahead and at the same time looking inquiringly back over his shoulder at Danny Shaylor.

He had seen something which wasn't the usual eddy or obstacle or floating log in the river.

I was sitting up at the front, but could see little directly ahead because of Raphael's body. Danny stood crouching at the stern, scanning forward carefully. For the moment he did not alter either speed or direction.

The river was now considerably narrower, perhaps 150 yards broad, and both banks were high and steep. It was midday and the sun was shining directly down into our miniature ravine. As ever, both slopes were solid with forest.

Danny throttled back and eased the tiller so that we began to move into the bank on our left.

Then, it seemed to me, for the first time I saw the Men of the West. They were perched in a row like monkeys along the length of a huge forest tree which lightning had laid horizontal from the river bank to well beyond midstream. There were ten of them and, in fact, only two were men, the others were three women with babies riding astride their hips and two young girls. They were tiny, they were naked apart from negligible bead aprons in the case of the women and G-strings for the men. Their faces had the frozen startlement of surprised monkeys and, at first, they did not move. Their bodies were a rich red-brown, their hair was black and cut in the usual pudding-basin style. They remained motionless for some time, and might well have been a vegetable growth parasitic to the tree.

We ran the dugout on to the small beach at the foot of a path winding up through the woods.

Then one of the women holding a baby found us figures of fun. She shot out her free arm involuntarily, pointing at us and uninhibitedly laughed loudly at our strangeness – a sort of jungle creature's cackle. The others became animated and chattered to each other, calling attention to our oddities.

We ignored them. We had a film to make, so we shuffled into single file to struggle up the steep trail leading to the village while Henry took hand-held shots from in front, the side and behind.

The Waikas hopped from their tree and accompanied us at a respectable distance.

Long afterwards Arthur Helliwell told me how he really felt as he gasped his way up that jungle path: 'As we walked up that long steep ascent I was apprehensive. There we were at the end of the line. I don't think too many white people had been there in the last hundred years, say. They just seemed to be watching us and they were only women and children mostly. And, you know, I was wondering what would happen when the warriors came back, because you know, these people have absolutely no regard for human life at all. They kill one another and forget it the next day. . . . I don't think any of us realised that we were dealing with such really primitive and, let's face it, savage people. The name Waika, of course, the literal translation of it means the "butchers", and these little people are named "butchers" because they are the most savage killers in Amazonas. And there we were among them. I think we must have all been out of our skulls.'

When we reached the top of the hill we saw a clearing which had been slashed and burnt out of the forest, with charred trees bereft of branches still standing at intervals. There were four huts, fairly new and in good order, and two of them were large enough to accommodate a number of families and their cooking hearths.

I asked Danny if the people would remember him? 'Sure,' he said laconically, 'they remember me.'

'Did you convert them?'

'Nope. I told them the gospel an' then left 'em mullin' it over in their minds.'

He said it was a small community, perhaps thirty or forty people altogether, and when I asked him why the village appeared to be deserted he said every able-bodied person would be away on the food quest, either hunting, gathering or working in their 'gardens' or plantations.

A very old lady staggered out of the forest with a huge pannier of firewood slung on her back from a wide band round her forehead. Apart from small children, she was the only woman completely naked. Her shape was fine and her shoulders square and broader than her slim hips. She had the wrinkled stretch marks across her thighs and lower abdomen caused by child bearing. But her deflated breasts had been sucked dry years ago. A tuft of black pubic hair feathered the cleft of her loose vulva. Fashion no longer forced her to depilate her withered cunny. Her legs and arms were fineboned. Her hair was round-cut and black and her lined face had a very Chinese look. She was the chief's mother and lived with him and his two wives and brother in the largest maloca. She was, perhaps, forty-five.

She dropped her pannier of kindling and disappeared into the hut.

We stopped on the hard-stamped ground in front of the large huts and produced our gifts. Everybody left in the village, except one, gathered round us and we dispensed fish hooks, nylon line, boiled sweets and plastic mouth organs.

Danny, more beneficially, had brought medicines – mainly dark, thick treacly stuff for the children to purge them of worms and other internal parasites. It was pathetic to watch the eagerness with which the young mothers (fourteen or fifteen years old) pushed their toddlers forward to receive the horrid jalap.

Arthur Helliwell had a *succès fou* with a miniature dictaphone, recording the women's chatter and then playing back their voices. None recognised their own voices, but found the voices of the others a source of giggling delight. They laughed and shouted like children at a party.

As we stood before the huts I asked Danny whether we had any chance of getting information on yopo.

'I very much doubt it,' he said.

'Couldn't somebody be persuaded to show us the tree or plant from which they make the stuff?'

'There's nobody here – except the chief, and he's not likely to do anything about it.'

'Why not?' I asked.

'Come and see,' said Danny and led the way into the largest hut.

Just inside the door a hammock had been slung – much smaller than ours – and swinging languidly in it was a naked Indian of maybe thirty. It was chief Nacoïshima.

'He says he's bewitched,' said Danny.

To the forest Indians there is no such thing as illness: any physical or mental ailment is the result of witchcraft. Nor do they accept the phenomenon of death by natural causes. Every death is an unnatural one caused either by physical violence or witchcraft.

'Who bewitched him?' I asked.

'It's a long story,' said Danny, 'and likely to lead to a bad blood feud.'

'Why is that?'

'It's this way,' Danny explained, 'Nicoïshima's father, an old man, died of what to us would be natural causes. To these Indians it was witchcraft, and they believed a man from a neighbouring village was responsible. They lay in wait for him and beheaded him with a machete in the forest. He was the brother of the two men we saw below the waterfall. They are scouting around for a chance to take their revenge on somebody in this village. In the meantime Black Tooth has fallen sick and believes himself to be under an evil spell cast by the witch doctor of the murdered man's village.'

'How long has he been like this?'

'He's lain in his hammock for three weeks. He just told me one of his witch doctors had treated him and had vomited something up which he reckoned was causing the bad spell, so he feels a bit better.'

'The witch doctor vomited it up?'

'Yes.'

'What was it?'

'He doesn't know.'

A wild and probably irresponsible notion came into my head. I looked at the apathetic chief in his hammock. A couple of feet away was his cooking hearth with two or three logs, their smouldering ends pushed together like spokes of a broken wheel. One of his wives was squatting by, cradling in her thin arms a poor, scabby, undernourished infant. She was the same young woman who had been standing on the fallen tree across the river and who had pointed at us so dramatically. Now she watched us two big white intruders standing by her husband's hammock and obviously discussing him as though neither she nor he were present. Her eyes were large and round, and she looked like an under-privileged monkey. I felt I wanted to do something which would at least give her hope.

'Danny,' I said, 'tell them I'm going to use white man's magic on Black Tooth.'

Danny looked a shade disapproving, but he spoke to them in Waika.

In my trouser pocket I had a tin of Boots' eau-de-Cologne pads, one of half a dozen my wife had insisted on my bringing to the hot sweaty jungle. I took out this flat tin with its printed flower pattern and pushed it into the chief's face. Such an artefact, quite unlike anything he had seen before, I judged would be an object of wonder to him. I took the lid off and offered the moist scented pads to his nose. I peeled off one of the damp lint circles and, pulling him over on to his belly, proceeded to rub the pad down his back from shoulder to buttocks. My movements were slightly exaggerated and theatrical. After about four rubs the white pad was almost black on the rubbing side, for he had obviously not had a wash for three weeks either. I showed it to him. His eyes glowed under the dark mat of hair. Then I rubbed him with the other side of the pad until that was black as well. I screwed it into a ball and deliberately thrust it into the golden ash in the centre of his fire. With a little splutter of steam it began to burn.

With all the showmanship I could muster, I stripped off another eau-de-Cologne pad and repeated the procedure. This time, when I thrust the dirty pellet into the fire I made a sudden flirt with my open fingers, as though I were casting out an evil spirit.

'Tell him,' I said to Danny, 'he will be cured within three days.'

Danny spoke to Black Tooth, but whether he passed on my opinion I do not know, nor did I have the courage to ask him; for what I had just done must have seemed as much like witchcraft to Danny Shaylor as when the chief's own practitioner had vomited or pretended to vomit the cause of Nacoïshima's being under a spell. To me, my action was a crude attempt at applied psychology, and my excuse for doing it is that somehow I felt a need to identify myself with these downtrodden creatures of the wild. Whether it was a sensible thing to do is another matter.

I gave Black Tooth a pocket-knife I had bought in Manaus, and he took it without a sign of hesitation or gratitude and shoved it into the hammock under his backside.

Danny left the hut and I followed him.

It had begun to rain, a dismal downpour which was to continue for a couple of hours.

The others had assembled in the adjoining large hut and were sitting on bamboo-slatted benches eating their lunch. Jesco called me to take tinned cheese, sardines and biscuit. The only two other men apart from Nacoïshima left behind in the village (they were sixteen or seventeen years old) sat around and watched; so did two very shapely young girls.

In my haversack pocket I had a pair of string-backed driving gloves my wife had bought me in Reading shortly before we all left for South America. I took one out and fitted it on to my hand, much to the puzzlement and then amusement of the two young men and two girls. One of the men caught hold of the glove and struggled to put it on. They all laughed loudly. The glove passed literally from hand to hand and soon disappeared. Bob Saunders' green forage cap was also tried on – and disappeared. 'I want my hat back,' he grumbled to me; 'And I want my glove back,' I said, no less determined.

The two maidens went out, and Bob Saunders and Pete Smith followed them with their still cameras, their eyes sparkling. Although it was pouring with rain, there was shelter outside beneath a verandah running the length of the hut, and if they didn't want to get wet the girls had only one other door into which they could retreat. They popped in and out of this door playing hide and seek from the cameras and giggling excitedly. Their red-brown bodies were things of beauty, their skin smooth and glowing, their limbs shapely and their firm breasts and thighs sculptural in their cool innocence.

Jesco went along the verandah to see the chief. Later he told me he had given Black Tooth a knife. 'Well, so did I!' I said. Arthur Helliwell, who was near by, said, 'I gave him a knife too!'

'Yes,' said Jesco, 'but the custom is to *exchange* presents. I didn't want anything for me, but I told him my father was a great chief – Danny told him for me – and I asked for something from him to my father. He gave me this –' and Jesco thrust forward a bit of wood, a bit of bone and a feather.

'What is it?' I asked.

'It's a rubbish,' said Jesco, screwing up his eyes. He was evidently disappointed and upset.

Bob and Peter came back into the hut; Danny came too. We sat around rather disconsolately. It stopped raining. It was all pretty dis-appointing and something of an anti-climax.

'I should like my glove back, before we go,' I said to Danny.

We began to collect our gear together.

'Stopped raining,' said Douglas, who had exhausted the possibilities as far as still pictures were concerned.

'Come on, then, let's go,' I said. Everybody moved out into the open space between the huts. It was about three o'clock and the sun was shining again.

'I haven't got my glove, yet, Danny,' I said.

'And I haven't got my hat,' said Bob Saunders.

'I sent Black Tooth his old feather an' bone back,' said Jesco.

'You did *what?*' I asked.

'I sent it back,' said Jesco with a grin.

'Come on!' I said urgently. 'Let's really get going.' The stupidity of our behaviour at last hit me. Here we were doing all the things which in the past had got other white intruders, from Fawcett to Calleri, knocked on the head. We knew what had happened to them, and yet our own behavioural patterns were so ingrained that we couldn't change them to save our lives. During that walk down the steep jungle path to the dugout canoe I felt apprehensive for the first time. When, as we neared the water's edge, Danny silently handed me my missing glove and Bob Saunders his hat, I felt my anxiety deepen.

An Indian came running down the track behind us. It was one of the two men left behind in the village. He held something in his hand. It was Jesco's bit of wood, feather and bone.

Jesco waved it away and turned angrily into the boat.

The man moved back up the hill and then shouted with crackling words.

The rest of us quickly scrambled into our places, and Raphael pushed the canoe stern first into the river. Danny pulled the starter cord and the engine roared. Raphael waded in, shoving the prow up-stream and then jumped aboard. Danny swung us round in a wide arc away from the fallen tree, and we headed with the current downstream.

Our brush with the primitive men had brought out some pretty primitive behaviour in us civilised animals; and we were now being driven on by another primeval motivator – fear. The Cuntinamo River flowed at round about four knots and that added to the push from the propeller meant we were travelling at something like fifteen miles per hour. With the jungle whizzing by on either bank, our apparent speed was more like fifty.

As we fled down to the first rapid I wondered how we should endure
the delay of stopping, off-loading and humping our gear through the
prickles and thorns. But, thankfully, Danny headed into the midst of
the white horses, and in a twink their tossing manes were all around us
and we were bucking down the cataract. There was less risk shooting
down than up, because even if the engine stopped, there was enough
way on to carry us through. At least, in theory. Half a dozen splashes
later we were into the smooth-running water again.

We took the next rapid in much the same way. The last one before
we reached the waterfall was that where the wide slanting rock formed
a dam. Danny throttled back and sent us at an easy glide into the brimming channel between the rocky cliff island and the bank until our
prow bumped the top of the sloping rock. It was like being in a canal
lock with the rock forming a natural gate. On the other side of the rock
cliff, and below us, the river roared and swept and tore over jagged
boulders. We off-loaded everything, including the motor, and carried
our gear piece by piece to a fairly quiet bay below the rapid. Then we
all came back to get the boat.

We lifted and heaved the front of the dugout until ten feet of it
protruded in the air over the rock dam. Then some of us scrambled
below (I was one, Jesco another) to find a foothold on the sloping rock
and then to swing on the canoe like boys on a branch to bring it see-
sawing over the dam.

As he moved into position from the top of the rock, Jesco, that experienced backwoodsman, slipped. His feet shot from under him, and
he landed squarely full length on his back. Without a pause, his huge
bulk skidded with the speed of a cake of soap down the sloping end of a
bath. Like a cat he twisted sideways as he tobogganed feet first towards
the boiling maelstrom.

I caught a glimpse of his startled eyes wide open as he passed my feet,
and his turned-up sombrero with BBC on it.

I thought, he's had it.

I couldn't believe that that terrific jounce had failed to break some
bone or other. And what would he be able to do for himself in the rapids
with a broken arm or leg?

By twisting sideways, he had managed to fetch up with a terrific
jolt against a flat rock protruding like a shark's fin from the edge of
the water. His feet went into the curdled foam at the river's edge.

Before he got to the bottom I was following him down with tiny,
quick, mincing steps to keep from sliding; and even as I reached him,
I was amazed to see him scramble to his feet.

I put my arms round him.

'Jesco! Jesco!' I cried, 'Are you all right?'

He pushed me off.

'Yes. I am O.K.'

'Nothing broken?'

'No. Perhaps bruised,' and he began to clamber gingerly like a bulky bear up to the overhanging dugout. There was no time for further solicitude, and we all set to work again, levering the boat as carefully as we could up to the delicate point of balance. When this was reached, those behind braced hard to prevent it darting headlong into the rapid, and we in front snatched at the thwarts to try and hold them as it ground past us. Its nose went into the bubbling water like a submarine doing a crashdive, and in a second it was full to within two inches of the gunnel. We were likely to have lost it but for the quick, deft efforts of Danny Shaylor and the two Indians up to their waists in foam, who, between them, shoved it up and rocked it, spilling out enough of the swamping river to make ordinary baling worth while.

After that there was nothing worth reporting until we reached the waterfall, where Paul, Hefty and the other Indian awaited us. We then went through the reverse of the process by which we had originally portaged the canoe above the falls. By the time we had manhandled it, rumbling like a dead-weight tram down the hill and into the water again, we were all in. Nobody spoke very much, and once arrived at Paul's village, we stripped off our shirts and sank exhausted into our hammocks. It was about five o'clock in the afternoon.

When I was able to think coherently I tried to sort out what we had achieved. Nothing about yopo, precious little worthwhile film of the Indians and not much film of the rapids either. We had found a clan of Waikas who, according to Jesco and compared with other Indians he had worked with, had 'given up', who seemed to have lost their reason for living. Now one of the worst crimes the missionaries commit (according to their detractors) is to cut the Indians loose from their cultural foundation, from the body of belief in the numinous which they have built up in millennia of jungle life and to wean them away from rites vital to their beliefs, such as endo-cannibalism or eating the powdered bones of one's ancestors in a sort of banana soup. But after encountering Nacoïshima and his wretched group of families it seemed to me that these Waika Indians were, in fact, quite capable of losing their own way.

I tried to look at their situation rationally: a belief in witchcraft which put the chief out of action and threw his clan into a crippling despondency; a belief in supernatural powers who could work death and destruction; an acceptance of illness as a reason for starting a decimating feud; all these seemed strong indications that the Waikas were no longer 'noble savages', even if they ever had been, but rather (still being rational and looking from a zoological point of view) a kind of men who had long got side-tracked from the main development of the species. They call themselves 'men' or 'people', *yanamamo*, and refer to their neighbours as monkeys; but to outsiders who seek their domains they never fully measure up to the description of men; to the missionaries an Indian whose soul has not been 'saved' is no better than a monkey; to a gold or diamond prospector an Indian is a dangerous jungle animal, and you'd better kill him before he kills you; to politicians an Indian is a pain in the neck, a nuisance. And what do you do with a nuisance? Get rid of it somehow, anyhow. What does it matter so long as you get rid of it?

When I had recuperated somewhat, and creaked stiffly out of my hammock, I talked to Paul with my elbows on a packing-case table and a hurricane lamp between us. The others (except Arthur and Jesco, who had gone to bed in another hut) were seated round us in the shadows. Paul gave me the impression that the Waikas were a tough assignment and that anyone who hoped to change their ways was in for a tremendous physical struggle as well as some good old soul wrestling, with exhortation and threats of doom and damnation in Hebrew-prophet style: Jeremiah would have found a niche here. You couldn't help liking the handsome Paul's quiet, serious way and his laconic Western country-style accent. He told me not to worry about our failure with yopo, but that next day he reckoned he'd be able to find some for us. He told us of the ways of the Waikas and of their spirit guides, whom they call 'hekurá'.

The making and use of yopo is directly concerned with the calling up of the hekurá. My impressions were as follows: the Waikas make yopo from at least three different plants, and the usable product takes the form of a fine dust or snuff. Because the active drug element in the powder is diluted, a Waika who wants to go for a 'trip' needs a helper to get sufficient quantities of yopo into his nasal and respiratory passages. A hollow bamboo cane about a metre long is applied to one nostril, and the helper blows clouds of this hallucination-producing powder into the tripper's nose. 'Oh, boy,' said Paul, 'you jus' ought to see 'em then! Their eyes pop an' begin to water. You think their blood vessels would break the way they heave an' throw up. Their noses run an' they slaver an' it comes out all black. Then they begin to shout. An' then they moan an' groan. Sometimes they make the calls of different forest animals like pig an' jaguar or any sort of animal noise according to what hekurá are coming. They jump up an' walk about, paddin' back and forward for hours – sometimes as much as fourteen hours. An' when they're comin' out of it, boy, are they fixed! They sure have the father an' mother of a hangover – an' do they feel sorry for themselves!'

I asked if the hekurá take human form. Sometimes they do, sometimes they are like animals, sometimes they may (unlike the Old Testament Spirit) be immanent in a great wind. There are benevolent and malevolent hekurá, the malevolent ones being those called up by your enemies to injure you. You can blow yopo against them to drive them away. Hekurá live in the mountains, and though they cannot abide earthly women, they do have surpassingly beautiful daughters, the hekurágnuma (gnuma is the Waika word for 'woman'). The hekurágnuma have lovely bodies embellished with painted designs. Their scent is delightful, and they are called upon to alleviate sickness and pain. (I thought of Hudson's jungle maiden Rima, and then how outraged people had tarred and feathered Epstein's statue of her set up in a London park.) Only initiated men can take yopo and thereby summon the hekurá. Such men are called hekurá themselves, and I got the impression that there is a strong similarity between western spiritualist mediums and the initiated hekurá. The western use of the word 'trip' to indicate being under the influence of hallucinatory drugs is significant: the yopo taker believes he makes journeys, covers vast distances, flies through the air to link up with his 'guides'.

I will insert here a strange story concerning a hekurá which I learned from another New Tribes missionary, Earl Hopkins, at Puerto Ayacucho. Earl told of this particular Indian who had exposed two children born to him deformed and had been threatened with imprisonment by the Venezuelan authorities if he did it again. 'I shall always do it,' he said, 'and you will never catch me, for I shall take yopo and disappear into the forest.' His third child was born deformed, and the Indian killed it and disappeared. But after about ten days' absence he turned up again, and one of the first people to see him was a New Tribes missionary to whom he related how he had been on a 'trip', flying through the air, and that 'I saw your captain shot'. The missionary was very puzzled by this assertion and asked the Indian to amplify. He knew, of course, that the Indian was using the word 'captain' in the sense of chief or headman. The Indian said, 'I watched your captain being shot from a bridge.' Outside news travels slowly to these areas at the back of beyond, and it wasn't until three days later that the missionary heard of the assassination of President John F. Kennedy. It is likely that the killing had been done when the Indian made his statement, so it is not impossible, though I would have said practically so, that he could have heard the news. But what to me appeared strangest about this story was the assertion that the shooting had been done 'from a bridge' – a belief held by many people contrary to the findings of the official Warren Report, and a theory which did not receive wide publicity until a long time after President Kennedy's death.

Our conversation about hekurá and yopo round the smoky hurricane lamp was cut short by a gigantic *miaow* from just outside the hut. We all pricked up our ears. It came again, *miaow-ow*. I thought at first it was Jesco or perhaps Peter Smith playing a joke. Then somebody said 'Jaguar!' Paul Dye picked up the lamp and opened the door. We grabbed machetes and followed him out. The night was black, with a presence you could feel – a sinister presence. There was a sudden rustling in the underbrush and then silence except for our nervous breathing.

'Yeah, jaguar,' said Paul, 'but it's gone now. Won't come back,' so we all trooped into the hut again and decided it was time to climb under our dusty mosquito nets into our hammocks. We had to be off early next morning, and Paul had promised to bring us to the 'yopo tree'.

CHAPTER SIXTEEN

Journey to the Waika: The Yopo Tree

At eight o'clock on a fine, rather grey-skied morning, being Thursday, 25th April, we left Paul's village with both canoes.

Arthur Helliwell had had a bad night, getting his breath only with continuous efforts; Jesco was bruised and limping rather more than usual; Douglas was hobbling; my right eye was 'sticky' and a little sore: we were, in fact, rather reminiscent of an army sick-parade but with no doctor. The two missionaries and the four Indian guides were in fine fettle, and Paul was well recovered from his jungle boil and using both hands. Bob Saunders was a bit morose and quiet, a humour which I put down to constipation. Peter Smith was spry and active as usual, his body now peppered all over with the dried blood spots of old *jejene* bites, with a sprinkle of new red ones in between: he had taken to wearing nothing but briefs because, he said, he felt it better to be like the Indians and see whether he couldn't build up some sort of immunity to the insect attack.

As we approached the first rapid I felt, with a little sinking of my stomach, that Paul was making for the bank. I'd hoped we were going to shoot all the rapids and not go through that humping again.

He said, 'Does anybody wan' to walk?'

I said, 'Are you going to shoot?'

'I reckon I will!'

Henry, who was sitting behind me, asked, 'Brian, do you want me to film from the bank?'

'Jolly good idea,' I said. So Henry picked up his bulky Arriflex camera and stepped off the canoe. He struggled into the leaves, and they closed after him.

Danny's canoe came up behind us, and we passed on the news of a slight delay to allow Henry to get into position.

After about fifteen minutes we saw a tiny Henry appear from the dense green growth about three hundred yards below us on the right.

We saw him flap his arms wide and slowly.

'Start up!' I called.

We in Paul's boat roared thrillingly through the rapid. We put into the bank and turned our heads to watch Danny slicing through the broken water. He drew up alongside us, and we waited for Henry.

At last his bloated face, red almost to blackness, thrust through the undergrowth, furious with suppressed anger and disgust. 'Ah wa'nt reddy!' he muttered.

'What?'

'*I wasn't reddy!*'

'What do you mean?' I asked, 'Didn't you wave your arms as a signal?'

'Ah wor o'ny showin' you where I was.'

So we in Paul's boat had flashed past him while he was still struggling to set the camera up on the tripod. He had managed to film Danny's boat, but 'at a stop Ah didn't know – an' wi' a gret dollop o' jungle mud on me filter!' He climbed back into our canoe, grumbling about our completely wasting his time and referring pointedly to 'some folk's' lack of gumption in not being able to understand his signals.

Of course, I realised that the 'some folks' was me, and I was content to take the blame without arguing, because I had failed to make a definite arrangement with him before he left us above the cataract. We resumed our journey with a sort of static of irritation in the midships of our canoe.

We drove under a large flock of fish-tailed birds circling over the river, probably the same as we had noticed coming up. Hefty, squatting in the nose of our canoe, called to Paul that he could see a black monkey. We all peered intently, but I could see nothing against the dark shadows and caverns of shade among the trees.

Paul asked if he should stop for the Indian to shoot the monkey with our 16-bore shot-gun. I gave a doubtful nod, and the engine was throttled back and the canoe slid in under the waterlogged forest branches. As the foliage brushed our heads and shoulders we were immediately showered with a million biting ants. The leaves and twigs were swarming with them. The scene was alive with that incessant running march and countermarch of theirs like one of those Italian Bersaglieri trotting brigades gone made. And, of course, they ran on us. But they also stopped to bite. I saw a frenzied Henry jumping about like a herring on a griddle as far as the restricted space between the canoe thwarts would allow. I was batting myself all over and still getting bitten on arms and legs and open neck and back. I dragged my shirt off, but this only exposed more skin for the ones still dropping down on us to fasten their nippers into. There were many lianas dangling about us, and I grabbed one to try and strap-hang the boat away from the bank. It was dry, lifeless, decrepit, and it snapped in my fingers only for a thousand ants to come draining out of its hollow interior. We were drenched in ants. Paul pulled away into mid-stream, and by this time Danny's canoe had overtaken and passed us.

It took us half an hour to get rid of the last of those ants, having collected dozens of bites in the process.

Fortunately, because of the hoo-ha, the monkey had had no difficulty in getting away. The gun wasn't even aimed, let alone fired.

At eleven thirty by my watch we overtook the other canoe pulled into the bank. Paul skilfully drew us in so that Hefty could catch their stern without our coming in contact with the vegetation. Both Danny's Indians were ashore and up a tree. They were hacking off with machetes clusters of egg-shaped fruit, each about five inches long. Our two Indians joined them. There were enough fruit for us to have one apiece. When banged on the boat's gunnel, the fruit cracked like an egg, and the brittle rind could be pulled apart. Inside were triangular seeds as big as the end of your thumb, cream coloured and covered with a sort of soft blancmange which we sucked away before spitting the harder core into the river. It was sweet to the taste, slightly acid and quite delicious. The Indians called the fruit *jowä*.

Shortly after we set off again we passed the island of the deserted village. Above the notched log, Jesco's plastic bag of sweets, fish hooks and mouth organs still hung at the top of the leaning pole. The Indians had avoided the place.

By midday we reached Shanamaña, the village of the two missionaries Cecil and Delora Neese with whom we had exchanged a boat. Mrs Neese offered us a salad of palm hearts, and I myself prepared a cauldron of oxtail soup from our packets on her butane-gas stove. Delora also gave us the usual iced tea, American apple pie and coffee. We were all touched by the missionaries' selfless hospitality. Getting stores from the outside world is a chancy, tedious and expensive business. We realised that what we took from the missionaries was for them a self-sacrifice, but to refuse would have hurt them and was out of the question.

After lunch, at about two thirty, Paul asked me if I still wanted to see a yopo tree. 'You bet,' I said. So Paul, Danny, the BBC party and Hefty the Makiritare Indian crossed the river in one of the outboard canoes. The sun was shining hotly as we chugged a little way downstream, but as soon as we turned into a shadowy jungle creek and scrambled ashore and entered the trees the gloom closed in. Hefty was leading us between tree boles and undergrowth along a narrow trail wide enough to admit only one person at a time. Even so, he had occasionally to hack away tendrils and creepers to open the path. But for the rustling of leaves and the rasp of our breathing the jungle was strangely silent at that dead time of the humid afternoon. It was a Turkish bathhouse with the over-ripe odour of rotting fruit.

After about ten minutes' exhausting padding along the rooty path, having got strung out a bit, we discovered Hefty had darted off to the left, and we all shunted up to see what was happening. Almost invisible among the leaves and lianas, Hefty was indicating with his machete a straight slender tree about fifty feet tall with foliage only at its top. It was free from parasitical creepers and about eight inches in diameter at the base. This was the tree from which bark could be stripped to make yopo.

Before anything else happened we had to set up our camera and microphone. Henry tested the light with his meter and said it was too dark to film. We looked about and saw a nearby tree already leaning at an angle of sixty degrees which appeared suitable to be chopped down to let in some light.

Paul, Peter Smith, Henry and Hefty took it in turns to fell the leaning tree with a machete. When a gash had been chipped out of it over half-way through it still showed no sign of falling. Its substance was iron hard, with a rich, light ochre-coloured set of outer rings and a dark mahogany brown core. When we glanced upwards it was obvious why the tree wouldn't fall. Its top was jammed into that of another tree whose trunk we could see thirty feet away.

Our woodcutters moved to the base of this new tree and started hacking. After ten minutes the crucial cut was arrived at and Hefty delivered this *coup-de-grâce*. Both trees plunged at once. We were standing, as we thought, out of danger behind their line of fall. Suddenly, the under-growth in our rear, together with a fallen log, began to move; a snaky rigging of lianas ripped along the forest floor threatening to overwhelm us with all its gummage; the two falling trees were pulling along a cordage and débris like that behind a launching liner, and we all skipped sideways and hopped madly to escape. A cloud of flittering leaves snowed all about us. There was a continuous shattering snapping of branches and twigs, and we peered anxiously through the explosive dusty fog to see if any of us was hurt. We were startled but uninjured.

With an unmoved expression on his face, Hefty retraced his steps to the yopo tree and made two horizontal cuts about three inches long and a yard apart. He inserted the blade of his machete in the top cut to prise up the bark. Then with one firm downward stroke he lifted away a neat ribbon of the tree's outer skin and handed it to Danny, who gave it to me. The inside of the bark had a glutinous, brownish skin, which I found moist and smelling like fresh rhubarb. I gave it back to Hefty. He put the bark strip on the ground, holding it firm with his foot so that he could scrape away the inside with the flat end of his machete. The blobby skin came away in a stringy fashion, sticking to his blade. He shook off the gummy skein on to a broad shiny leaf he had plucked for the purpose. Then he removed three more pieces of bark and scraped them as before. He collected about half a pound of this raw material for yopo-making and wrapped it up into a neat leaf parcel so that I could take it back to the hovercraft scientists.

Hefty told Danny and Paul that the next stages in the manufacture of the drug were as follows. First you dried the material quickly over a fire until it went hard. If you left it damp for more than a day the makings would go bad. When dry you pounded and ground the brittle substance between stones until you achieved a fine powder. In this state, your yopo was ready for use.

I asked Danny if he had ever seen this tree before.

'No, I haven't,' he said, 'this is the first time I've actually seen it.'

'What do they themselves call the tree?'

Danny spoke to the Indian in Waika.

Hefty said, '*Ebená*' and Danny repeated the word, '*Ebená*'. I wanted to be quite sure, and I asked if that was the name in the Waika language, and Danny said yes.

Conrad Gorinsky had particularly asked me, if we ever found the yopo plant, to bring back leaves to help in its botanical identification. Here the leaves were situated at the very top of the tree, fifty feet above ground, but Danny passed our request to Hefty, who did a monkey jack-knife from ground to foliage in about twenty seconds flat and cast down two great sprigs of leaves which we parcelled up with the yopo material.

On our way back, the canoe was once more driven into the bank, and Hefty went ashore alone into the forest. After a few minutes he returned with bunches of a plant rather like Creeping Jenny. The Indians also use this for making yopo, and their name for it is in Waika *cowari*.

A third substance which they use to produce hallucinations, we were unable to procure. I understood from Paul that it was obtained in similar fashion to the other two from the fruit or pod of a tree they call *jisiyomö*.

I have since been told by Conrad and others that the inhalant dusts or snuffs which the Indians use for their 'trips' contain the active alkaloids of dimothyltriptammine and bufotenine and that the plants belong to the genus *Piptadenia* or *Virola*. My impression is that the Indians still hold secrets which neither we nor the scientists know – and perhaps will never know.

We left the village of Shanamaña in the late afternoon and reached Coshalowateri by dusk and spent the night there.

Next day, Friday, 26th April, we started late. Arthur Helliwell and Douglas Botting didn't want to wait a day at that hell-hole Esmeralda and decided to turn up the Orinoco to visit Mavaca three hours away: Danny agreed to take them in his boat. The rest of us headed for Tama Tama with Paul. We, too, had no intention of stopping at Esmeralda, which we passed after nightfall, anyway.

It was nine o'clock at night and pitch dark before we reached Tama Tama. There were flash lights on the tiny rocky beach 'shining like good deeds in a naughty world', and before we even started to climb over the thwarts and cocked-up nose of our dugout I heard a young woman's voice saying, 'That's the man I want to see!' It was Paul's wife.

Interlude to Inquire into the Fate of the Amazon Women

THE three most intriguing mysteries in all South America are El Dorado, the Lost Cities and the Amazon Women.

El Dorado, I'm afraid, will never be found, for it just does not exist outside men's minds; the most arduous seeker after Lost Cities, Colonel Fawcett, never found one, while a casual jungle wanderer, the American Hiram Bingham, accidentally stumbled over the most famous of them all, Macchu Picchu, not sixty years ago; such cities, marvels of masonry hidden like Sleeping Beauty's palace under centuries of foliage and jungle creepers, will continue to be found; indeed, an old film acquaintance of mine, called Robert Cundy, was in at the discovery of the most recent of them within the last five years, the Peruvian lost city of Pajaten; but the Amazon Women – shall we ever get to the bottom of that particular travellers' tale?

My overnight stop at Tama Tama leads me to believe that there is perhaps a solution to the mystery of the women-who-live-without-husbands.

In fact, when you come to think of it, the lot of the primitive Indian women among such tribes as the Waikas is so depressed, so subject to casual beating even to the point of broken bones, or death, so chattel-like with one tribe's men continually snitching the other's marriageable girls and wives that here, I would have thought, was the ideal forcing ground for a revolt and running away of a group of like-minded women. The situation is worse than it was in Victorian and Edwardian England, and even that produced the suffragettes.

The postulation, therefore, of a group of women driven to revolt by the blind, cruel stupidity of Man, to rid themselves of a slavemaster whose two main requirements have always been work and that they should open their legs, is not so far-fetched. Our Saturday spent as a sort of holiday at Tama Tama before the hovercraft picked us up on the Sunday morning brought me personally to grips with this fascinating puzzle.

Pat Dye, Paul's wife, had led us by flashlight in a steep scramble up a narrow path bordered by rustling grass to a mud house with thatched roof, the empty home of some missionaries on furlough in the States. There were several rooms downstairs and a loft reached by a ladder. We quickly put up our hammocks and mosquito nets before descending the hill again to Paul's home where Pat had prepared a dinner of spaghetti bolognese steaming in a Pyrex dish. It all seemed to appear like magic with the exact number of places laid. But then one suddenly remembered that these sequestered missionary families are bound close by radio, and that even as we left Shanamaña, Pat Dye would hear how many were in the dugout and what time they could be expected at Tama Tama.

Dorothy Dye was there, a splendid matronly woman who, after the slaughter of her husband, had lived on herself in the jungle with her three children, a modern Amazon. Now she serves at Tama Tama as a nurse and midwife. Whenever I happened to be in Paul Dye's home during that forty-eight hours it always seemed that Dorothy, his mother, was coming in through the back door announcing the delivery of another Indian baby.

Pat Dye was the very pretty young woman who had spoken to me when we first landed from the hovercraft. She reminded me of the fresh cotton-frocked girls of American western films – feeding the men, calling her husband 'honey' and everybody else 'sir'.

On the Saturday, Jesco and the rest of us wandered round the hill of Tama Tama doing some desultory exploration. Our imagination had been sparked off after an early lunch with two middle-aged missionaries, Mr and Mrs Kilham. (There were three curiously named families at Tama Tama, Paul had told us – Catchem, Kilham and Dye.) The Kilhams' home overlooked the Orinoco, from which the fish had come for our main dish which we found an obstacle to conversation, for it filled our mouths with dozens of tiny Y-shaped bones. Mr Kilham, however, managed to cope with them and told us he had farmed most of his life in South Dakota, but his elder brother now had 'the home farm'. After lunch he showed us stone axe heads and pottery found at

Tama Tama. Some mission schoolboys came in with other fragments of ceramics, thin, delicate and having sophisticated artistic designs. These pots excited Jesco out of all recognition. He rushed us to the top of Tama Tama hill, led by the schoolboys, to a known pottery digging, and sure enough we were able to pick up, after a little scrabbling, bits of angular earthenware – though none as fine as those we had already seen. The boys said that over the hill towards the jungle there was a long gully strewn with flat-faced rocks on which were engravings. We followed them through the chest-high brush, ignoring the *jejenes* in our excitement. My impression of Tama Tama was that the site had been a natural for a people looking for a home which they could easily fortify. It was surrounded on three sides by river and on the fourth side by the gully or ditch from which earth had been carried up to make or to extend the hill which medieval European castle builders called the 'motte' or 'donjon'. The ditch has been somewhat cleared by the missionaries in a defeated attempt to start an aeroplane runway: the boulders which spread out from the ditch into the forest are so huge that only dynamite and massive machines could hope to shift them. No doubt this work will be accomplished in time, but when it is, it will destroy some remarkable archaeological evidence. Whether this evidence, as Jesco thought, is a link in the story of the Amazon women, is a matter for speculation.

The designs on the weathered rocks are old, but how old, it would be difficult without ancillary evidence to suggest. The motifs most repeated are the concentric circles with a centre dot, and a kind of double cross. There is one huge rock, over man height, with a much larger and more sophisticated interlacing pattern contained inside a rectangle two feet square. When I had first landed at Tama Tama I had been shown a boulder by the river's brink with a much worn double-spiral pattern. Later that Saturday afternoon, I crossed the river with Jesco, Henry and two younger Shaylor brothers, Mike and John, to trade for pots of curare from the Piaroa Indians. Not more than 400 yards away from Tama Tama in the Piaroa village we found another carving. It was on a rock twelve feet high, with mud houses built within a foot either side so that the design was impossible to photograph. I copied it into my notebook, remarking its association with the concentric rings and dot.

It was all very tantalising. It reinforced my convictions that the present Waika, Piaroa and Makiritare tribes around this junction of the Casiquiare and the Orinoco are more primitive than Indian peoples who have passed this way before. A young Makiritare lad (dressed in

European mission clothes), whom we questioned earlier by the pottery site, had some interesting things to say. Speech exchange was difficult, for he had a little Spanish, and our nearest to that was Jesco's Portuguese. In addition, because he was converted, the youth was reluctant to speak about the old ways and beliefs of his pagan fathers. Nevertheless, he told Jesco that he had heard of a tribe of Indian women who lived without husbands, but being a Christian, he didn't want to talk about it. On being pressed, he said the older people of his tribe knew more about the women. He also told us that the pagan Indians believed Tama Tama to be haunted and that for many years no one would go near the place until the Americans bought it.

These scraps of information led Jesco into expounding his theory of the Amazon women, a theory which (it seems to me) may well be near the truth.

The classical Amazons were a race of warrior-women led by a queen (Shakespeare calls her Hippolyta in *A Midsummer Night's Dream*) who, better to draw the bow, were said to cut off their right breast, hence their name, Amazon. Such a race intrigued, irritated and frequently roused the scorn of ancient male authors because of their rejection of men except during a short period each year when the Amazons required and allowed temporary husbands to do duty at stud. Such a role, while titillating to men at first sight, is soon seen in its proper perspective as a severe blow to the male ego. It's the men who are being used as chattels.

The South American Amazons, be they mythical, a mistake or real, had sufficient impact to imprint their name on what many acknowledge to be the greatest river in the world. This fact alone makes their story worth the investigation, for names have power, and place names, particularly, express the fundamental attitudes of men.

There have always been two versions of the South American Amazons story: one writes off the warrior women as a mistake or a tall story; the other vouches for the truth of their existence. The version insisting on their truth starts with the advantage of having appeared first, but more important, comes from the pen of an eye witness, and what's more, a witness who by his calling of a clerk in holy orders ought to gain credibility.

Let us examine, then, the story of the man who saw it all, the man who was there, Friar Gaspar de Carvajal. An expedition had set off from Quito in 1539 to discover the Land of Cinnamon and, if possible, El Dorado. It was led by Gonzalo Pizarro, a brother of the Conqueror of Peru. A one-eyed Spanish Knight, Don Francisco de Orellana, spent 'over forty thousand gold pesos' fitting out himself and his twenty-three followers, only to find that the expedition had set off from Quito without him. Orellana, left high and dry, 'was somewhat embarrassed as to what he should do,' says Carvajal, who himself had started with Pizarro and the main body. Nevertheless, Orellana decided to follow, 'suffering many hardships, both from hunger and from fights which the Indians forced upon him' until, like a belated Don Quixote 'when he overtook the said Gonzalo Pizarro he still had left only a sword and a shield, and his companions likewise . . . and although all I have told you up to now I neither saw nor took part in, still I gathered up information from all those who came with the said Captain [Orellana], because I was with the said Gonzalo Pizarro and I saw the other and his companions come in in the manner that I have said; but what I shall tell from here on will be as an eyewitness and as a man to whom God chose to give a part in such a strange and hitherto never experienced voyage of discovery'.

Orellana, together with Carvajal and fifty-six other men, was sent off ahead in a brigantine whose building had been supervised by the one-eyed knight. Later chroniclers have castigated Orellana for continuing down the river in what they call his desertion of Pizarro; but Carvajal (who was, after all, there) suggests there was an agreed split, Orellana saying to Pizarro 'in case he did not come back, Pizarro should not be concerned about him; and thereupon the said Governor [Pizarro] told him to do whatever he thought best'.

One thing is certain: Orellana was one of the most energetic, resourceful, brave and likeable of men. He carried his fifty-odd followers through incredible dangers, near disasters, running fights with ferocious Indians for days on end and finally brought the survivors out into the Atlantic and then to Margarita. There is never any suggestion in Carvajal's narrative of mutiny or plotting against the leader; and in his dealings with the Indians, Orellana showed himself sensible and humane. What is more, he had a number of practical qualities which probably made him the one man who could have successfully brought off this transnavigation of an unknown continent: not least of these was a facility to speak the Indian tongues, 'his understanding of the language,' says Carvajal, 'was, next to God, the deciding factor by virtue of which we did not perish somewhere along the river'.

At a point near the confluence of the Putumayu River with the Amazon, Francisco Orellana held a pow-wow with Indian chiefs who, says Fray Carvajal, 'told him that if we were going to visit the Amurians, whom they call Coniupuyara in their tongue, which means "grand mistresses", to be careful about what we were doing, for we were few in number and they many, for they would kill us; and they counselled us not to stop in their country, for right here they would give us everything we might need'. A few pages earlier in his journal, the priest had recorded, 'It was here that they informed us of the existence of the Amazons and of the wealth further down the river, and the one who gave us this information was an Indian overlord named Aparia, an old man who said he had been in that country.'

These are the very first written references by western observers to the existence of the Amazon women.

Having heard about the Amazons, the expeditionaries might well be disposed to expect seeing them: would such an expectation colour their judgement? The point to consider here is that before ever Europeans came to South America there were current among Indians reports of 'women without husbands'. Whether legendary at this time or not, such reports (so students are coming more and more to believe) nearly always have a foundation in fact.

In June 1542 at a point on the north bank of the river about half-way between modern Manaus and the sea, Carvajal had his first sight of the Amazons.

Some three weeks before the encounter, the expeditionaries had been told by an Indian they had captured that they had entered lands whose people paid tribute to the Amazons. On Monday, 31st May 1542 they had put ashore at 'a medium-sized village' between 100 and 200 miles east of modern Manaus. They were astonished to see a very large public square in the middle of which 'was a hewn tree trunk ten feet in girth, there being represented and carved in relief thereon a walled city with its inclosure and a gate. At this gate then were two towers, very tall and having windows, and each tower had a door, the two facing each other, and at each door were two columns, and this entire structure that I am telling about rested upon two very fierce lions, which turned their glances backward as though suspicious of each other, holding between their forepaws and claws the entire structure, in the middle of which was a round open space: in the centre of this space there was a hole through which they offered and poured out *chicha* for the Sun, for this is the wine which they drink, and the Sun is the one whom they worship and consider as their god. In short, the construction was a thing well worth seeing, and the Captain and all of us, marvelling at such a great thing, asked an Indian who was seized here by us what that was, or as a reminder of what they kept that thing in the square, and the Indian answered that they were subjects and tributaries of the

Amazons and that the only service which they rendered them consisted in supplying them with plumes of parrots and macaws for the linings of the roofs of the buildings which constitute their places of worship, and that all the villages which they had were of that kind, and that they had that thing there as a reminder, and that they worshipped it as a thing which was the emblem of their mistress, who is the one who rules over all the land of the aforesaid women.'

Continuing downriver, landing before nightfall to seek suitable quarters, always skirmishing with the Indians, whose villages they used as pantries and posting stations, on Thursday, 24th June 1542 they 'came suddenly upon the excellent land and dominion of the Amazons. The said villages had been forewarned and knew of our coming, in consequence whereof they came out on the water to meet us, in no friendly mood, and, when they had come close to the Captain, he would have liked to induce them to accept peace, and so he began to speak to them and call them, but they laughed and mocked us and came up close to us and told us to keep going and added that down below they were waiting for us, and that they were to seize us all and take us to the Amazons. The Captain, angered at the arrogance of the Indians, gave orders to shoot at them with the crossbows and arquebuses, so that they might reflect and become aware that we had wherewith to assail them; and in this way damage was inflicted on them and they turned about towards the village to give the news of what they had seen; as for us, we did not fail to proceed and draw close to the villages.'

Orellana attempted to beach his two brigantines (they had built another on the way) and in doing so aroused a hornets' nest of battling Indians. 'Our companions,' says Carvajal, 'jumped into the water, which came up to their chests: here was fought a very serious and hazardous battle, because the Indians were there mixed in among our Spaniards, who defended themselves so courageously that it was a marvellous thing to behold. More than an hour was taken up by this fight, for the Indians did not lose spirit, rather it seemed as if it was being doubled in them, although they saw many of their own number killed, and they passed over them and they merely kept retreating and coming back again. I want it to be known what the reason was why these Indians defended themselves in this manner. It must be explained that they are the subjects of, and tributaries to, the Amazons, and, our coming having been made known to them, they went to them to ask help, and there came as many as ten or twelve of them, for we ourselves saw these women, who were there fighting in front of all the Indian men as women captains, and these latter fought so courageously that the Indian men did not dare to turn their backs, and anyone who did turn his back they killed with clubs right there before us, and this is the reason why the Indians kept up their defence for so long. These women are very white and tall, and have hair very long and braided and wound about the head, and they are very robust and go about naked, but with their privy parts covered, with their bows and arrows in their hands, doing as much fighting as ten Indian men, and indeed there was one woman among these who shot an arrow a span deep into one of the brigantines, and others less deep, so that our brigantines looked like porcupines.

'To come back to our situation and our fight: Our Lord was pleased to give courage and strength to our companions, who killed seven or eight (for these we actually saw) of the Amazons, whereupon the Indians lost heart, and they were defeated and routed with considerable damage to their persons; and because there were many warriors coming from the other villages to give aid and as they were again giving their calls, the Captain ordered the men to get into the boats with very great haste, for he did not wish to jeopardise the lives of all, and so they got into the boats, not without some trouble, because already the Indians were beginning to fight again, and besides this there was approaching on the water a great fleet of canoes, and so we pushed out into the river and got away from the shore.

'In this village just mentioned,' says Carvajal, 'there was captured an Indian trumpeter, who had been attached to the fighting force and who was about thirty years of age, who, when he had been captured, started in to tell the Captain many things about the country farther inland, and the Captain took him along.'

A little lower down the river Orellana's men wished to put into what appeared to be a deserted village to recuperate and possibly get food. Orellana was against it, but the men (including Carvajal) urged it and the captain gave way. The Indians were waiting in ambush. The priest writes, 'Out of all of us, in this village they hit no one but me, for they planted an arrow shot right in one of my eyes, in such a way that the arrow went through to the other side, from which wound I have lost the eye and even now I am not without suffering and not free from pain, although Our Lord, without my deserving it, has been kind enough to grant me life so that I can mend my ways and serve Him better than I have done hitherto.'

Before the expeditionaries reached the mouth of the river, the indefatigable Don Francisco de Orellana had extracted from the Indian 'trumpeter' captured during the battle with the Amazons a vocabulary of new words for use in questioning the prisoner. Carvajal says, 'The Captain took aside the Indian who had been captured farther back, because he now understood him by means of a list of words that he had made, and asked him of what place he was a native: the Indian answered that he was from that village where he had been seized; the Captain asked him what the name of the overlord of this land was, and the Indian replied that his name was Couynco [or, in another version, Quenyuc] and that he was a very great overlord and that his rule extended to where we were, and that, as I have already said, was a stretch of one hundred and fifty leagues.

'The Captain asked him what women those were who had come to help them and fight against us; the Indian said that they were certain women who resided in the interior of the country, a seven-day journey from the shore, and that it was because this overlord Couynco was subject to them that they had come to watch over the shore.

'The Captain asked him if these women were married: the Indian said they were not.

'The Captain asked him about how they lived: the Indian replied first that, as he had already said, they were off in the interior of the land and that he had been there many times and had seen their customs and mode of living, for as their vassal he was in the habit of going there to carry tribute whenever the overlord sent him.

'The Captain asked if these women were numerous: the Indian said that they were, and that he knew by name seventy villages, and named them before those of us who were there present, and he added that he had been in several of them.

'The Captain asked him if the houses in these villages were built of straw: the Indian said they were not, but out of stone and with regular doors, and that from one village to another went roads closed off on one side and on the other with guards stationed at intervals along them so that no one might enter without paying duties.

'The Captain asked if these women bore children: the Indian answered that they did.

'The Captain asked him how, not being married and there being no man residing among them, they became pregnant: he said that these Indian women consorted with Indian men at times, and, when that desire came to them, they assembled a great horde of warriors and went off to make war on a very great overlord whose residence is not far from the land of these women, and by force they brought them to their own country and kept them with them for the time that suited their caprice, and after they found themselves pregnant they sent them back to their country without doing them any harm; and afterwards, when the time came for them to have children, if they gave birth to male children, they killed them and sent them to their fathers, and, if female children, they raised them with great solemnity and instructed them in the arts of war. He said furthermore that among all these women there was one ruling mistress who subjected and held under her hand and jurisdiction all the rest, which mistress went by the name of Coñori.'

After giving the answers to further questions about houses, temples for worship of the Sun, dress, domestic livestock, customs and so on, Carvajal writes, 'All that this Indian told us and more besides had been told to us six leagues from Quito, because concerning these women there were a great many reports.'

The evidence put forward by Friar Gaspar de Carvajal on the subject of the Amazons is of two kinds, eye-witness and hearsay. We should remember that ninety per cent of the evidence used by historians to build up a picture of any but the most recent past is hearsay, so we don't have to reject out of hand all of what Carvajal reports that he heard.

To deal with the hearsay first: Carvajal heard of a numerous tribe of warrior women living without husbands who perpetuated themselves by annually taking exogamous mates, by doing away with sons born from the union and by retaining and training up the daughters to their single, warlike way of life. Their ruler was a queen called Coñori, and their material culture (clothes, artefacts, houses, villages) was further advanced than that of neighbouring Indians. Carvajal got none of this information first-hand: it came through his leader Orellana acting as an interpreter.

What Carvajal *saw* with his own eyes was a fierce attack on Orellana's two boats when they attempted to land on the north bank of the Amazon at a spot about 500 miles east of present-day Manaus. At the forefront of the attack were ten or twelve very white, tall, robust women; they differed from the Indians they led in having very long hair braided and wound round their heads; they were naked except for their genitals; Orellana's men killed eight or nine of these women.

Now we can (if we want to) say first that Carvajal was lying. Considering his priestly calling, that his leader and surviving comrades could substantiate or deny his account, and the fact that his general reportage, where it can be checked today, is accurate (including such apparent travellers' tales as his first reporting of the strange phenomenon occurring at the confluence of the 'black' River Negro and the 'white' Amazon, where the two waters run with a sharp dividing line for miles), in my opinion one cannot accuse him of deliberate falsity.

So we can then say Carvajal and his companions were mistaken, that either what they thought were Amazon women were really men with long hair (and some Indian men *do* grow their hair long) or they were merely wives helping their husbands to fight. But the Friar's report also says that these particular fighters differed from the rest in being 'very white' and 'tall'; also they had their long hair braided and wound round their heads – a fashion I have never heard of among forest Indian men. Presumably Carvajal also saw breasts (he says they were naked except that their 'privy parts' were covered), which would leave him in no doubt as to the sex of the warriors. Finally, that women among jungle Indians should take up arms is extraordinary: among Amazonas Indians war is man's prerogative and the touching of arms by women so interdicted as to be regarded as a taboo.

My first contention is that there exists *prima facie* evidence which (if one could find later traces of such warrior women) would lead one to accept Carvajal's report that Orellana's expeditionaries did in fact come into contact with the 'Amazons'.

My second contention is that Jesco has uncovered just these later traces of the fighting-women-without-husbands.

Jesco has spent the last fifteen years of his life among the wild Indians of the upper Xingú, a mighty tributary of the Amazon flowing from the south and joining the main stream opposite the lands where, according to Carvajal, the Amazons lived. The Xingú is a river of wild cataracts and waterfalls impossible to navigate from the Amazon. Parallel to the Xingú and a little farther west, but still opposite the traditional Amazon lands, is another great tributary, the Tapajos. But the Tapajos is more amenable to navigation.

Now the Xingú Indians have a tradition that once a tribe of armed women, whom they called Yamaricumá, came down from the north probably by way of the Tapajos river. They start the story by saying, 'One upon a time there lived the tribe of the Yamaricumá. The men stayed away for many days and sent no fish to the women. So the women made bows and arrows from the forest and learned how to use them. They learned to live without their men.'

Along the River Tapajos the Indians have for hundreds of years traded unusual and highly valued amulets in the form of green stone frogs. Writing in 1744, La Condamine says, 'Many Indians tell of certain green stones known as Amazon stones with the power to ward off evil spirits and grant fertility which were given to their fathers by the women-without-husbands.' Any southern migration from the traditional Amazon lands would almost inevitably have to come by way of the Tapajos, and a feasible continuation of the route is across the Serra Formosa and down the Manitsaua Missu River to its junction with the Xingú – the very area where the story of the Yamaricumá is today to be found.

In this remote and inaccessible region (guarded by jungle, rapids and swamps) just where the Manitsaua and Xingú meet is an outpost set up by the fathers of modern Brazilian Indian protection, the brothers Villas Boas. It is called Diauarum. Here Jesco has lived, off and on, for many years. When the first attempts were made to clear the jungle for an air-strip at Diauarum the workers found traces of a man-made defensive moat protecting the landward side of the peninsula formed by a bend in the river. Later, the rains washed up finely designed ceramics of a much higher quality than those used by local Indians. There was an earthenware triangular loin-cloth worn by women of a matriarchal society – a ritual object that men must not touch: if they did they would never be capable of hunting or fishing successfully again. Today, a miniature fibre form of this, known as the *uluri*, is worn by all Indian women in the Xingú. The *uluri* is such a tiny triangle that it hides nothing and could never have been designed as a cunny concealer. The suspicion is that it began as some sort of ritual object.

One of the tribes hereabout (numbering fewer than 100) is the Suyá. Jesco lived with them alone for a year, learning their ways and language. The Suyá say that the warrior women came in two big groups. One of these groups settled on the Suyá River by a lake which became known, and still is known, as the Yamaricumá lake. The other group settled on the Tanguro River, where are found rocks with the concentric circle symbols believed to be sun symbols. And we remember Carvajal's account of the great carved tree bole 'which was the emblem of their mistress' and 'through which they offered and poured out *chicha* for the Sun'.

Anything which to a forest Indian is against his ordered way of life or untraditional he calls 'ugly'. The settled Xingú Indians called the women who came to live by the Yamaricumá lake 'ugly' because they fought back and had no use for permanent husbands. In time the women disappeared. According to the Suyá, they had been eaten up by alligators.

There is no known Indian tradition as to what happened to the second group of women from the north, the ones who had settled on the Tanguro River.

At that time a tribe called Aura lived on the banks of the Tanguro.

Today the Auras are unique among Xingú Indians for a number of reasons, not least that their women are makers of fine decorated pots, some of them quite huge. Neighbouring tribes have been known to kidnap Aura women in order to introduce their pottery-making skill into the tribe. What is perhaps even more significant in setting the Auras apart from their neighbours, the Aura *women* have a language personal to themselves which the men do not use.

But the most exciting group of clues which suggests a connection between the modern Auras and the Amazon women is to be found in a unique ceremony. Jesco had the good fortune to film this ceremony, which happens once, perhaps twice, in a lifetime. In this ceremony only the women take part. They call it the dance of the Yamaricumá and say that it was taught to them a long while ago by a tribe of warrior women of that name.

All Indian women know they must never touch the bow and arrow or the spear, and they must never take part in fighting. Yet on one special occasion, at the death of an Aura princess, they do all this and more in a complete reversal of the roles of the sexes. They wear (some of them) the feather headdress peculiar to men; they are led in the dance by a woman so decked out and carrying weapons, a woman unique among Xingú Indians, for she is an Aura priestess.

The triangular *uluri* is worn by all the participants, and the sophisticated pots decorated with the triangular symbol also play a significant part. Some of the hugest, great straight-sided bowls, a foot deep and three feet across, are set out on the dance square between the village huts in a particular pattern – an extended triangle.

The climax of the ceremony is something so unusual and out of character that one is forced to believe that an extraordinary event gave rise to it. It is a ceremonial fight between the women of the Auras and women invited from a neighbouring tribe.

One after another, pairs of women and girls kick up clouds of dust, wrestling in a way more ritual than in earnest. What strong reason can there be behind such a tradition which, because of 'civilised' encroachments in the Xingú, is unlikely ever to be seen again, and now only remains recorded on a unique film? Can it be that these Aura women are acting out battles symbolic of those that tradition says were engaged in by the women-without-husbands? Or, perhaps more likely, is this Yamaricumá fighting the expression of a folk memory of warlike training once given to Amazon daughters? And the name Yamaricumá – could the first part be identical with the local name for Amazons given by chief Aparia to Carvajal 'Amuri-ans' with a form of the jungle Indians' word for woman, i.e. 'gnuma' tacked on? Amuri-gnuma?

Whether one accepts in whole or in part the theory I have outlined here, I believe that there is enough evidence to show that without further archaeological and historical research one cannot yet dismiss the Amazon women as characters of fable, legend or travellers' tales.

Traditions of the women-without-husbands are found along the Amazon from within six leagues of Quito (Carvajal) to sixty leagues from the river's mouth (Raleigh, in his *Discovery of Guiana*). Writing in 1596, Raleigh quoted as his source a 'Casique or Lord of People' who 'had been in the river and beyond it also' and who said the Amazons lived south of the river. We ourselves heard from the young Makiritare Indian of women-without-husbands known to peoples living in the area of Tama Tama, where the Casiquiare Canal joins Orinoco to Amazon. At the time when the first evidence was being collected and written down – the second half of the sixteenth century – nobody claimed that the Amazons were still in the upper reaches of either the Amazon or Orinoco. If we collate and compare the local traditions from 1539 to the present day we get the definite impression of a migration down the Amazon, and/or down the Negro from the northern end of the Casiquiare Canal, to a region on the north bank of the Amazon about opposite the Tapajos tributary, a migration which continues south to the Yamaricumá lake on the Suyá River and to the Tanguro River.

Are the circular sun symbols and other carvings on the rocks at Tama Tama the starting point of the wanderings of the Amazon women, and did they finally assimilate with men of the Aura tribe on the upper Xingú River?

This tantalising problem is all the more intriguing because, at present, we cannot know for certain what the true answer is. What a quest to fire the imagination of a latter-day Colonel Fawcett! But then, a Fawcett would only wish to search if he believed that Amazons in their pristine state, taking lovers once a year, were yet to be found. And who can tell but that, somewhere in those vast impenetrable woods, there still exist congeries, offshoots left behind, of those naked, white, long-haired, statuesque beauties – the women-who-live-without-husbands?

And that on a night of the full moon they wait by the shores of a secret lake to enjoy their lovers in a communal marriage, of which modern wife-swapping is but the last kick and survivor of an urge once common to our 'fruit-picking primate ancestors' before they jumped down from the trees and finally turned their backs on the forest?

CHAPTER SEVENTEEN

Arthur Helliwell's Chest

On Sunday, 28th April at nine in the morning the hovercraft picked us up and we left Tama Tama. For me there was a real feeling of sadness as I said goodbye to Paul and Danny, to Pat Dye and Dorothy Dye, to Peg and Robert Shaylor, all of whom, one realised, we should never meet again. Everybody came down to the beach to wave us off.

We said goodbye, too, to blue cloud-capped Duida, and to hell-hole Esmeralda, that inferno of gnats.

We entered once again our jungle tunnel.

By nine thirty a.m. tall, monkish mountains peered over the jungle wall on our left with cowls of white cloud about their shoulders. Here and there, on both banks we glimpsed settlements of four or five mud-walled huts with corrugated tin or aluminium roofs – always where an outcrop of boulders occurs forcing a natural abatement of the jungle. The River Orinoco was here about 300 yards wide, and we skimmed and bounced steadily at speed over the smooth water. I wrote with my diary on my knee, 'More low jungle-covered hills. Bright sunshine, high dense clouds, full brimming river. Jungle, jungle, jungle – same as ever. No bird life, no animal life, everything for miles ahead driven away by the hovercraft's roar and crackle. Colonel Leal hasn't shaved for days and now is black-avised with a quarter-inch long full set and, wearing his képi, looks more like Fidel Castro than ever. 11.25 Very high mountain on right about 12,000 feet with cloud all along its flat topped plateau, appears to be two-thirds metallic bare rock. Boulders protruding from the surface of the river. 12.15 rendezvous with Castillo's boat and the scientists by a riverside rock as big as a backyard. Beyond the rock, open savannah pimpled with termite cones. Lunch of warm sardines, warm cheese, rye biscuits and oily butter. David Smithers promised us beer off the ice at our next stop. We thought it a weak joke. Left the rock at 12.50 with a litter of sardine tins, pilchard cans and paper wrappings and the thought "Who cares if we don't keep Amazonas tidy?" Sun blazing. Temperature in the hovercraft 96°. Skin prickling on forearms from sunburn and *jejene* bites. Across the gangway, Arthur Helliwell looks a sick man. Turned right up the Orinoco's tributary the Rio Ventuari. More savannah. 2 p.m. arrived at trading station of the feudal overlord of these parts, Nestor Gonzalez, king of the river and millionaire. Beer off the ice. BEER OFF THE ICE!'

It was true after all. Nestor (in appearance a middle-aged, tropical-suited George Raft) was prepared to let us drink all we could pay for. It was rather expensive, having to be transported all that way, round the Great Rapid, but we sank one frost-misted bottle after another on the verandah of his Spanish colonial, stone-built estancia. In front was a runaway garden of palm fronds and fleshy leafage hiding a sort of water tower which housed Nestor's low-suite pink porcelain flush closet and shower, which we were to be allowed to use. On the left of the garden was his company store, and just beyond it a tall stone-built crude-rubber warehouse some of us were to sling our hammocks in. All these buildings were situated well up from the river's brink in an open region with more savannah and rocky outcrops than we had seen before. There was an expansive view up the wide river with blue mountains in the distance. It all looked quite paradisiacal and was called on some maps Yacuary and on others Las Carmelitas.

Just up from the wide sandy beach where the hovercraft was moored stood a large palm-thatched, open-sided shed. The scientists, Douglas Botting, the hovercraft crew and Robin Hanbury-Tenison were quartered here. The BBC crew and Arthur Helliwell were billeted in the rubber warehouse.

The warehouse was dark as the black hole of Calcutta, its sluggish atmosphere heavy with the unchanging, stinking pot-pourri of raw rubber blocks and hemp sacks. At night it was rat and bat infested, and when you shone a torch you were likely to attract gigantic flying beetles and monstrous hairy moths. They hung on the outside of your mosquito net like glibbering creatures menacing you with waving antennae, demanding horror parts in your waking nightmare.

That first evening the 'leaders' (David Smithers informed us) were commanded to have dinner with Nestor Gonzalez: the 'other ranks' were to feast at the *cantina* in the Caboclo village. This would be the pattern during the five days we were due to stay at Las Carmelitas.

The pattern was rudely broken. We 'leaders' (David, Arthur Helliwell, Graham Clarke, Mike Eden, Robin Tenison and myself) were seated at table over our candles and vintage wines: we had reached the nuts and grapes when a file of figures grumbled on to the verandah like a peasants' revolt. It was our 'other ranks' who stared in at us with all the grievance of a starving mob inopportunely asked why they don't eat cake.

Wafted out on an aroma of cigar-smoke, I had hardly stepped on to the verandah when Bob Saunders assaulted me with a blow-by-blow description of the squalor of the *cantina*, the crudity of the rough table and benches, the sickening smell and fouler taste of the communal bowl of hash served up by a corpulent and none too clean Indian mammy in the shadows thrown by a smoky oil lamp.

'*Cantina*!' he snitted (this is a portmanteau word I am forced to invent to cover the exigencies of his voice and expression – it is compounded of 'sneered' and 'gritted'), 'never again! Never! I shall not eat there again!'

Henry Farrar joined in the general grumbling rumble, and I asked Peter Smith what he thought.

'Pretty bad, Brian, pretty bad.'

'O.K.,' I said. 'I'll eat there tomorrow, and one of you can take my place here.'

David Smithers couldn't help but hear us, and he said he didn't think my plan was possible because we might offend Nestor.

'Well, I'm sorry, David,' I said, 'he'll have to be offended.' So we drifted off to our sleeping quarters.

That night in the rubber warehouse was one of the worst I ever remember. The rope fastening the foot end of my hammock shared a ring in the wall with the rope fastening Arthur's head end. We were that close. I could hear his every laboured breath – or failure to take breath. In the dark, in the oppressive stench and heat, I came to understand the meaning of that cliché 'to hang on somebody's every breath' – for that's what I found myself doing with Arthur. In his struggle for air he would sometimes appear to stop breathing for five minutes at a time and I would think, 'God! he's gone,' when a gasp and rattle would bring him back to life again. In between those silences from Arthur I would hear all kinds of suggestive rustlings, noises of creatures – one had no idea what – palping, scuttering, sliding about floor and walls. What made it all the more suggestively frightening was that when we had returned to our night quarters Jesco had been horrified to find a vampire bat, spotlighted by his torch, hooked on to his mosquito net. I have a horror of snakes and bats. There was something grotesque about the way Jesco disposed of this night visitor. The vampire bat isn't all that big, its body perhaps little larger than a well-fed mouse, and it doesn't sink its fangs into your throat. The vampire works much more stealthily, scraping gently at the skin of a big toe, perhaps, which you've stretched out to touch your net, carefully abrading the skin and smearing the wound with its saliva containing an anti-coagulant so that your blood continues to flow freely and the vampire laps its fill. In the morning you may wake weak with loss of blood, but by far the greatest risk is rabies. That's what the real vampire bat can pass on, not the Dracula quality of becoming a vampire yourself. As I say, there was something grotesque, macabre, in the way Jesco disposed of the vampire bat. As we stood back in the darkness gazing, I felt the panic horror of the sentries on the ramparts at Elsinore when surprised by Hamlet's father's ghost, *'Shall I strike at it with my partisan?'* cried Marcellus. But there was nothing at hand to hit the vampire with. Action was urgent if the bat wasn't to fly free, a menace from the shadows. Jesco snatched up a large tin of Johnson's Baby Powder and smothered the startled creature from wing-tip to wing-tip, from mousy snout to stumpy rump. The surprised ghost of a bat was immobilised, and somehow Jesco had bundled it up and got it outside.

So bats were part of the imagined hobgoblins outside the security of my mosquito net as Arthur fought for breath. Sometimes he rambled deliriously. Sometimes he moaned. Frequently he puffed and coughed. I vowed to myself that if he survived that night I would take positive steps to get him medical treatment, and I believed there was a way to do it.

I heard Arthur staggering out of his hammock at first light. Quickly, I nipped out from under my net and went after Bob Saunders, still slumbering in the porch to the warehouse. The previous evening I had noticed Nestor Gonzalez' receiving and transmitting radio.

'Bob,' I said, 'Are you awake?'

'Yes, Brian.'

'Look! We've got to get Arthur to a doctor. If we don't, he's going to die.'

'Where is he?'

'Outside, shaving. Bloody old war horse – he'll never give in. He'll just drop in his tracks. We've got to stop him.'

'Sure – what do you suggest?'

'Nestor Gonzalez' radio. Can you call up Paul Johnstone at Ayacucho and get him to fly a doctor up here?'

'Where to?'

'I don't know. There must be an air-strip somewhere. We can find that out from Nestor. But for God's sake don't let Arthur know.'

'O.K. Soon as I'm washed and shaved.'

An hour later Bob pulled me aside like a conspirator and said, 'I've fixed it. Paul is flying up this morning and bringing a doctor. Apparently the nearest air-strip is downriver, a two-hour trip by outboard.'

'He can't do it,' I said, 'the hovercraft will have to take him.'

Bob grinned pityingly. 'Well, you'll have to work on *them*,' he said, 'and the best of British luck.'

I regarded the situation as being so serious that I was even prepared to hire the hovercraft out of my film-programme budget to take Arthur to the air-strip. However, David Smithers and Graham Clarke realised Arthur's grave need of attention and agreed to use the hovercraft to get him to La Sabañita, as the three or four huts at the air-strip were called. 'And what's more, David,' I said, 'I reckon we shouldn't let him come back here. He ought to go on with the Cessna to Ayacucho and be treated in hospital there. We can pick him up after we've shot the rapids.'

David's eyes bulged. 'Don't think he'll do that,' he said.

After breakfast I broke the news to Arthur about what I had done. He didn't protest, he didn't say very much at all, and I think in his heart of hearts he was relieved.

So we all (less the scientists) bundled into the hovercraft and within an hour were nearing La Sabañita. It was twelve noon, the hour of our rendezvous with Paul. Little, bright-eyed Jim Sweeney was manning the craft's radio, and he indicated having linked up with Paul's plane.

'Pilot wants us to land,' he reported. 'Says the air-strip has pools of water. Doesn't think its suitable for a touchdown.'

This was a shock. The next air-strip was at Santa Barbara where the Ventuari meets the Orinoco. I doubted the hovercraft would go that far.

We caught sight of the Cessna flying towards us. The plane broke away and banked over the jungle on our left. We saw a steep slope with a path leading to a well-built bungalow in the trees. A quarter of a mile farther downstream the jungle stopped and savannah began. Here at the river's edge stood the usual collection of mud-walled tin-roofed huts.

We gingerly landed by the huts, and I jumped out with Graham Clarke; Julio Castillo led the way, for he knew Sabañita and the 'location of the air-strip. The three of us ran strung out across a baked clay trail through a few huts and then across the savannah and between the ant-hills. The track led towards the clump of jungle on our left. We wanted to get to the strip as soon as possible and not to keep Paul aimlessly flying in circles waiting until we signalled whether he might land or not.

Castillo entered the trees. Graham followed him. I was still panting among the termite cones. It was much farther than I had thought.

The track became sandy and appeared to have two well-worn wheel ruts, four or five feet apart. 'Funny,' I thought, 'Wheels and vehicles in these sequestered parts? Surely not.'

I jogged into the oppressive foliage, fuggy as a steam-heated greenhouse. Ahead of me I saw something moving on the track. It was neither Castillo nor Graham, who by this time were well out in front. It was much too small, anyway. Then, in the forest gloom, I saw that it was a bird, a walking-type bird, with the general appearance of a small emu. Its body was egg-shaped, its neck and beak long and graceful, its legs like stilts. The darting head, neck, sides and underbody were a dark rich red colour, so dark as to be almost black, but a colour which shaded imperceptibly into the upper body's egg-shaped pink. When it turned to watch me I saw its breast and under-neck had a speckle of blue. It was a beautiful bird, and as I quickened my steps to catch up, it stretched its strides the longer. For the best part of a mile that bird kept twenty paces – sometimes more, never less – ahead of me. Its movements were beautiful to watch as it lifted and delicately dropped its long thin legs, feathering its extended toes together on the lift and splaying them out as the foot reached the sandy ground. When it felt I was getting too close it tightened its wings by its sides, hunched its shoulders, pushed its neck straight forward and ran like a sprinter.

The bird stopped and then leapt sideways into the bush. Something was coming down the trail towards us. I had the shock of my life. It was a battered old army issue Willys jeep. A big man in a boiler suit was crouched over the wheel. He was past sixty. The jeep pulled up and I saw, crowded under the canvas cover at the back, Castillo, Graham, Paul Johnstone the air pilot and a dark young man in white laboratory coat hugging a black bag. No need to ask who he was. They pulled me unceremoniously in and the jungle-ravaged vehicle coughed its way back and then side-tracked towards its lair – an open palm-thatched shed standing near the smart bungalow we had seen previously from the river.

Obviously, Paul had taken a chance and landed, and the owner of the bungalow, on hearing the plane, had immediately jumped in his jeep to enjoy to the full the excitement of an unexpected visitor.

By this time Arthur Helliwell had come labouring up, and we all moved through the mosquito-netted door into the bungalow. Paul introduced the young Venezuelan doctor, and Gustavo X, the owner of the bungalow, introduced himself. He was a very tall blue-eyed Scandinavian-looking man with a leathery skin rather like one of those gangling Swedish Kings who live on bicycles. Later, I found out a little more about him. To all intents and purposes he was a hermit, a man who for reasons of his own had opted out of Western city life and preferred to live sequestered and alone, except for the Indians. While Arthur stripped off to the waist and the doctor sounded and tapped his chest, I nosed round Señor X's home.

It was really only one room built to withstand tropical extremes of weather and insect life. The roof was palm thatch, and immediately below the eaves, all the way round, was a three-foot band of mosquito netting, so the air was cool and insect free. The floor was smooth concrete. Down either long side wall ran a narrow bench, waist height, littered with everything imaginable: tinned food, cleaning powders, condiments and spices, bandages, great wads of surgical cotton wool, bottles of rum (Colonial St Theresa), whisky (Johnny Walker), a ·45 Smith and Wesson revolver (loaded), an electric soldering iron, a bag of tools open and spilled out, a two-two rifle and a shot-gun, a wireless receiver and transmitter. In the middle of the floor was a table with the remains of a meal on it. Under it were two cardboard cartons stuffed with paperbacks – Pelicans, Penguins, Peregrines, thrillers. Señor X told me he read them all in rotation and then started again, having forgotten enough to make the repetition painless. His hammock, an Indian one (more intricately woven, fringed and finer than ours), was slung from two roof posts which allowed him to recline alongside his radio. He told me that although he preferred his life as a recluse, he did, in fact, speak by radio almost every evening with friends in Caracas.

He had been a civil engineer working both in Venezuela and the States, and partly because of that, I suppose, his jungle home had all 'mod cons'. At the far end from the door there was a kitchen sink with running water, a butane gas ring and a large refrigerator. To the left of the sink a door led into his bathroom with shower, wash hand basin and low flush suite in cream porcelain. He had engineered his own water supply, collecting the almost daily tropical showers in a V-shaped shiny aluminium catchment area with gutter between. The water ran down into a filter and a tank and was thence piped to the house.

One was curious to know why he should have chosen to retire to the heart of the forest and live alone. He had been married, he told me, but he and his wife parted – no fighting, still friends – but she loved Caracas and he wanted to get away. He felt strongly for the plight of the Indians: 'Everybody exploits them,' he said in his gentle sad voice; and he doctored them for diarrhoea and intestinal parasites, skin diseases and so on. Outside, he had an old dugout canoe filled with soil brought from quite a distance – there was no soil suitable for his purpose near by – and in it he was growing tomatoes. The fruit were ripe and, before we left, Julio Castillo cadged a handful from him.

I heard afterwards that Señor X had been moved to leave society because of a stroke of fate: he had had a cancer of the bowel necessitating the removal of a large part of his intestine so that now his waste matter was eliminated from his side into a plastic bag. Life as a recluse was his way of coping with it.

After twenty minutes the young dark doctor folded his stethoscope and snapped up his bag. I asked Paul Johnstone, who acted as interpreter, what the verdict was.

Arthur's condition was serious, and he ought to go into hospital in Ayacucho at once for observation, treatment and rest.

I asked Arthur if he would go with Paul in the plane.

He simply shook his head.

'Arthur,' I said, 'you've *got* to go. You'll kill yourself staying in this lot.'

'I can't go, Brian,' he said quietly, 'I've got to be in that hovercraft when it goes over the rapids. My paper sent me all this way for that purpose. I just can't flunk it. I've got to go.'

The others chipped in, everybody trying to persuade him to fly to Ayacucho and the nearest hospital. It was no use.

Bob Saunders had come prepared to go in the plane on the first leg to Caracas. He would take all the film we had exposed so far and air-freight it to London. Then he would fly back and rejoin us at Puerto Ayacucho. In this way Paul's journey would not be entirely wasted.

We said our goodbyes, and Señor X took Paul, the doctor and Bob in his jeep to the air-strip. The rest of us walked dismally back to Saba-ñita and the hovercraft. On the way I saw the strange bird again together with a huge stork which stood staring at us disapprovingly like a frock-coated Edwardian stockbroker as though we had trespassed into his Surrey estate. Julio Castillo said the small bird was a *Gruya* and the stork he called *Galson Sordado*. Both were pets of a young Indian boy.

It was five minutes past two when we arrived back at Las Carmelitas. I asked Jesco if he had anything in his medical kit to give to Arthur. He went away to his own dark corner of the Black Hole and returned with a disposable plastic syringe and a wide-spectrum penicillin injection we had bought in Manaus. We persuaded Arthur to have a jab. I suppose his resistance was lowered because he felt bad about all the trouble taken and his refusal not to benefit by it. He agreed to be injected. He pulled off his shirt. At the drop of a hat, Jesco injected him in his left arm then and there, standing in his casual wear – football shorts.

That night he coughed much less and he seemed much improved.

CHAPTER EIGHTEEN

Dicing with Death

On the morning of 2nd May at nine o'clock we left Yacuary or Las Carmelitas with some relief and pleasure.

I had gone with Arthur Helliwell to Smokey Joe's (the *Cantina*) for breakfast of watery porridge, rye biscuits and coffee which was tepid, bitter, black and undrinkable. I pointed out to Arthur the incongruity of the 'props' on the stained adobe walls. There was a wooden-pegged hat rack with a pale blue, part unwound toilet roll thrust on one peg, a wide-brimmed worker's straw hat on another and a guitar hanging from a third. By the hat rack, on the same wall, hung a gaudy print, all blues and reds, of the Virgin Mary, immediately above a poster showing a matador about to deliver the *coup-de-grâce* to a charging bull. On the adjoining wall was another gaudy religious print of a large hand, the hand of Christ with bloody nail wound, supporting one of the four apostles on each finger and the Virgin on the thumb. Next to this was a glossy Nestor R. Gonzalez calendar having a large coloured photograph of a white 'model', nude, kneeling and pushing her bottom backwards and her bosom forwards. The caption was *Perlas Lindas*, 'beautiful pearls' though her string of beads was the last thing one would notice. I never sorted out which I liked least, the salacious business humour of the trader's calendar or the religious prints. A last print behind us depicted the sleeping infant Jesus with a large oriole, and in the background a cross and ladder – the shape of things to come. As Arthur Helliwell remarked when we pushed away from table, 'If you did this to a theatre set in Stoke-on-Trent even, they'd say, "Come off it. Aren't you overdoing it a bit?" '

At midday, after an uneventful three-hour trip, we ran up out of the river on to a wide expanse of grass-grown beach at San Fernando de Atabapo. San Fernando has the air of a real frontier outpost, the same unchanging air it has had for the last 300 years. The plaza had been mapped out, and the rollo, with Bolívar's bust, stood at the centre of a diagonal of paths. And there was a splendid newish nunnery and church, but the rest were timeless adobe buildings weather stained and tin-roofed.

After landing, I slung my hammock in a whitewashed warehouse along with Arthur Helliwell, Jesco and Graham Clarke our hovercraft pilot. The others found shelter at the military barracks across the way. Round the corner from our warehouse there was actually a shop – *a shop* which sold cold drinks – we really were nearing civilisation.

During the hot afternoon I lay in my hammock pumping sweat at every pore, but at last fell asleep.

After a couple of hours I awoke and went to find Jesco, who had been on a tour of discovery round San Fernando and declared that he now knew of a 'fine Brazilian restaurant' where he felt we ought to dine. So Jesco, Arthur Helliwell, Peter Smith, Henry Farrar, Douglas Botting, John Thornes, David Harris and I strolled up the rutted streets accompanied by dogs and hens to the 'Brazilian restaurant', a shack, about half a mile away. We all sat round a large table facing a tureen which turned out to be a broth of chicken bones. We had hardly had time to contemplate our helpings when a violent rainstorm started. Water began to trickle through the roof at three points and was collected in aluminium cooking pots and a white enamel chamber pot. Then, without warning, the electric lights went out.

Obviously, the generator had been shorted, shocked by a rude intrusion of rain water.

We were left rather nonplussed round the table in pitch black except for the points of glowing cigarettes.

A brown arm and a hand thrust a saucer with a lighted candle into our midst. As the fat flame lolled this way and that, we were overlooked from the walls by our shadows, swaying to right and left, in an attempt to peer over our shoulders. Then a rickety vapour lamp was produced which made our shadows steady as guardsmen but kept us on tenterhooks by continually appearing to be at the point of expiring.

Frantic pumping restored its hissing vigour for a time, but it was clear that most of the air was leaving by way of a leak.

The rain hammered down on the tin roof and, if anything, got worse. The trickles became cataracts, and a shift system was needed to change the pots catching the floods. There was only one thing now in our minds – how to get home – if you could call the warehouse home. After an hour of unremitting downpour stronger than if you'd been standing directly under a fire-hose our host produced a solution. He had a long tarpaulin. If we walked out into the night, two by two, holding the tarpaulin above our heads we could do it.

So the eight of us caught the last tarpaulin home.

Those in front got wet anyway, from the beating rain; those in the middle soon realised the danger of the water collected on top. Underfoot, the 'road' was like a First World War Flanders battlefield for unevenness, holes and a sliding greasy surface. Most of us had flashlights. One of them pooled with illumination a grotesque sight – a frog or toad fully ten inches high. He was so big he looked like one of those pottery imitations people put in their gardens along with gnomes and mushrooms. He stared like a pop-eyed athlete caught in mid press-up, his dark skin glistening with wet. The tarpaulin stopped while everyone gaped, then went into gear again and caterpillared its way through mud and pools. Half-way home we were joined by another passenger. Conrad Gorinsky must have been marooned like us by the sudden storm. He was sheltering in a shack doorway when he saw this unbelievable creature crocodiling through the inky wet with flashlight eyes all round and voices emanating from its belly and behind. With a leap and a yell he dived under the last tarpaulin home. Being taller than most, he pushed up a sagging pool and swished it into the night.

When we arrived at our warehouse it's doubtful whether we were much better off than if we had simply walked bareheaded through the storm.

I draped my sodden pants and shirt over my hammock ropes and rolled into bed.

After breakfast next morning we drifted down to the river's brink to wave off the scientists – all of them this time, including Mike Eden, who had been condemned to the galley, Castillo's boat, for the very last stage of their trip. They would take it as far as it could go, namely the landing at Samariapo. From Samariapo to Puerto Ayacucho they would be conveyed with their cases of specimens along the road which circumvents the Great Rapids, a distance of some eighty kilometres. Graham Clarke was progressively shedding the hovercraft's load.

Even as the boat puttered away, I saw Graham come hurrying from the buildings, calling my name.

His news surprised me. We had been scheduled to stay another night at San Fernando, but the rain had pushed Graham into changing his plans. As I have reported, when we first landed, the hovercraft had been driven up the flat savannah well clear of the water and, in fact, just beyond the dump of fuel drums waiting for us. At first light the crew had been disturbed to see a foot of water round the fuel drums and the hovercraft's stern awash. The Orinoco had risen that much in a single night. Of course, at this very point it was joined by its huge tributary, the Atabapo, and was easily a mile wide.

Graham told me he had decided to leave in less than half an hour, by ten a.m., for Isla Raton (Mouse Island) just above Samariapo and the beginning of the Great Rapid. Henry, Arthur and I went hotfoot towards the warehouse to unsling our hammocks and pack our gear. Before we reached the buildings a Cessna aeroplane swooped out of the sky and landed behind some trees. There was no time at the moment to inquire who it might be. Henry, Peter and I scrambled our personal gear together and carted it and our cameras down to the water-logged hovercraft. The news had evidently got round that we were leaving, and a large crowd had gathered, with more coming every minute.

Pushing through the throng came Bob Saunders, followed by two men and a girl. Seeing Bob was something of a surprise. 'Did you get to Caracas all right?' I asked.

'Sure, Brian,' he said.

'Get the film sent off?'

'Oh, yes. No trouble at all.' He looked just as though he had stepped out of a first-class hotel – brilliant white shirt, neat tie, pants with a knife-edge crease. He introduced us to his companions. The girl was a coloured American Peace Corps worker, a nurse at the San Fernando hospital. Her name was Pearl. The two men were also Americans, poles apart in their lives, but somehow, when you think about it, like the two sides of one and the same coin. One, Earl Hopkins, a New Tribes Missionary from Puerto Ayacucho who later told me the yopo story of the Indian who 'saw' President Kennedy's assassination; the other a wild and worldly bush pilot whose name was Tex.

They had all flown from Ayacucho following the line of the river, and Bob had evidently been more than shaken by his view of the rapids from some 400 feet.

'Brian,' he said, 'I don't want to frighten you, but I think they're impassable.'

'They'd better not be,' I said, 'otherwise we'll lose the climax to our film.'

'No, seriously,' Bob said, 'they stretch for the best part of half an hour's flying, must be fifty miles. I've never seen anything like it – waterfalls, whirlpools, rocks – the lot.'

'Well, there's nothing we can do now,' I said, 'Graham's decided to set off at ten o'clock.'

'Will you shoot 'em today?'

'I don't really know. I expect so. I've got the feeling he's going to have a bash.'

Bob shook his head. Tex, the tough-looking bush pilot, said, 'Boy, yo' sure got some chore ahead of yo'.'

Pearl and the missionary, the other two locals, looked at us pityingly. They were curious and interested by the strange mechanical monster lying 'midst her skirts half in and half out of the river, but you could tell by their faces what they thought of our chances.

I tried to get a little more information from Graham, who, for the first time, seemed a bit preoccupied, a bit worried, and who was impatient to get everyone aboard. However, he did take time out to tell me that he had been in radio communication with Puerto Ayacucho and that a huge Venezuelan Air Force helicopter had already arrived there from Caracas to co-operate with the hovercraft. The arrangements as they had stood were for us to have waited at San Fernando until the helicopter arrived; but Graham, influenced by the unexpected rise in the river overnight, had tentatively decided to shoot the Great Rapid that day. It was a momentous decision and literally meant opting for 'a tide, which taken at the flood' might well 'lead on to fortune'. He had therefore arranged to proceed downriver as far as Isla Raton, where he could rendezvous with the Venezuelan helicopter and then be taken for a reconnaissance flight over the rapids.

I passed on this information to Bob and Tex, his pilot, and agreed that they should fly to Isla Raton, so that when we all met there we could once more size up the situation. I knew that Graham Clarke was itching to lighten the hovercraft of every superfluous ounce of weight, and I didn't want any mischance to prevent our having a cameraman aboard.

Suddenly I heard Graham calling, 'Get aboard, gentlemen, please! Lift off in three minutes.'

At ten a.m. exactly, the hovercraft blew out her flaccid skirts, skittishly splattered the water from her behind, slewed round like a house in an earthquake and roared on to the surface of the bulging river.

By eleven thirty we had drawn alongside Isla Raton, a large island in the Orinoco where, these days, the Dutch Fathers have a well-organised plantation scheme with sugar cane in regimented rows and a proper irrigation system using water pumped up from the river. It was all ship-shape and regular like a pattern of bulb fields – quite un-South American. The bank was about ten feet above our heads, and Robin Tenison had scarcely tied us up to a tree when we heard the hollow metallic *clopper* of a helicopter. The pilot had seen us and was flying upstream and right over our heads. His machine was an American Bell thirteen seater, its huge bloated body with a long narrow tail giving it the appearance of a gigantic dragonfly. It flapped low and out of sight.

We scrambled up the clay bank and through a young corn plantation to the combined football pitch and air-strip. There were no flight regulations or airport procedure here: the helicopter was already putting down, while behind her, like an impudent urchin mocking a grave signior's portentous gait, jigged Tex's Cessna. The cheeky Tex skimmed alongside the trees bumping down once, firmly, and then fetching round the still twisting blades of the whirly-bird as though he were driving a motor-bike.

Three splendidly attired Venezuelan Air Force officers dismounted proudly – latter-day conquistadors. They were dark, young and handsome. One of them very aristocratic in the old Spanish way, and intense. We were told later that he was the captain and never flew without a bible to hand. Their uniform was stunning against the jungle green and baked ground drab: it was a sort of well-tailored boiler suit in old-gold with large, flamboyant United States-type badges and flashes. A maximum-survival suiting, we were informed. Certainly it would have been visible miles away against a forest background.

Graham Clarke, Stuart Syrad and David Smithers quickly button-holed the air crew. As a result of their confabulation, only five expedition members were to be taken for a 'look-see' over the rapids. The BBC was allowed one representative only, and I decided that the seat must go to Henry Farrar as cameraman. He would not only be able to see the conditions under which he would have to film the hovercraft when it came to attempt the rapids, he could also take his Arriflex and film the dangers which we would then be able to cut into our documentary as a foretaste for viewers of what the hovercraft would be up against.

Nevertheless I must confess to feeling a little aggrieved at not being able to go myself – after all, the helicopter *was* a thirteen seater. Still,

Tex was there with his Cessna, hired by Bob Saunders on behalf of the BBC, and I asked him to take Peter, Jesco, Arthur Helliwell and me for a private view. We followed the chopper after an interval of about ten minutes and had hardly left Isla Raton behind when we reached the first set of rapids. They certainly looked spectacular. The river was split apart into numerous channels like a skein of silver wool. Bare rocks and granite boulders the size of hills separated the various channels, and one saw everywhere the ripples of white water which from the air mean rapids. As Tex came skidding down the sky almost to water level, and well below the dome-shaped tops of the surrounding boulder-hills, I could see the massive bulk and thrust of the mighty river as it fought insensately to get through or past or over the many obstacles.

We saw no sign of the helicopter. We banked up and down the sky, craning our necks to right and left, with no success. We were a little alarmed to see a column of smoke beyond some trees and open savannah perhaps six miles away. Tex (running low on fuel) asked what he should do. 'Fly back if we can't locate the chopper,' I said.

So we landed back at Isla Raton near the football-pitch goal posts. No helicopter. We made our way to a trestle table under an open roof where David Smithers and the others left behind were lunching on the usual expedition fare of corned beef, tinned salmon, sardines and dry biscuits – plus a smelly river fish with a big head donated by the Fathers. We joined in. David believed that the helicopter would have gone all the way to Puerto Ayacucho and that there was no cause to worry.

This proved true, for at two fifteen the chopper noisily returned and we were informed that Graham Clarke and his two advisers, Stuart Syrad and Robin Tenison, had decided to shoot the rapids that very afternoon – in fact at three p.m., in three-quarters of an hour's time.

Now, at last, we were faced with the moment of truth. This was where you tightened your belt and consulted with yourself what kind of man you were.

My wife says that I am incapable of recognising danger when I see it. This may be true, but what I had seen for myself of the Great Rapids was certainly daunting, certainly dangerous. Yet when I asked Graham what he thought of our chances he said, 'There are two separate sets of rapids. They're tricky. Yes, there are one or two bad patches. We shall have to get lined up properly. Still, we've got to go. It's too far back the way we came to Manaus.'

I got the distinct impression that circumstances made it impossible to turn back. Somehow, we felt we had to stand up and be counted; at least, I did. In a way we were like small boys who just had to take a 'dare'. There we were, representing the battered old tail-tweaked British Lion watched by Americans, Venezuelans and, at home, at least by Arthur's faithful followers, the readers of the *People*.

Graham gave instructions that only two BBC representatives could be allowed in the hovercraft in its attempt to shoot the rapids, and I was asked who I wanted to have aboard. There was really no choice: Jesco had to go as our second cameraman, and I had to go to direct him – it was as simple as that. Unbeknown to me, Peter Smith had already asked Graham if he could go and I had to over-rule the permission already given. Peter, very disappointed, took his recording gear off to the helicopter. Our other spare gear, camera boxes, tripod and film were loaded by Bob aboard Tex's Cessna. Henry Farrar and Douglas Botting made their way to the waiting chopper. At two minutes to three Graham sounded the hovercraft klaxon.

I have always been a lover of Old Icelandic literature, particularly the ancient ballads: they are packed with pithy wisdom. There's one ballad poem which tells how the mischief-maker of the gods, Loki, once borrowed Freya's feather flying coat to visit Giantland to try to locate Thor's stolen hammer. When Loki flew back into Asgard the impatient Thor caught him while still on the wing and shouted: 'Hey! Give me your news from up there! By the time a man's sat down he's twisting his story! Give him a chance to lie down and he really will lie!' On this principle I shall tell the story of our fight with the Great Rapids using my diary account which I wrote less than twelve hours after the adventure finished.

It begins, '4th May. Yesterday, eleven of us men encountered an experience which I can most nearly liken to going over the Niagara Falls in a barrel – and lived. The eleven, in order of seating in the hovercraft starting from the front of the bus, so to speak, and numbering off from left to right, were Julio Castillo (Orinoco river pilot); Robin Hanbury-Tenison (campmaster and map reader); Stuart Syrad (Royal Marines Captain and second hovercraft pilot); Graham Clarke (hovercraft captain and pilot of the hovercraft); in the second row, myself (BBC television film director); Wolf Jesco Baron von Puttkamer (Brazilian film cameraman); John Hoyland (hovercraft engineer); James A. Sweeney (hovercraft engineer); in the third row, Arthur Helliwell (columnist of the *People* Sunday newspaper); Lt-Colonel Evilio Colmenares Leal (Venezuelan Army); and David Smithers (journalist and expedition business manager).

'I am writing this account at 3.30 a.m. by my watch, lying in bed at the Amazonas hotel, Puerto Ayacucho – said by Smithers to be a rundown flea pit, but to me seeming to be the height of luxury after the hovels we have slept in over the past three weeks.

'Graham sounded the hovercraft klaxon. The men I have enumerated above went on board and took their seats. There could be no standing up, no moving about. "In fact," said Graham, "I am going to strap myself in," and proceeded to do so.

'Julio Castillo, nervous, asked me for rum since he had always found me a source of it in the past. I reached for a bottle, but the hovercraft crew said "no", so he got none.

'We started off with fairly clear weather, a lot of high cloud and a smooth river.

'None of us, except Graham and Stuart, had been over rapids of any size in the hovercraft before, so there was a feeling of nervous expectation in the air.

' "What instructions did you give the helicopter, Brian?" Graham asked me. I had previously told Henry to get every type of shot he could – high, low, back, front, tracking alongside, tracking behind, crossing – everything in the book. This wasn't what Graham meant. He was wondering about instructions for starting. In the scramble, I had in fact said nothing to the pilot, partly because the helicopter appeared to be working principally for the *Geographical* part of the enterprise, favouring Doug Botting, the stills cameraman, and partly because I expected everybody knew that the chopper must get airborne as soon as the hovercraft left moorings.

'I pointed out something of this to Graham and then looked anxiously back through my window for signs of the machine.

' "About five minutes to go before we reach the first rapid," said Graham.

'I looked back through the window again at the empty sky.

'Then I saw the hard black spot of the dragonfly body coming up in the distance on our port quarter. I told Graham.

'Two minutes later I reported, "Helicopter alongside," and so she was, looming very large on my left about forty feet away and twenty feet above the water. I could see, with satisfaction, Henry our cameraman and Douglas Botting plainly framed in the two large open side windows. Both had cameras to their eyes.

'We could see through the spray-splashed front windows of the hovercraft (the windscreen wipers were clearing some of the wash away) a line of broken water ahead. Jesco, beside me, put his camera to his eye and I braced myself against the seat in front of me with my knees and hugged him tightly to give him support.

'The hovercraft seemed to be sucked into the outer rim of a maelstrom of smooth, hard water as the great river was constricted between rocks. We plunged over the edge of the flow at tremendous speed and I doubt that none of us was ready for what happened next.

'If you imagine driving a bus over a river bank into a raging torrent, I reckon you have something like it. The whole front of the hovercraft dived down into the waves and tons of red-brown river blotted out the front windows. There was a deafening crash below us and I thought we had struck a rock and weren't ever coming up again. The red-brown light persisted for an eternity, and in the first flash I saw Graham, tense-faced, fighting the joystick and foot rudder-controls with a look of great surprise on his face. The other three men in front of us were flung bodily forward on to the browned-out panes. Two roaring waves geysered in through the two open slide windows on my left, drenching me to the skin (I remember feeling aggrieved as though somebody for no reason at all had put his foot in my face); at the same time a deluge of water, a gigantic flood, poured in through the window on Graham's right and he looked like somebody sitting in a mountain torrent; the craft lurched violently away to my right and Jesco was wrenched from my grip. His camera rocketed out of his hand up to the roof and he himself tried to catch it, succeeding in breaking its fall with his right hand and landed awash on the floor under the back of the pilot's seat with me on top of him.

" 'Get up, Jesco!" I yelled, "Keep filming!"

'We scrambled back into our seats and I slid my window shut. Julio Castillo closed his in front of me. Jesco retrieved his camera and put his eye to it.

'By this time the craft had reared out of the water, and as we looked through the windscreen we saw a similar surf mountain ahead of us to the one we had just come through.

' "Stand by!" yelled Syrad, "Another coming!"

'I got my right arm round Jesco and gripped him till he squelched. "Film when I yell *now*!"

'At the brink of the waterchute I got my lips to his ear – for there seemed to be an infernal hullaballoo in the craft, what with the normal roar of the engine, the *whaa-wharr* of the reverse pitch of the propeller, and the waves outside – and shouted "Now!"

'Again we pitched headlong over the brink and again the nose of the craft dived deep into the boiling, foaming river; again the windows were blanked off by a comber of red-brown opaqueness and one saw the pilot and his helpers struggling like actors in the foreground of some science-fiction film with the unreal, unbelievable scene in back-projection beyond them. This time, the craft gave a stomach-turning skid sideways away from us to the right, and as we breached like a whale coming from the bottom of the ocean, rising solidly at tremendous speed up out of the cauliflower of billows, I saw rocks flashing past the starboard windows – rather with the effect of near objects seen blurred from the wet windows of a fast-moving railway train on a rainy day.

'Flying above us, Tex, the pilot from Texas, saw this dangerous sideways drift as he flew over. Afterwards, he described the situation to me as he felt it in his slow John Wayne drawl –" 'Jeez', Ah says to myself, 'Jeez Captain' an' 'bawg' Ah says – Ah use 'bawg' sometimes if'n Ah'm gettin' excited. 'Bawg, Capt'n', Ah says, 'you better stawp that craft driftin' into them rawks or you be a dead capt'n. An Ah don' mahnd admittin', Ah wuz jus' a little excited – an' Ah wuz shoutin'! An' Ah wuz lookin' fur a place to land mah plane on the Colombia side o' that river, 'cuz we wuz goin' to have to fish some purty wet Englishmen out o' that water. Yes sir! Ah'd seen that ship disappear completely under them waves – an' Ah tell you it was sump'n'! But boy-ee – it wuz them rawks Ah was afeared of – an' Ah saw we wuz flyin' out o' gas on both our tanks, but Ah couldn't leave. Ah says to Bawb, 'We'll jus' stick aroun' a leetle longer – cuz if'n he hits them rawks – that's curtains!' "

'If we had hit the rocks, a touch would have been enough, for the plenum chamber which holds in the cushion of air is like a curved crinoline of thin aluminium. Even an unwary foot stepping on it is likely to go through. Had it brushed a boulder, it would have crumpled like tinfoil and all the lift would have gone from that punctured side. The craft wouldn't necessarily have sunk, for there is a bouyancy tank divided into twelve water-tight compartments on which it would float. But any control from the driving-seat would have been lost and she would have slid and tossed and spun and bobbed with every twist and eddy of the river like a cork or a child's paper boat hurtling down a flooded gutter.

'But she *didn't* graze the rocks and Graham still had control as we slowly rose to daylight from the smothering torrent of foaming light-ale surf. As we rode the billows and could see out again, I shouted to Jesco to rewind his camera ready for whatever came next. I glanced behind me at the other occupants to see if there were any likely reaction shots. I saw Colonel Evilio Colmenares Leal standing like a strap-hanging passenger in a bus – one arm above his head – and he was drenched from the top of his round pill-box nebbed cap to his canvas jungle boots. His wet uniform was clinging to his body with odd lumps protruding at breast pockets and thigh pocket where he had stuffed papers and what-not. His eyes were round and sparkling, and there was a look of exhilaration and elation on his swarthy dark-brown face. "Well – Meester Brans'on!" he shouted. "You like?"

' "Yes, Colonel!" I yelled, "I like!"'

'Immediately behind me, Arthur Helliwell, the *People* columnist, was sitting grasping our seat back with his left hand, and in his right, his note-taking tape recorder into which he was talking fast. Over the last three weeks his grey hair had grown long and was curling upwards from the nape of his neck beneath the wide brim of his planter's hat with wrapped-around, gay-spotted, and now sweat-discoloured bandana. His sprouting grey sidewhiskers and moustache and mild blue eyes completed the picture of the Southern colonel. What he was saying was lost in the din, but the tape recorder was picking it up and I knew the deathless prose would appear in the *People* come Sunday – if we got out in one piece.

'I looked behind me again and saw David Smithers with Douglas Botting's pet parrot clinging awkwardly to his left shoulder. Anything less like Long John Sliver was scarcely imaginable. The gorgeous blue and red bird was bedraggled with water: in its fright it had become speechless, using all its energy to haul itself by beak and claw up Smithers' dank shirt on to his upper arm. Smithers may not have looked like Long John Silver, but in one respect he bore a striking resemblance to the lamented Robert Newton who played that fearsome character in the film – particularly on those occasions when he leaned forward confidentially and croaked "Jim, laad!" *Then* his eyes would bulge out of his head with a clear ring of white round the starting pupils. So looked David Smithers' eyes behind his horn-rimmed glasses: the epitome of a wild surmise. He was soaking wet and talking fifteen to the dozen into his tape machine.'

Of course, I could not hear what David was saying, but he played the recording over to me afterwards, and it was going like this: 'My goodness! We are going into the most boiling cauldron of water I have ever seen! Fantastic! We shall . . . this is fantastic! Leaping, jerking and jumping, everything is falling over! Tremendous bumps! But we are all right! I hear some breaking glass, but I can't see anything . . . the whole craft is inundated with water. Waves came right up over us, I

wouldn't have believed it possible. . . . *Going down! Down! Crash!*
We can't survive this. It must go down, it must, the craft must sink!
How can we live in this? Great brown waters have obscured the windows, the water is pouring in through the windows! We're soaked to
the skin, hanging on for grim death! *Down* . . . we've had it this time,
we must have had it, the water's in, we're soaking, completely flooded
out! *O.K. We're going!* One of the windows is smashed right through.
The Colonel's holding it on, and worse is yet to come! I'm not even
sure what I'm recording or if this is being recorded at all, because the
tape recorder's been absolutely soaked, drenched in water! I am
absolutely certain that no craft of any kind has been subjected to such
strain as this craft is being. . . . An aeroplane is circling around overhead. They must think every moment will be our last! Actually I think
so myself. Nothing so far can compare with this: not the insects,
nor the Indians, nor the discomforts, nor the sickness – all are absolutely
nothing compared with this test of gruelling endurance. . . . Pray
heaven we don't prang on any of these fantastic rocks! But if we do, the
helicopter will be able to pull us out – I hope. Though we probably
wouldn't survive that long. With these currents and these rocks we'd
be smashed to bits in a moment. . . . *Down we go! Down! Smash!*
Water is pouring in on us. Tremendous! Down we go, gosh, up and
smash down and up, smash down and up, and smash and up and
down we go! It's like a witch's cauldron, nothing but a hovercraft
could be in this a second and live! Huge rocks looming out at us! Here
we go, over to port side! For survival's sake filming has to stop, everything else must stop! Over to port side, now to starboard side. Brian's
clutching Jesco round the waist to hold him. Already his camera has
smashed down once and is probably broken. . . . Oh, my goodness!
Another lot, *bash!* The parrot that got loose has snuggled up behind
me for company and is pecking my shirt. It's pathetic! I can't do anything about it. I am just holding on for my own health's sake. I can't
help it. She wants to be looked after. I've got the parrot on my shoulder.
I can't bear the poor thing suffering like this. . . . The parrot is pecking
at my ear, wanting comfort. *All right, parrot!* She doesn't understand
what's happening!'

Another eye witness of our descent down that first stretch of the
Maipures Rapids was Douglas Botting in the helicopter. He, too,
recorded his impressions next day. He said, 'Well, we watched you
depart with some degree of emotion, which we never expressed, but we
were not convinced that we were going to see you again, because both
Henry and I had been over the Maipures Rapids that morning and

neither of us felt that a hovercraft could, in fact, go through that tempest of water. . . . We watched you go at great speed towards this huge chute of water – I suppose an eight- or nine-foot drop of water. *We* could see this. *We* could see what was in store for you, even though *you* couldn't, and it was rather like photographing a snake eating or about to eat a frog. It was a moment of a mesmeric sort of frozen horror. And then you went down and I was photographing this, therefore my vision was simply a small rectangle in the viewfinder of the camera. But it seemed to me that you went down at an angle of about forty-five degrees. You went down until it was impossible to see your windscreen because of water – not just spray I think, but actual river water. . . . And then it seemed a very great age indeed before anything else happened. You disappeared in the water. The spray enveloped the rest of the hovercraft, and both Henry and I, without speaking to each other, were convinced you had gone. . . . Then the craft struggled like some harpooned whale, and in a great sort of defiant gesture, surged upwards and shook itself like a dog. By this time we were at a different angle, circling over, and it seemed that you had lost all momentum, and I gather in fact that the forward speed had been stopped abruptly by the shock of the impact, even though the engines were running and that you were then sliding sideways down this rather beautiful, immensely powerful chute of water, like a log out of control, and again I thought, well this must be it. It can't go on.'

But it did go on.

Not, however, before we had gained a period of respite. There is a stretch of calmish water between the Maipures (at the beginning of the Great Rapids) and the Atures. And for a description of what happened I return to my own diary.

'During this calmer stretch – it lasts about ten miles – Graham Clarke left the hot seat and Stuart Syrad drove. Graham sat on the front step facing backwards and said to me, "You see, Brian, what I meant by saying nobody could stand up?" He was referring to my request at the start that Jesco might be allowed to move about at the front, the better to film reaction shots. Our experiences made an answer unnecessary.

'The weather suddenly changed, as it does frequently along these mighty rivers. A cloud dropped down, a noisy frying of rain penetrated – or seemed to – above the noise of the smooth-running engine. The front windows cleared and smudged as the wipers crossed and returned. But even when they cleared, you seemed to be looking into a cloud, and the thought occurred to me to say to Graham, "Shouldn't you wait for the weather to lift?" But I kept it to myself and we still skimmed on.

'The *pratico* (Julio Castillo), by now, I am afraid, too confused to be of any help, Robin Tenison and Stuart Syrad were peering this way and that through the front windows and Graham (back in the driver's seat) was asking anxiously, "Which way? Which way?"

'The helicopter had disappeared and even had she been forty feet away, as at first, she would have been difficult to discern through the mist.

'Graham Clarke slowed down and began to slew the hovercraft round. No one but a fool would have kept going forward in that hell's kitchen.'

Douglas Botting has recorded his impressions of this time: 'To me it was just a grey blanket over an entire circular landscape. We rose and ascended from the river to get on to the Atures Rapids and we left you behind and very quickly you vanished into this grey London-type smog. We hung around for a long time (it seemed to me) and realised that you weren't coming. I think it was then that, in that small community of the pilots and Henry and myself, and Peter, that there was some anxiety because we could no longer see you; we no longer knew what was happening; and I think all sorts of things crossed our minds. In mine, I think it was an explosion.'

Down there in the fog (according to my diary) 'we hung about for a very short time after which the cloud cleared as quickly as it had closed about us. I stared ahead and saw blue sky. We were moving downstream again.'

I saw in front of us, stretching right across the visible river, what appeared to be the tossing white manes of the horses of a packed cavalry charge. Before you could blink, we were in the *mellay* and it seemed that a stampede of war-steeds was trampling right over us. We dropped at the nose and the watery brown-out was on us and as Douglas saw 'you came very, very near to disaster. . . . I don't think you had gone over an eight-foot drop or anything like that – you had just *nosed in*. It seemed an age before you began this process of rearing up, shaking off the weight of water, wallowing, rolling, God knows what. . . . We came near in and for the first time I could see the people inside the craft – the first three or four in the front – that must have been Graham, Stuart, Robin and Julio. And it was like a tram in a Keystone Cop film, going round bends: everybody was rolling and shaking about in the most incredible manner – and this was merely in choppy water as it seemed to us from above. A moment of horror was, when again in fairly calm water and going at great speed, you seemed bent on a course leading to total destruction. There were three flattish, black rocks. A foreshortening occurs when you are doing a landscape from above. It seemed to me that you inevitably must pile up on those rocks. It seemed to me that in fact you *did* go over them because I could see the rocks beneath where the hovercraft had gone. But if you *had* gone over them you would probably have ascended them and then found yourself at the top of a little cliff and I think the whole hovercraft would then have become airborne – which would have been very interesting from a photographic point of view and disastrous from the point of view of any further progress on your journey.'

What the pilot said was, 'On the rest of the trip, the main hazard was not being able to pick up rocks due to bad visibility: the first wave that had hit the craft had pushed the port windscreen wiper out of position. I could have used it, but it would have burned out the motor before the end of the trip. The centre windscreen wiper was not working as efficiently as it might, and this would probably have packed up at any time, so we were left with really just the starboard wiper, which limited the vision, and the others were used purely to have a quick look and then switch off again. As regards going over the rocks, I know we went over at least one flat rock which appeared very quickly. There was a wave ahead, and it looked as though there was rock there. But to turn right and avoid it – well, there was another solid rock which definitely *was* there, so I decided to go over this flat-rock-with-the-wave – and in actual fact, I don't think anybody realised we had been over one. Apart from this difficulty of seeing the rocks, the main problem was the fact that it seemed to be such a long time without any break: concentrating all the time until we reached Puerto Ayacucho.'

My own impression of the Atures Rapids is that after the first bad waterfall there was nothing so frightening as at the beginning. The ride was rough, but it was also exhilarating. For those who were watching us, other emotions came into play. Douglas said, 'I know my emotions were curious ones: you seemed like some small animal that one wanted to look after and encourage and give some affection to. You were this little Isle of Wight-run craft, with some 2000 miles of Amazonas waters behind it, still there, still busying along like a waterboatman, and so diminished by the colossal landscape of water, savannah and river, and forest, and mountains beyond the savannah – you just became a courageous little flea on the back of this terrain. And really, it was then that one began to feel very proud. One was proud for *it*, and for the people in it – and sorry that we hadn't been able to share this experience and be part of the team that had gone through. As the helicopter banked to photograph you coming into the jetty at Puerto Ayacucho the Venezuelan pilot did the nearest thing he could to a victory roll in a helicopter and turned the thing almost on its side! I've never been in such a steep turn in an aircraft, and we had great fears of dropping through the portholes straight vertically down into the river!'

Envoi

WELL, as old Kaspar said in the poem, 'It was a famous victory,' but what it all adds up to, I am hard pushed to say.

The day after we shot the Great Rapids we of the BBC party said goodbye to our expeditionary friends and flew off to Caracas. One memorable vignette on the plane from Puerto Ayacucho: we five men shared four facing double seats with one other passenger – a striking young woman with the complexion and beauty of a porcelain shepherdess. She looked, in her chic tailored clothes, like something straight from the ornate portals of an expensive Paris couturier's. She spoke Spanish, so we had difficulty in following her. There was something about her behaviour, a sort of careless freedom, which didn't quite go with her dress and make-up. For instance, she borrowed Bob Saunders' comb and proceeded to arrange her hair. Then she produced her bombshell. Through Jesco she let it be known that she was a Makiritare Indian. This seemed impossible. We indicated as much, shaking our heads. She opened her handbag and produced evidence: photographs, snapshots of herself, perhaps five years ago, at a mission school in a Makiritare village. Then she admitted that her father was a Frenchman. Still – ! Half-way to Caracas, at San Fernando de Apure, she left us, and we craned our necks to watch her graceful gait as she strolled from the airport buildings, alone.

Our friends in the hovercraft spent a couple of days resting at Ayacucho and then set off again at high speed and, breasting the broad and ever-broadening waters of the Orinoco, sped out into the open sea and the nearby island of Trinidad. It took them no more than two days, and there the expedition ended in a mellifluous melange of rum fumes, calypsos, fat toothy grins and steel bands.

We are all back at our old jobs. Myself, once more settled in my semi-detached in Ealing (we moved back from Henley into the Smoke), going by tube each day to my office along with the other harassed nine-to-fivers. Sometimes, as I stare po-faced at my reflection in the black window opposite, the tunnel wall turning it into a mirror, I see an almost white-haired middle-aged man staggering through the dank foliage of an Amazon rain forest, plagued with the flies, exhausted with sweating, anxious about what lurks in the shadows or in the eddies of the mud-coloured river – and I think, 'Can that have been me?'

Index

A Guide to Indian Tribes, People, Places, Rivers, Rapids and General Subjects

918.7
B821g

Branston.

The last great journey on earth.

January 1972

A

918.7
B821g

Branston.

The last great
journey on

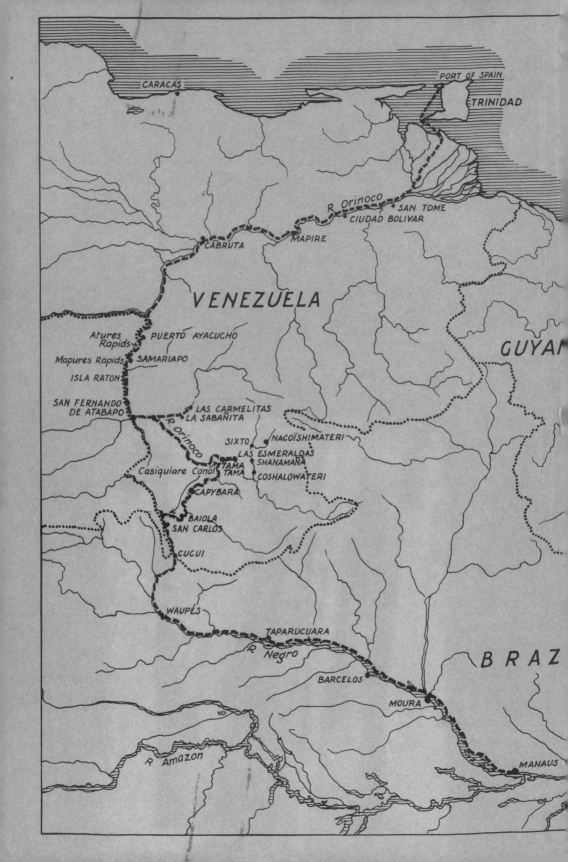